DATE DUE

CONFESSIONS OF A PR MAN

CONFESSIONS OF A PR MAN
ROBERT J. WOOD
WITH MAX GUNTHER

NAL BOOKS

NEW AMERICAN LIBRARY

NEW YORK AND SCARBOROUGH, ONTARIO

Published simultaneously in Canada by The New American Library of Canada Limited.

 NAL BOOKS TRADEMARK REG. U.S. PAT. OFF. AND FOREIGN COUNTRIES
REGISTERED TRADEMARK—MARCA REGISTRADA
HECHO EN CHICAGO, U.S.A.

SIGNET, SIGNET CLASSIC, MENTOR, ONYX, PLUME, MERIDIAN and
NAL BOOKS are published in the United States by NAL PENGUIN INC.,
1633 Broadway, New York, New York 10019,
in Canada by The New American Library of Canada Limited,
81 Mack Avenue, Scarborough, Ontario M1L 1M8

Library of Congress Cataloging-in-Publication Data

First Printing, June, 1988

1 2 3 4 5 6 7 8 9

PRINTED IN THE UNITED STATES OF AMERICA

CONTENTS

INTRODUCTION

PUBLIC RELATIONS:
WHAT IT IS AND WHY I'VE LIKED IT

MY BAPTISM of fire in the public-relations profession took place in the summer of 1945. That was a long time ago, but the story still has direct relevance today. It illustrates at least three important characteristics of PR.

To begin with, the story demonstrates the sheer fun that can be had in this profession. Second, it illustrates the risks that one must face from time to time—risks which, in my opinion, can enhance the fun. And third, it shows how effective a good PR effort can be, even in the hands of a relative newcomer.

The story also marks the beginning of my personal tale. If you want to know why I became a PR man and devoted my life to the profession, you will find the answers in this 1945 adventure. That is why I've chosen to begin the book with it.

In June 1945, I was a young public-relations officer in the Air Force, stationed at MacDill Field, outside Tampa, Florida. I was responsible for the PR affairs of the Third Bomber Command. For three years I supervised the PR officers of sixteen air bases—a most valuable experience.

One day in mid-June I received a call from Captain Arthur Vandenberg, Jr., who was PR chief of the Third Air Force. He said he had just heard from Washington that August 1 had been designated Air Force Day. The brass in Washington wanted the day to be marked by parades and other celebrations around the country, to show the taxpayers what a valuable outfit the Air Force was.

Arthur said he himself would spend Air Force Day in Washington, since that was where the most elaborate promotion was planned, and it was expected to generate national media coverage. This national promotion was to be supplemented with local affairs at various Air Force bases. Arthur asked me if I would arrange something to stir up people in our part of Florida. He thought a straightforward military parade would be enough—some Air Force equipment, maybe a few captured Japanese or German planes.

I said I would do my best, and spent a couple of days thinking it over. This was the first time in my young career that I had been handed a big promotional campaign and told to produce it on my own. As I saw it, there were two ways to go. There was the safe way—I could do exactly what Arthur suggested, run a simple parade, get a few pictures in the local papers, and come out of the venture no bigger than when I started. Or I could take a risk and try for a triumph.

I didn't have any great fund of experience on which to base a decision. But some instinct told me to take the risk.

What kind of promotion would be more interesting than a parade and display of military equipment? I recalled reading about a demonstration of parachute jumping that had generated a good deal of public interest and media coverage a couple of months back. So I got on the phone and started making inquiries. How could I arrange to have a planeload of paratroopers jump over MacDill Field on Air Force Day?

I was referred from one officer to another. When I ran into resistance, I invented a story that opened doors instantly. I said a demonstration jump had the support of Lieutenant General Lewis Brereton, who was famed for leading paratroop combat units in Europe during the Second World War. The fact was that I had never talked to Brereton, but his name worked magic. "We'll do anything for Lewie!" one officer said, promising to set up the jump for me.

The lie was a risk, of course. But so was the whole project. If it went wrong, I alone would be responsible.

My ideas grew more grandiose, and so did the level of risk. I arranged for formation flights of fighter and bomber planes, demonstrations of target bombing, and other exciting events. I did it all without getting approval from anybody. And, to please Arthur Vandenberg, I did set up a traditional parade.

Then things started to unravel—not an uncommon occurrence in a complex promotion. First of all, I was told MacDill Field lacked a big enough drop zone for my proposed parachuting display. After some frantic phone calls I was able to get my large and growing promotion moved to Drew Field, which was on the other side of Tampa and had a better layout for the paratroopers.

Then two of the parachuting officers came around about a week in advance to inspect the drop zone. In my talks with them I had envisioned a relatively modest demonstration—a few paratroopers jumping out of one plane. I was astounded to learn that their vision was vastly more exciting. Maybe I had oversold them. They were planning to descend on Drew Field with 8 officers and 142 enlisted men jumping out of 9 planes from only 800 feet.

But the officers almost called everything off when they saw the drop zone at Drew. It was a wilderness of tree stumps and a swamp—they wouldn't stage the jump unless these two potential problems were taken care of. The stumps had to be removed, and during the jump, enlisted men had to be stationed around the swamp to prevent possible drownings of paratroopers.

Once again I had to make a desperate move. I managed to talk Drew Field's commanding officer into removing the stumps and guarding the swamp. But I wasn't yet through testing his good nature. After the parachuting officers left, I gave him some more troublesome news. The nine planeloads of jumpers— one hundred and fifty men all told—would be arriving in Tampa two days before their jump and would need meals and a place to stay.

"Where are you planning to put them up?" the Drew Field chief asked me.

"Well," I said, gulping, "I thought it would make sense to have them stay at Drew."

"Oh?" He sounded startled. Then he said, "Well, all right, I guess it's possible. But whose budget is going to cover the cost?"

My neck was already far out. Another inch wouldn't make any difference. I promptly replied, "Third Air Force."

That satisfied the man. The fact was that I had no idea who was going to pay for the paratroopers' room and board.

Shortly after that, I had to increase my risk still more. I was called into the office of my boss and a wonderful guy, Joseph H. Atkinson, commanding general of the Third Bomber Command. He remarked that he had been reading a lot of news stories and hearing a lot of radio reports on the coming Air Force Day promotion, and to his surprise he was prominently quoted in all of them. What or who was the source of these stories?

I was, of course. I had generated a steady stream of press releases and other material on the August 1 promotion, and the media coverage had been excellent. I explained to General Atkinson that I had quoted him copiously because I felt Third Bomber Command ought to get credit for what was promising to be a gala occasion in the Tampa area.

The general accepted that, but added, "There's one thing that worries me, Lieutenant. These stories of yours make it sound as though this whole thing was my idea. If that's the way you want to play it, fine. But suppose there's an accident. Suppose some soldiers or civilians are hurt or killed? Who will be held responsible?"

I bared another inch of my neck for the axe and said, "General Lynch, sir." I was referring to one of the top brass at Third Air Force.

The truth was that General Atkinson would be held responsible. It was his military career that was on the line—and if his career went down the drain, mine would follow. But I dared not tell him this. I was afraid he might call off the whole promotion.

My blood pressure continued to rise as August 1 approached. I was working frantic eighteen-hour days, trying to hold the soaring enterprise together. One additional chore I had was to write a speech for General Atkinson. I had arranged for him to speak at a lunch of Tampa business and civic leaders on the day of the gala about the impact of strategic bombing. Much of my material came from a British military report.

To save some desperately needed time, I constructed the

speech partly by means of scissors and paste, snipping passages out of the British report and pasting them directly into the general's speaking notes.

The great day arrived with the enterprise still patched together. The main airborne events—the parachuting and so on—were scheduled for the afternoon. At midday General Atkinson and I went to the downtown lunch. I sat back to listen as he began the speech. Then I sat bolt upright. I realized that I had made an embarrassing mistake.

I had presented the general with a speech that was peppered with Britishisms—"petrol" for gasoline, and so on.

That could have thrown some speakers and resulted in a public-relations disaster. Luckily for me, General Atkinson kept his cool. The speech received a standing ovation.

Then we got into the general's staff car and set out for Drew Field, but it wasn't going to be an easy trip. Ten miles away from the field, we ran into bumper-to-bumper traffic. We had to turn off the highway and drive across fields to make headway.

The news media had predicted a crowd of some 10,000 people at the affair. By two o'clock, more than 35,000 had already passed through the gates of Drew Field. In the end, some 5,000 people had to be turned away.

From the point of view of drawing crowds, my promotion was evidently a success. But then a brand-new problem loomed up.

The problem, like some others, grew out of the very success of the enterprise. People had wanted to be a part of it. Like the paratroopers who wanted to come in nine planes when I only asked for one, participants had kept adding to the program's size and scope to make roles for themselves.

One man who had done this was Brigadier General Thomas Blackburn, chief of the Third Fighter Command. He had suggested that one of his P-51 fighter planes lay a smokescreen in the north end of the drop zone immediately before the jump. This would make a dramatic backdrop for the parachute jumpers, he argued, and would increase the likelihood of good media coverage. There would be both movie newsreel cameras and still photographers at the gala, so I liked the idea. But I had a question.

"Suppose the smoke blows into the drop zone?" I asked.

"Hardly likely," Blackburn promised me confidently. "The prevailing winds around here are in the other direction."

So I said okay. And now the climactic hour was here. I stood and watched eagerly as the P-51 swooped through, trailing thick smoke.

Unfortunately, the prevailing north wind wasn't prevailing that day. Instead of blowing away, the smoke covered the drop zone. A paratroop officer, describing the events over a public-address system, said the jumpers would now have to use instruments to find their way to the ground safely, but their safety couldn't be guaranteed. Some might get hurt. The crowd gasped.

My heart rate rose to what felt like several hundred beats a minute.

To my enormous relief, the exercise went off beautifully. So did the rest of the gala. It went so well, in fact, that it not only made a big splash in the local news but completely upstaged the Washington celebration, which was supposed to have been the big national event of the day.

A few days later General Atkinson and I were playing golf on a course in Tampa. At about the fifth hole, when we were waiting to tee off, I told him the truth about the responsibility for the promotion at Drew Field. He was completely silent for about two minutes and then got up to tee off. Without looking up, he said, "Lieutenant, let's not bring this up ever again."

We never did.

The brass in Washington sent General Atkinson a medal and letter of commendation for helping to make Air Force Day so big a success. Instead of receiving a medal, I learned that I was capable of staging a big, complex promotion, holding it together, and making it work.

I also got my first real taste of professional risk, and I found that I loved it, along with everything else about PR. There was no doubt in my mind—this was the profession for me.

This book is a collection of true stories drawn from my long lifetime of experiences and observations in the public-relations business. There are 65 of these stories in the book. Each illustrates a point worth making about this profession. Almost every story includes the names of the participants, many of which you will recognize. Some of the stories are dramatic, some funny, some sad, and all, I hope, are instructive.

I can think of several reasons you might have picked up this book. Perhaps you have reached a crossroads in your life and are trying to make a choice of career, either as a young man or woman starting out or as an older person looking for something new to try. You are wondering whether public relations is the field for you. Very well—I have written this book partly with you in mind. I think you are going to find it helpful.

Or perhaps you are an executive, asking questions about PR as it may relate to your own company or business. You wonder, maybe, whether public relations can solve a certain problem for you, or whether it can be useful in a broader, more general way in improving the circumstances in which you operate. Can PR provide more recognition for your company, your product or your service? Can it help you introduce a new product or service or put more zoom into an old one? Can it influence public opinion or legislation in your favor? The book answers all these questions and many more that you may not have thought to ask.

Or it may be that you are simply curious about this profession and want to learn more about it. I've often thought it odd that public relations, which spends a lot of energy making companies, products, people, and ideas well known, has never done a particularly good job of making itself well known or understood. PR is rather mysterious to many—including the chief executive officers of some companies with large PR staffs.

I've met many a CEO who didn't know exactly what his or her own PR people were doing or what they could be asked to do. Often a CEO will inherit a public-relations staff from a previous CEO—and let the potentially good staff sit, barely or inadequately used, or used for the wrong assignments.

Often, too, public-relations people are hired by executives who don't know anything about PR, or how to identify a solidly qualified PR professional. I've known men and women with high-sounding titles—Public Relations Director, Vice President of Communications, and so on—whom I wouldn't even have hired for an entry-level job. Many companies put lawyers into top PR jobs—which makes as much sense as hiring a railroad engineer to fly an airplane.

My hope is that this book will fill some of the gaps in the business world's general knowledge of what public relations is, what it does, and how it does it.

Let me pause now to present my credentials briefly. Who is Robert J. Wood, and why should you pay attention to and accept what he says about public relations?

I've been a public-relations man virtually all my adult life, except for a necessary period of training as a newspaperman. That early training took place on the *Herald-Journal* and Associated Press in Syracuse, New York. Then came the war. After that, at the request of General Omar Bradley, I took a PR job with the Veterans Administration in Chicago. I worked there a short time, then joined the Chicago office of Carl Byoir (pronounced *buyer*) & Associates.

I stayed on Byoir's payroll for the next thirty-seven years. I became a vice president in 1951, executive vice president in 1961, president in 1965, chief executive officer in 1976, and chairman in 1981. I retired from Byoir in mid-1984. When I took over as president in 1965, Byoir had 125 employees representing 30 clients. When I stepped aside as CEO in 1983, the organization had a staff of 396 serving 239 clients.

I can hardly think of a better vantage point from which to have watched and participated in the continuing development of public relations over these four eventful decades. When I joined it, the Byoir organization was already one of the biggest and best-known PR agencies in the nation. Though it was finally destroyed in the mid-1980s after a disastrous merger—a story I will tell at the end of the book—it achieved a worldwide reputation before that unhappy event.

During my time there the Byoir organization counted among its clients some of the biggest and most powerful corporations, trade associations, and government agencies in the nation—indeed, in the world. I worked directly and actively with the chief executive officers of more than sixty of those clients. The Byoir

organization and I were involved in some of the most passionately debated issues of our times—issues such as racial equality,
atomic energy, mass transportation, and mass financing. In 1982
I was actively supervising twenty-one accounts, including such
blue-chip clients as RCA, Hughes Aircraft, ITT, Hallmark,
Arthur Andersen, A&P, Borg-Warner, American Bankers Association, and Kodak. You'll find stories about all these clients
in the book.

But not all our work involved big issues or larger-than-life
clients. We also got into some trivial episodes and some downright silly ones. But that's public relations. I'll lay it all out for
you.

The book will also convey, I hope, my basic optimism about
PR, a profession that is gaining respect in the general business
community. It used to be that PR budgets were among the first
to be cut in hard times. But during the 1981-1982 recession,
public-relations budgets actually increased overall for the first
time.

Business people are coming to understand that if good public-
relations advice is useful in good times, it is absolutely essential
when things go wrong, as some of the stories you are about to
read clearly illustrate.

Being a member of this profession has been not only a source
of pride, as my Air Force Day adventure illustrates, but also a
source of endless fun. It may be, in fact, that fun is the major
reward most people derive from the profession. My boss, Carl
Byoir, told me once that he was in PR mainly for the fun. The
stories I'm about to tell will show why he could make that
statement.

CHAPTER 1

EASY AND NOT-SO-EASY CLIENTS

The first thing a PR professional must learn is how to get along with clients and earn their respect. This requirement presents a variety of problems.

Some days, some clients are impossible to please.
Every public-relations professional must learn to take
this fact of life in stride.

—A story of RCA

DAVID SARNOFF was a man who impressed himself vividly on the memory of everybody he met. Not everybody liked him, but nobody ever forgot him.

He was the longtime chairman and chief executive officer of RCA, as well as the main founding genius of the NBC Radio and TV networks. He was a man of short stature, and some thought this might explain why his ego was big. During the Second World War he had been helpful to President Roosevelt in handling certain communications matters, and the president had conferred on him the title of General. He insisted on being addressed as General Sarnoff ever afterward.

He was not easy to please, and we at Byoir sometimes found it a struggle to satisfy him.

The General, as we always called him, enjoyed giving major speeches—perhaps six a year. We usually managed to get good coverage for him. But one day in the early 1960s, I learned that "good" wasn't going to be nearly enough.

The General had arranged to give a major speech in Atlanta about communications in the year 2000. We had done our usual thorough job of preparation—had arranged a press conference, prepared solidly informative press kits, and so on. But two days before the speech, I received a worried call from Ken Kilbon, Sarnoff's speech writer. Ken told me that the General considered his Atlanta speech the most important of his life and

3

wanted it reported on the front page of *The New York Times*. If it wasn't, the General had promised, heads would roll.

Ken and I knew well, of course, that you don't get front-page space on any major newspaper just by asking for it, nor is there any amount of money that can buy it. All we could do was hope. But the speech did have genuine news importance. At least that much was in our favor. As long as no major national or international news broke on the day of the speech, we had an outside chance of getting our front-page slot. But if there was a devastating earthquake somewhere or a major international figure was assassinated that day, then the General and his speech would be rudely banished to the back pages.

The day before the speech, I called the *Times*'s chief editor, Turner Catledge. I told him about the speech and I believe impressed him with its significance, but of course he would not make any commitment. He agreed only to read the copy I offered to send him.

On the day of the speech, I kept turning on radio news reports to find out if any major stories were breaking, but by enormous good luck, it was a fairly dull day. Nobody got assassinated, the stock market didn't crash, and the occupants of the White House and Congress seemed to be spending the day sleeping.

The suspense mounted as evening came. I knew that the bulldog edition of the next morning's *Times* would be available at about a quarter of nine. I asked the head of Byoir's financial news department to grab that edition fresh off the press and call me at home before the ink had a chance to dry.

I had no interest in dinner that night; Ken Kilbon told me later that he'd had no appetite either.

The call came about nine o'clock. The nub of the message was, "Break out the champagne!"

Not only was our story on the front page, but there was also a one-column picture of the General. I immediately called Ken at home with the good news. We were sure the General would be happy over the success of our efforts.

The next morning I saw with delight that the story and photo remained on the front page through all editions of the *Times*. Our victory was complete!

I phoned Ken as soon as I arrived at my office. "The General must be ecstatic!" I said.

Ken paused before replying. My heart skipped a beat. Finally, Ken said, "Well, Bob, I may be about to ruin your day. Maybe your whole week.".

"*What*? You mean he isn't happy?"

"I'm afraid not. I just left his office. He told me he's disappointed because the story isn't on the upper fold."

The message is loudest when it comes from the top.
— A story of Howard Hughes

Senator Owen Brewster of Maine was not gentle with Howard Hughes. But Hughes had the last laugh—with a little help from his PR counsel.

During the Second World War, the Army had asked Hughes to develop a gigantic transport plane that could carry 900 troops. His aircraft company had come up with a six-engined, oceangoing monster made of plywood. Its official name was the *Hercules*, but everybody called it the *Spruce Goose* when Hughes wasn't listening. The single test model sat in Long Beach, California, and had never been flown.

After the war, Hughes was summoned to hearings in the United States Senate. "You spent $11 million of the taxpayers' money," Senator Brewster roared at him, "and as far as anybody knows, that thing won't even fly!"

Hughes tried to explain that the war had ended before his development work on the *Hercules* was complete. Virtually all military development projects, not just his transport plane, had come to a screeching halt. But Brewster and some other senators were in no mood to let Hughes off the hook. They roughed him up.

Stung and angry, Hughes momentarily lost his cool. When a group of reporters buttonholed him outside the hearing room, he made a statement that he later regretted. "If the Hercules won't fly," he said bitterly, "I will leave the United States for good."

We at Byoir, as Hughes's PR counsel, also regretted the statement. It put a sharp cutting edge on an otherwise dull story about military procurement. Before we knew what hit us, newspapers and magazines were full of articles about the fat wartime profits raked in by military contractors. Hughes and his *Spruce Goose* figured in these stories prominently.

Before leaving Washington, Hughes called William Utley, the Byoir account executive in charge of the Hughes operations, and told him to set up a lavish press party. Writers and reporters from major publications were to be flown to California, shown the *Spruce Goose*, and given Hughes' side of the story. I was working in Byoir's Chicago office and was given the assignment of rounding up some key Chicago press people for the affair.

"Will Hughes himself show up at this party?" I asked Utley.
"I doubt it."
"But it won't be half as effective without him."
"Don't I know it," Utley agreed gloomily. "But Hughes rarely turns up at press parties."

Hughes at that time—the late 1940s—was not the recluse he was to become, disliking even shaking hands with people for fear of picking up germs. In the 1940s he was sociable enough, particularly with beautiful movie stars. His lack of enthusiasm for press affairs, though, was becoming a major problem for Byoir. As Utley and I both knew, journalists aren't particularly interested in going to an affair where they will be handed canned statements by a bunch of PR people. What any good journalist wants is to hear the story directly from the top executives involved—preferably *the* top executive.

"I think you ought to push Hughes on this," I told Utley.
"I've tried. He won't come."

"Try one more time. Without him, all that's going to happen is we'll get a lot of new wisecracking stories about the *Goose*."

Utley sighed. "Okay. I'll give it one more shot."

Somehow, Utley did it. Hughes resisted at first, then capitulated. And not grudgingly, either.

This was an element of Hughes's complicated character that I admired as long as I knew him—he never did things halfway. Once he decided on a course of action, he waded into it with a whole heart and on a grand scale.

Having decided to participate in our California press party, he proceeded to make it a more spectacular success than either Utley or I had dared dream of. He showed up early for our opening reception at the Los Angeles Biltmore—one of the few times I ever knew him to attend a press party—and stood at the entrance with Utley and shook hands with more than a hundred writers and reporters as they entered.

When they were all in the reception room, he turned to Utley and asked, "Bill, what are we giving these people?"

Utley replied, "Oh, the usual. Martinis, scotch—"

"No," said Hughes, "I mean what are we giving them as gifts?"

"Gifts? Why, we hadn't planned on anything like that."

"I'll tell you what I want you to do," Hughes said. "I want each of these people to get a gold cigarette case and matching lighter. And then I want you to find out from each of them what their favorite booze is, and I want a case delivered to everybody's home."

"But you're talking about 115 people!" Utley said, astonished. "Do you know what that would cost?"

"Did I ask what it would cost?" Hughes replied. He then left the hotel.

As it turned out, the total bill for the gifts was some $12,000, an enormous sum in the 1940s—roughly the average price of a three-bedroom suburban home.

On Sunday morning, the journalists were herded into motorboats, and we chugged out into the ocean off Long Beach. As we stared, fascinated, the *Spruce Goose* taxied past us majestically with Howard Hughes himself at the controls. It was obviously too big to fly. Its wingspan was just one inch short of 320 feet—longer than a football field. It was the biggest wingspan of any airplane in history.

Hughes taxied out into open water. Then, suddenly, the huge craft gathered speed, went bounding across the ocean, and lifted into the air as we gaped in amazement.

Hughes flew only a thousand yards and never ventured higher than seventy feet. But that was enough. His point was made.

There are four postscripts to this story.

Postscript 1: The *Spruce Goose* never flew again.

Postscript 2: As far as I know, Howard Hughes never attended another press party.

Postscript 3: At my suggestion, Utley hired the George Gallup organization to poll public attitudes toward Hughes one week after the *Spruce Goose* proved itself. It turned out that our press gathering—with Hughes's help—had promoted a lot of goodwill. Some 94 percent of the people polled said they were much more inclined to side with Howard Hughes than with Senator Brewster.

Postscript 4: Owen Brewster lost his next bid for reelection to the Senate. His opponent's campaign fund was enriched by a generous contribution from Howard Hughes.

Appearances are deceiving, as are early signs and omens. Never jump to conclusions about how well something is going until all the returns are in.
                    —A story of Black & White Scotch
                        and a worrisome moment

John Malloy, sales vice president of Black & White Scotch, owned by Fleischman Distilling, was looking for an agency to handle public relations for his brand of whiskey. He contacted

Byoir in the early 1970's, telling us he had made similar contacts with four other large PR outfits, and he invited us to submit a proposal and put ourselves in competition for his company's business.

And he was talking about big business. Black & White had been the best-selling Scotch whiskey in the United States for about five years after the Second World War, but had then gone into a decline that lasted for twenty years. The main reason for the decline, John and his colleagues agreed, was ineffective use of public relations and promotion. The management was determined to shore up this weakness by making a substantial investment in PR for at least the next three years.

John was aware that the Byoir organization had represented Schenley for some twenty years and had played a key role in moving Dewar's Scotch into the number-two spot. When we said we were interested, we were scheduled to appear before a decision-making group in about ten days and, like our four competitors, given one hour to make our pitch.

We worked hard to prepare a strong, well-organized proposal. On the appointed day, two colleagues and I walked into the Black & White boardroom to face the jury. Eight members of B&W's top management came to the meeting, among them Frank Fitzmaurice, the president and CEO.

We began our pitch by talking about some successful Byoir campaigns of the past—concentrating, of course, on promotions involving products similar to B&W's. Then we shifted quickly into recommendations of specific promotions and publicity ideas that we felt would help achieve B&W's goals.

Some of our ideas were creative—for example, we proposed to find a genuine Scottish chef and send him on a multicity tour of the nation. At each city he would appear on local TV and talk about fine cooking, with special emphasis on Scottish dishes and on recipes using Scotch whiskey. A B&W bottle would be prominently in view during his appearance.

But as we began unveiling this and other ideas, I felt an inexplicable chill in the air. The chill emanated from the top man, Frank Fitzmaurice, who looked impatient, annoyed, and fidgety. He grimaced, rubbed his forehead and his jaw, poured glass after glass of ice water.

I reacted with growing embarrassment. This was by no means the first such presentation I had ever made in my PR career, and I had the experience to know we had a good, stimulating proposal. Why was Fitzmaurice being so discourteous? Couldn't he at least wait and hear us out before turning thumbs down?

I became so discouraged that I was strongly tempted to cut our proposal short, thank the executives for their time, and leave. But I plowed through patiently to the end.

When our formal proposal was complete, I asked if there were any questions. Frank Fitzmaurice was the first to respond. He apologized for his seeming inattention and fidgety behavior— the reason, he said, was a splitting headache. He added with a grin that the headache was not the result of a hangover from overindulgence in his company's product; nor did it have anything to do with our presentation. It was just a headache that had come mysteriously and, he hoped, would soon depart the same way.

He then said, "You invited us to ask questions, but as far as I'm concerned, I have no questions. You guys get my vote."

To my astonishment, it was as simple as that. The contract was signed the next day.

And incidentally, our promotion involving the Scottish chef was a thundering success. Carolyn Walden of our radio-TV department arranged the tour and then accompanied the chef to his many city stops. They were welcomed everywhere. And the effort sold a lot of B&W Scotch. Within a few months of our going to work, the long slide of B&W was halted.

Try not to let clients tell you how to do your job.
          —A story of Dr. Willard Libby, Carbon 14,
                              and cosmic rays

During my first three years with the Byoir organization I kept in regular touch with about fifty scientists at the University of Chicago. The University was a Byoir client, and my job was to stay abreast of what the scientists were working on and generate media coverage when newsworthy developments cropped up. One of the more interesting of these people was Dr. Willard Libby, a physicist who was eventually to win a Nobel Prize for his work on some aspects of radioactivity.

One day he told me about some experiments with a substance called Carbon 14. He had determined that the rate of radioactive decay in Carbon 14 could be measured with precision. Such measurements, he said, could be used as a basis for fixing the age of fossils, bones, and other archaeological finds. Specifically, he could measure the age of any material up to 30,000 years within 200 years.

"You mean you can fix the age more exactly than ever before?" I asked. My news sense was shouting *"Story!"*

Dr. Libby replied, "Yes, much more exactly than has ever been possible up to now."

"This Carbon 14, then—it's a sort of atomic clock?"

"Yes."

Dr. Libby then went on to talk excitedly of another outgrowth of his radioactivity research. He had discovered, he said, that the level of cosmic radiation—that is, the natural radioactivity impinging on the earth from elsewhere in the universe—had remained constant for at least 25,000 years. He had data to back up his statement. His data seemed to disprove an earlier theory, widely accepted until then, that the level of cosmic radiation fluctuated.

This new theory about cosmic radiation didn't stimulate my news sense to any great degree, but I reacted politely.

As was customary, I agreed to delay releasing any story to the media at large until Dr. Libby had published his findings in the scientific press. I went back to my office, wrote a story that conveyed my fascination with the "atomic clock" breakthrough, and sent the draft to Dr. Libby for his approval.

He phoned me the next day and asked me to come and see him. When I got to his office, he said I'd written my story upside-down—I had led off with the Carbon 14 part of it and followed with the cosmic ray part. Dr. Libby said it ought to be the other way around, for the cosmic ray discovery was far more significant to the world of science than the business about the atomic clock.

I told him my article was intended for the general press—the newspapers, magazines, and radio and TV reports aimed at the lay public. My news sense told me almost beyond a doubt, I said, that the atomic clock story would get more attention from all those editors and their readers and listeners than would the cosmic ray story. In a good press release, as in any good news story, the most important, startling, and eye-catching material always should come first.

Dr. Libby and I debated the question for about half an hour and I couldn't budge him. I was relatively new at the game then, and there was a limit to my license to argue with clients. So I gave up, went back to my office, and rewrote the piece his way.

He called me promptly after seeing this second draft to say that he liked it fine. I told him we would be sending it out to the news media on Thursday for release the following morning, in exactly the form he had approved. I warned him, however, that we would have no control over what happened to it after it left our hands. Editors would be free, as always, to perform surgery on it in any way they liked. Dr. Libby said he understood.

The story won widespread coverage on the day of its release, making the front pages of most major newspapers. I couldn't help grinning when I saw that virtually every paper had restructured the story in the way I had originally built it. The Carbon 14 material came first in almost every story and of course was featured in all the headlines. The cosmic ray business was banished to the end of the piece and in many cases was cut down to a couple of offhand paragraphs.

Over the next ten days we were bombarded with requests for more information, for interviews with Dr. Libby, for photo sessions. *Life, Look*, and other big magazines sent crews around. Everybody wanted to talk about atomic clocks; hardly anyone seemed to care about cosmic rays. In addition, archaeologists and other scientists from all over the world phoned and wrote to find out more about carbon dating and to ask if they could send samples to be subjected to the process.

When things finally quieted down, I received one more phone call from Dr. Libby. He said the past hectic weeks had been for him both a new experience and a lesson. "I'll make you a promise, Mr. Wood," he said. "From now on, I'll take care of the lab, and you take care of the public relations."

That's a lesson that some clients learn more readily than others. But even when they learn it grudgingly, it's a lesson you should never stop trying to teach.

Don't be downhearted when people fail to appreciate your efforts. It's the nature of the business.
—A story of S. C. Johnson and a new shampoo

This is a story about—I'm not sure what I want to call it. Ingratitude, perhaps? Lack of appreciation? Fear? The reason I don't know is that I was never able to fathom the motives of the man and woman I'm going to tell you about.

At any rate, it is the story of a time when the Byoir organization put forth a prodigious effort with what I and others thought were outstanding results. But not everybody sang our praises, and one reason I tell the story is because it illustrates a sometimes frustrating fact about public relations.

Though there are times when a PR effort produces results that show up quickly and can be seen and measured, that doesn't happen often. More commonly, the results of public relations develop slowly and are at least partly subjective. One person may look at these results and say, "Wonderful!" while another person may say, "So what?" In public relations, there will be many times when you feel you deserve a pat on the back but don't get one.

What do you do then? Just take it in stride. Shrug, go on about your business, and be patient. Those slow-developing results *will* develop in time if you have done your job right. And finally, a day will come when you will be able to say, "See? *There* are the results!"

Byoir had gone to work for S. C. Johnson & Son, Inc., of Racine, Wisconsin, popularly known as Johnson's Wax, back in 1951 and had helped introduce a lot of appealing new consumer products to the market. One of our most successful promotions for Johnson—indeed, for anybody—took place in 1978. It was the kickoff promotion for Agree, a new shampoo for women.

The Johnson people, who assigned this job in the spring, said they wanted Agree to hit the market with a major splash in late June. We were told not to worry about the budget. Sam Johnson, the "& Son" of the firm, who had taken over the CEO title from his father, considered Agree the most important new venture his company had undertaken in many years.

We were given two specific objectives:—to create that introductory splash, beginning with a major, newsmaking press conference of some kind, and then to work with the Johnson marketing people until Agree had seized 4 percent of the $800-million-a-year women's shampoo market. Our promotion was to be the opening shot of the entire campaign, we were told. It would come before any advertising or other selling efforts.

It made us happy, of course, to know the Johnson people were willing to put that much faith in us. It also provided a tough challenge. The kickoff promotion had to be *good*.

After a few creative sessions, we began to develop an idea. We asked choreographer Peter Gennaro if he would be interested in creating a show for our press affair—something involving hair or hairstyles, of course. He was not only interested, he was enthusiastic. He quickly refined our idea into a show to be called "Sixty Years of Dancin' Hair." Couples would demonstrate the popular dances of each era, and they would of course be appropriately dressed and coiffed.

Peter suggested further that the affair be held at New York New York, a popular discothèque of the 1970s, the successor of the old Toots Shor Restaurant. It was roomy enough for the hugh crowd we hoped to gather. We planned to invite a large cluster of Hollywood celebrities, particularly those known for their dancing talents, as well as executives of leading stores and store chains where Agree would be sold. Needless to say, we hoped to attract a big press, radio, and TV contingent too.

Advance preparations went swimmingly. It was expensive, but our instructions from Johnson were that we shouldn't worry about money, so we didn't—at least, not all the time. Ginger Rogers agreed to be mistress of ceremonies, and among the dancers we snagged were Ruby Keeler, Alice Faye, Alexis Smith, Virginia Mayo, Gloria Dehaven, Yvonne De Carlo, Peter Lawford, Bob Fosse, and George Murphy—a largely middle-aged but certainly stellar group. Most of them would be demonstrating dances of which they had personal memories.

The level of enthusiasm was stunningly high as the big day approached—the highest I've seen in the many promotions I've been involved in. What we had here wasn't just another new-product introduction but a show-biz event. The aging film stars we had assembled were participating not just for the money but because they felt the bash would be fun. They *enjoyed* performing those old dances and reliving memories of days gone by.

If the idea of our party was that attractive to the participants, I thought, how would it go over with the media and their readers and viewers? Could it be we had a genuine PR triumph coming up?

I thought it was possible—but then my optimism was dampened by a wet blanket.

Josh Henderson (not his real name), Johnson's public-relations chief, came to New York shortly before the big day, along with a woman he had recently hired for his staff. They attended a rehearsal of the show on the afternoon before our party. The woman remarked that, in her opinion, Ginger Rogers wasn't the best mistress of ceremonies we could have found.

Several people heard the remark and it quickly got back to Ginger Rogers, who exploded. She spoke to Peter Gennaro, who immediately urged Josh Henderson to keep his new woman staffer out of Ginger Rogers's sight. Henderson agreed, and the storm seemed to blow over.

I forgot all about it the next day, when our press party was the roaring suceess I had hoped for. It began at noon and lasted five hours. Some 300 media people had been attracted to it, and I knew we were going to get incredible coverage. I could feel it in the air.

At about half past three, the formal part of the program ended, but the music continued and many of the guests started to dance just for the fun of it. Feeling exhilarated but exhausted, I started to head back to my office when Josh Henderson buttonholed me and took me into an empty room. He thanked me, Gene Oliva, Elaine Benvenuto, Carolyn Walden, and the rest of the Byoir staff for a press party that exceeded his highest hopes. About ten of us had been actively involved, and I said I would pass on his comments to the others. And to show his appreciation in a more direct way, Henderson proposed to return to New York in a week or two and take us all out to dinner and a Broadway play.

Back at the office, I passed this on to the group. For days we basked in the glory of a job well done. The coverage in the press and on radio and TV was massive. We were bombarded with phone calls, letters, and memos from various Johnson people in Racine, expressing their thanks.

But after about two weeks had gone by, I started to wonder about that dinner-and-theater evening. Josh Henderson had never set a date for it—indeed, he had never mentioned it again. I was puzzled.

I happened to talk to Josh by phone one day on another matter, and at the end of the conversation I found what I hoped was a graceful way to bring up the planned New York evening. I had told the Byoir group to be ready for it, I said. When did Josh think it would be?

He muttered vaguely about work pressures. He didn't know when he would be able to make it to New York.

Some kind of chill was being transmitted along the phone lines from Racine. I didn't understand it. He had been effervescent with gratitude two weeks back when he had proposed the evening on the town, but now all the effervescence was gone. What had happened? Had I said or done something to irritate him? I couldn't think of anything. Mystified and disturbed, I said good-bye to Josh and hung up.

A couple of days later, by chance, a Byoir staffer, in Racine on an unrelated mission, heard the explanation. The woman on Henderson's staff who had critized Ginger Rogers had continued to criticize other participants and other aspects of our press party. Somehow she had convinced Josh that it was all sizzle and no steak.

I don't know to this day what caused her to view the affair so negatively. As I said, judgments of a public-relations effort often are at least partly subjective in nature. People review a press party in the same way they might review a play or a book, and it is by no means unusual for reviewers to have sharply different opinions. The woman was certainly entitled to make her own assessment of our effort and to state her views. But I was perturbed by Josh's apparent about-face—and its suddenness. What can she have told him to change his mind so quickly and completely? It is a question that still puzzles me today.

I told the Byoir staff team, of course, to forget about the proposed evening on the town.

We went on with the job of introducing Agree to the public, developing various promotions to follow our opening splash. One of the more successful was a promotion involving college homecoming queens and scholarships. And in a very short time, tangible results began to flow in.

As these results piled up, we were less and less at the mercy of subjective reviews. If somebody accused us of producing a lot of sizzle, we were now in a position to say, "Look for yourself. *There* is the steak."

A steak is a steak—it isn't subjective. You don't have to convince people it's there. It can't be argued away or reviewed out of existence.

One of our biggest steaks was an accounting of the sheer

volume of TV, radio, and print coverage we got for Agree and the various Agree promotions during our first eight months on the job. By actual count, the total circulation of our story in print media alone during those eight months was 484 million.

But our juiciest steak was the marketing history of Agree itself. At the end of eight months the new shampoo had a total market share of not 4 percent, the original objective, but a full 6 percent.

In the end, it was one of the most successful new-product introductions Byoir ever handled. If you can get objective results like that, you can shrug off bad reviews.

After you've been in the PR business for a time, you develop hunches about people. While these intuitive feelings shouldn't be your only basis for action, you should always listen to them.
— A story of John DeLorean and a star-crossed relationship

John DeLorean, a former General Motors executive who at one time had been spoken of as a candidate to become the giant automaker's CEO, announced in the early 1980s that he was going to found his own company. It was to manufacture pricey sports cars, and its main plant would be near Belfast, Northern Ireland.

The British government was enthusiastic. The new plant offered a promise of economic revival in a chronically depressed region. The government therefore arranged many millions of dollars' worth of financing for DeLorean's new company.

Before the first car rolled off the assembly line, however, DeLorean ran out of money. When he went back to London for more, a more frugal leadership was in control and the answer was no.

So DeLorean turned to the private investment community, not only in Europe but also in New York and Hollywood. But by this time the press and broadcast media were turning unfriendly. Reporters on both sides of the Atlantic enjoyed pointing out the contrast between John DeLorean's public poor-mouthing and his jet-set private life. Not much was written about the DeLorean car, and what was published was mostly negative. (This was too bad; the car was actually a pretty good one.) Amid all this unfriendly comment, the dashing manufacturer couldn't find the financial backing he needed.

So he turned to Carl Byoir & Associates, which, he had been told, enjoyed a reputation for helping clients in trouble. Bob Henkel, one of our executive vice presidents, and I went to see him at his office on Park Avenue. He explained his problems and his number-one need—a more friendly reception in the international financial community. With our offices all over the world, and our wide experience with this sort of assignment, we believed we could help. Together we signed a one-year contract with a budget of $135,000.

We did help. Over the next four months we developed some good publicity in both the United States and Europe. We worked up feature stories on both the man and his car, some of which appeared in the general media and some in specialized publications read by car lovers. We set up some one-on-one interviews between the urbane entrepreneur and top magazine, newspaper, and TV people. We produced a short film for TV use. And we began to regain for DeLorean a better image in the business press.

He seemed satisfied, but it was hard to tell. I began to have uneasy feelings about him. He seemed preoccupied, unable or unwilling to focus on PR activities during some of our meetings. At one meeting he seemed particularly tense, and I sensed that he had problems, perhaps big ones, he wasn't telling us about.

Then the nature of our relationship abruptly changed.

We received a phone call from David Scott, one of the top public-relations executives of the Ford Motor Company. Scott said his company was planning to hire outside PR counsel and wondered if we would like to make a presentation. There were to be several other PR agencies in the running. We were happy to take a crack at it.

Ford's main reason for hiring outside help was to promote its new car models, particularly in the local media. So in presentation we emphasized our record of success in other new-product introduction campaigns. We said nothing about our relationship with DeLorean or with an older and pricier client, Alfa Romeo. We doubted Ford would consider either DeLorean's or Alfa Romeo's cars competitors of its own popular-priced models. We assumed, in any case, that Ford knew about our work for these two clients. There had never been any secret about either—how could there be? Our client list was distributed far and wide.

We won the competition. Dave Scott, when he phoned to tell us the good news a few days after our presentation, said Ford had in mind a budget in the neighborhood of $500,000 a year for our work.

Then he brought up the subject of our other automotive clients. He asked me exactly what the relationships were. I said we had worked for Alfa Romeo for about two years and DeLorean for four months, and I explained our feeling that neither company could be considered a competitor in Ford's segment of the market.

In the case of Alfa Romeo, Scott agreed. But he said he and his colleagues would object to our continuing a relationship with DeLorean if we were to sign a contract with Ford. I said I'd get back to him.

It was a quandary with no perfect solutions. Whatever I did would be wrong. We had a contract with John DeLorean, and if he wished to hold us to it, of course we would honor it. On the other hand, I felt he would understand our enthusiasm for a $500,000 budget. The Ford contract was nearly $400,000 bigger than the DeLorean one.

Furthermore, we had that strong hunch that he was having problems we didn't know about, and that if we stuck with him, we might land in some hidden quagmire ourselves.

I called DeLorean, told him about the offer from Ford, and said we would honor our contract. He was irritated at first but after a few minutes simply asked in his preoccupied way if we would recommend another PR agency for him. I recommended three. DeLorean and Byoir parted amicably.

I was tempted to remind him that he was a bit overdue on a $35,000 payment that he owed us, but I decided in the end to leave that to our accounting department.

We went to work for Ford. DeLorean hired another PR agency, but a few months later the roof fell in on him. It became evident that his money woes were considerably worse than he had been letting on. He managed to produce some cars at last, but they sold poorly, particularly in the United States. His company finally went belly up.

And we never did collect that $35,000.

Some companies and some executives have an innate sense of good public relations.
—A story of Hallmark Cards and a bird's nest

Hallmark Cards was founded by Joyce Hall, who acted as its CEO for many years. His son, Donald, took over the CEO post from him in time. Both men had an innate sense of good public relations and it was a pleasure to work with them.

As a purveyor of sentimental greeting cards, Hallmark, more than most companies, had to take the greatest care not to present a public image of coldness or excessive attention to the bottom line. The company not only avoided such an image but leaned over backward in the opposite direction.

When its hometown, Kansas City, Missouri, was hit by disastrous floods one spring in the early 1950s, the city's economy felt the impact heavily. The record-breaking floods made national news, causing people all over the country to rethink plans that had involved Kansas City. Business conventions were canceled; vacationers went elsewhere; hotel and restaurant business slumped dramatically; companies that had planned to establish offices or plants in Kansas City made new plans.

At the time Hallmark had been a Byoir client for several years. Joyce Hall called to say he wanted the Byoir organization to help counteract his home city's disastrous PR. Our fees and expenses, he said, would be paid entirely by Hallmark.

A team of ten Byoir media specialists was immediately dispatched to Kansas City for two weeks. They developed a series of stories and photos to demonstrate that Kansas City was cleaning up fast after the flood and would emerge better than ever.

It wasn't easy, but in time we got the needed results. Canceled conventions were rescheduled; hotels and restaurants filled up again; and Kansas City was back to its old, bustling self.

And Hallmark picked up the tab. That was the kind of company it was.

On another occasion some years later, Hallmark started to build a warehouse and distribution center in New Jersey. The steel skeleton was just about complete when somebody discovered that a pair of birds had built a nest in a corner. There were eggs in the nest.

Hallmark ordered all construction stopped immediately. It stayed stopped until the birds finished raising their family and flew away.

The story had an appropriately happy and sentimental ending. After the birds had departed and just before construction resumed, a hurricane blasted through the area. If the building's walls and roof had been partially installed at the time, there would probably have been heavy damage. As it was, the steel skeleton presented no face to the winds, and there was no damage at all. Kindness had been rewarded!

This story charmed a journalist named Max Gunther when he heard of it in the middle 1960s. Max was a freelance who wrote for many magazines, among them the *Saturday Evening Post*, which enjoyed enormous power and prestige until its death in 1969. The *Post*'s editors had asked Max to write an article on what they called the "love industry"—companies that earned income from the public's yearning for romance. So Max wanted to talk to a company that made Valentine cards and the name Hallmark came to mind. When he learned that Hallmark was a Byoir client, he dropped in at Byoir's New York office to do some preliminary probing, and one of our staff members told him the story about the bird.

The story grabbed him. He wrote it into his article on the love industry.

"This bird story really brings a tear to the eye," an editor commented sourly after reading it. "It sounds too goody-goody to be true."

Max responded that he had checked it with three independent sources, and named them. They were the Byoir staff member who was known and liked at the *Post*; a Hallmark executive; and a woman named Joy Perry, member of a birdwatching club that had monitored the Hallmark episode.

"But it reads like a fairy tale," the editor grumbled. "Virtue gets rewarded and all that."

"Exactly!" Max said. "It's a story about a company that not only sells sentiment but practices it. Nothing could be more relevant to my piece. Listen, if you whack this little anecdote out of this piece, I'll never forgive you!"

The anecdote survived uncut.

Hallmark was the kind of client every public relations counselor loves to work for.

And some companies and executives don't *have an innate sense of good public relations.*
—A story of Borg-Warner and a riverbank town

Borg-Warner Chemical produced thermoplastics that were used to make telephones, automobile parts, football helmets, and hundreds of other products. In 1976, when the company decided to build a new plant, it sent a team out to acquire a site.

I don't think I've ever seen a job which, from a PR point of view, was more thoroughly botched.

The site-acquisition team was headed by a man I'll call Larry Ellis, an old-fashioned, hard-driving engineer-executive who was intensely loyal to his company and guided by the motto "Get the job done, whatever . . ." It didn't matter to him if people's toes got stepped on. With no sense of public relations, he established a goal, fixed his eyes on it, and charged straight at it like a bull.

The company's requirements for its new plant site were specific and not easy to fulfill. Polymers to be used in the plant were made by suppliers that were mainly located along the Mississippi River in Louisiana. So Borg-Warner wanted its new plant to be on the river, allowing polymers to be delivered to the plant by barge. The polymers, in liquid form, would then be pumped directly from barge to plant through pipes.

Larry Ellis and his team found a site that satisfied all the engineering requirements admirably. The problem was that this site wasn't empty land. It was occupied—by the tiny town of Saverton, Missouri.

But it didn't trouble Larry that a town was in his path. He saw a quick way to solve that problem. He would simply buy the town.

Without telling either us at Byoir or Borg-Warner's own public-relations department, he and his team began very quietly buying up options on Saverton residents' property. There were only a few hundred residents, most of them were poor and happy to get the money. The team collected some 200 options— about half the town. Borg-Warner's name wasn't used; the transactions were handled through a third party.

There was a small Methodist church and cemetery in the proposed plant site, but not even this troubled the PR-blind Larry Ellis. He envisioned tearing down the church and moving the graves somewhere else.

About ten miles north of Saverton was Mark Twain's hometown, Hannibal. The Hannibal newspaper got wind of the mysterious buying-up of Saverton properties and started to investigate. Borg-Warner stayed hidden behind its buying agent, but the newspaper did find clues pointing to a large company and a proposed new chemical plant. It began to publish stories full of dark forebodings.

Nothing could have been more badly handled.

Byoir's account executive serving Borg-Warner, Bob Kelly, was stunned when news of this project finally began to reach his ears. He had some earnest and worried talks with Doug Mueller, Borg-Warner's PR chief. Doug, too, recognized the potentially disastrous scope of the PR mistakes that were being made down there in Saverton.

With Doug's backing, Bob Kelly went to a meeting at the company's headquarters in Parkersburg, West Virginia. At this meeting, attended by executives of Borg-Warner Chemical and by Larry Ellis and his team, Bob spoke in the strongest possible terms of the PR nightmare being created at the proposed new plant site. Bob predicted that when the public found out what the company was up to, there would be a tremendous outcry. All the makings were there for an image of a huge company cynically squashing a tiny town—and worse, doing it secretly. When the public finally asked about the secrecy, the answer was going to seem all too obvious—the intended plant was to be a noxious one, spilling poisonous chemicals into the air and the river.

Bob urged that a concerted public relations effort be initiated right away to kill this image before it got too difficult to handle. He suggested that the company immediately tell the local media candidly of its plans, emphasizing the fact that the new plant would create jobs in a chronically depressed region. Another move he suggested was that civic leaders and journalists be taken on trips to other, similar Borg-Warner plants, which were strikingly clean and odor-free. The fact is that manufacture of thermoplastics, carefully engineered, does not create any significant pollution hazard.

But Larry Ellis and his team laughed Bob Kelly out of the room. They didn't need PR people in their way, they said.

The outcome was every bit as bad as Bob predicted. As the facts about the proposed plant dribbled out into the open one by one, a tidal wave of protest arose. The Missouri Environmental Protection Agency was in the forefront of the protest, vociferously backed by individual environmentalists, clean-up-the-river groups, fishing interests, and a varied group of area residents who were unhappy over the sneaky way Borg-Warner had gone about acquiring the site. These people demanded that the United States Army Corps of Engineers hold hearings and make a thorough study of the whole project before letting it go ahead. The proceedings dragged on for a year and seemed likely to go on for all eternity. Finally, Borg-Warner announced that it was abandoning the Saverton site.

When the president of Borg-Warner Chemical came to New York some time later, he was frankly apologetic. "We made a mistake not listening to you people," he admitted. "And a very expensive mistake it was, too."

The company found another site, in Mississippi. This time, all Bob Kelly's recommendations, plus a few new ones, were carried out. The local citizenry welcomed the new plant with open arms. And Borg-Warner has since expanded the plant several times, with never a word of protest.

Some executives are natural-born performers. They aren't common. When you run into one, be grateful.
—A story of Robert Maynard Hutchins and a radio show

Robert Maynard Hutchins was chancellor of the University of Chicago, where the first successful atomic pile was built in the early 1940's. In 1947, Hutchins learned of something called the Smyth Report, and it filled him with fear and rage.

This report, written by a Princeton physics professor, Harold D. Smyth, described in detail how to build an atomic pile. For reasons that have never been well explained, the United States Atomic Energy Commission quietly released this document for world distribution in 1945, shortly after the Japanese surrendered. It was translated into Russian, Chinese, and other languages.

When Dr. Hutchins learned of this casual distribution, he was horrified, for the building of an atomic pile is a necessary precursor to the making of an atomic bomb.

In 1947, the United States was the only nation in the world capable of making such a bomb but Hutchins predicted that this monopoly would soon end. (It did—in Russia—just two years later.) Hutchins felt it was essential that people everywhere be made aware of the terrible dangers that lay ahead in a world where nuclear weapons capability can spread from one nation to another.

And so he called me to his office. The university was a Byoir client, and one of my earliest assignments after joining Byoir's Chicago office had been to work with Hutchins, for whom I developed tremendous respect. Hutchins told me of his concern over the Smyth Report, saying it was the worst blunder in United States history and that his fears should be made public. We agreed that a good start would be an article under his byline, placed in a major magazine, followed if possible by a talk or interview on network radio (TV at the time was only in its infancy).

I went to work. I will always remember this assignment because it gave me an opportunity to see a natural-born performer in action. Dr. Hutchins was a man of awesome poise and fluency, a very tall and handsome man who, if he had chosen, could have made his living as an actor or radio-TV announcer.

Early in 1948 Byoir's magazine department in New York placed Hutchins's byliner with *American* magazine, which had only a few more years to live but at the time was one of the biggest national publications. The article, titled "The Bomb Secret Is Out!" passionately set forth Hutchins's view that the only way to avoid a global nuclear holocaust would be to establish a world government.

Meanwhile, I had been working on the radio angle. I'd called a man named Bill Ray, head of NBC radio news in Chicago, and asked him if he'd like to put Hutchins on the air. Bill said he would suggest the idea to his New York headquarters and call me back.

A few days went by. Then *American* hit the newsstands, and

the Hutchins article made a satisfyingly big splash—helped along, of course, by our press releases sent to hundreds of other publications in the United States and Europe. The day after the magazine was published, Bill Ray called me back.

His call came about two in the afternoon. He said New York wanted Hutchins as the lead guest on the NBC network's "World News Roundup" at six o'clock that night, in a segment to be broadcast live from Chicago. Bill gave me some very careful instructions. What he wanted from Hutchins was a two-minute statement, covering the chancellor's fears about the Smyth Report and his urgent call for a world government. "And when I say two minutes, I mean *exactly* two minutes," Bill said. "I don't mean two minutes five seconds, and I don't mean one minute fifty seconds. Got it?"

"Got it," I said. "Two minutes."

"Right. Now one last thing. Have your man here at our studio at five-forty for a dry run."

"Five-forty. Right. See you then."

And a young public-relations man started hustling. I called Vesta Orlich, Hutchins's secretary (later his second wife). She got him out of a meeting, and returned to the phone to tell me that Hutchins wanted to do the radio appearance and wanted me to prepare that two-minute statement.

"Send it over here as fast as you can," Vesta said.

"Okay. And be sure he gets to the studio by five-forty."

"I'll do my best," she promised.

I sat down at my typewriter. It wasn't an easy assignment, boiling down Hutchins's *American* piece into a statement of exactly two minutes' duration. It took me an hour. It was about 3:30 when I folded the typed statement, put it in an envelope, sealed it, and dispatched a messenger to rush it to Hutchins's office.

I arrived at the NBC studios at about 5:30 and checked to make sure there hadn't been any last-minute problems, but everything was on schedule. At 5:40, the time when Hutchins had been instructed to present himself, I went out to the reception desk to meet him.

He wasn't there.

Nor was he there at a 5:45.

Nor was he there at 5:50. There were now just ten minutes to go until airtime. I was getting soaked with perspiration.

At about 5:52, Bill Ray came out to the reception area and asked, "Where is he?"

"I don't know," I said helplessly. "A traffic jam, maybe."

"If he isn't here in another two minutes, we'll have to cancel him."

Hutchins finally showed up at 5:54. He was perfectly calm, unhurried. He muttered something about traffic but seemed serenely confident that this minor hitch wouldn't interfere with his radio appearance. I hustled him to the studio, but there was no longer time for the dry run Bill Ray had talked about. The studio staff showed Hutchins to a chair and introduced him to the announcer. They were jittery. He was entirely relaxed.

He reached into a pocket and pulled out my envelope. When I saw it, I almost fainted. It was still sealed.

With the greatest deliberation, he opened the envelope, pulled out the statement, and read it silently to himself—as coolly as if there were two hours, rather than two minutes, to go till airtime. He changed a couple of words, then sat back to wait for his cue.

The news show began. Hutchins was introduced and proceeded to read that statement absolutely flawlessly. It was as smooth a performance as any I've ever seen. He didn't just read it in a mechanical way—his voice was rich with cadence, and he paused for emphasis exactly as I would have coached him if given the chance.

He kept his eye on the studio clock, adjusting his speaking pace by it. He finished the statement in precisely two minutes.

He was a natural-born performer. I haven't met many others. Unfortunately, the breed is rare.

*As a public-relations professional, you will often hear
wonderful stories that are told to you, unfortunately,
in confidence. You must respect that confidence no
matter how much it hurts.*
　　—a story of Enrico Fermi and Benito Mussolini

I sat on a perfectly fantastic story for about forty years. There
were many times when I wanted to tell it to journalists I liked,
for it was a story that didn't deserve to die in the dark. But I had
promised never to tell it during the lifetime of the man who was
its main protagonist. He was a client, and I felt bound to respect
his wish.

The man died of cancer in 1955. I still sat on the story. I am
not entirely sure why. I am now about to tell it for the first time
in public. Afterward, we'll look briefly at the importance of
keeping promises in the world of public relations. Treasure your
reputation for integrity. It may be the most important piece of
professional equipment you possess.

The story I sat on had to do with Dr. Enrico Fermi, the great
Italian physicist who produced the world's first self-sustaining
nuclear chain reaction at the University of Chicago, and ushered
in the atomic age on December 2, 1942. Dr. Fermi's work in
Chicago was largely responsible for the fact that America developed a working atomic bomb just one step ahead of Nazi Germany. Our bombing of Hiroshima and Nagasaki has been loudly
lamented since, but most United States military strategists believe those bombs saved a million American lives by making an
invasion of Japan unnecessary.

The outcome of the war could have been hideously different.
We almost didn't get the services of Dr. Fermi.

Early in my career with Byoir, one of my duties was to develop
stories about scientists who were associated with the University
of Chicago. While on that beat, I heard the remarkable story
from one of his colleagues, of Dr. Fermi's escape from Italy just

before the Second World War. I later checked the details with Fermi himself, but this was the story he didn't want released in his lifetime.

Fermi, born in 1902, was a young physicist at the University of Rome when Benito Mussolini reached the peak of his power in Italy. Fermi, absorbed in his world of science, had scant interest in politics, belonged to no political organizations, and made no fist-shaking speeches. But, on the few occasions when he was heard to express political views, he made no secret of his dislike of fascism.

As Fermi's fame in the scientific world grew, so did Mussolini's worries about him. The dictator didn't want to lose this brilliant young man to some other country. And so, on Mussolini's orders, Fermi was made a prisoner of Rome—free to go about his daily work but not to leave the city. He was guarded night and day.

His unhappiness with this situation grew as Adolf Hitler and the Nazi party gained increasing power in Germany during the middle 1930s. Fermi read more and more news stories about the Nazis' treatment of Jews and feared that similar racism might spread into Italy, since Hitler and Mussolini were becoming more closely allied. Fermi's fear was personal, for his wife was Jewish. Under the Nazi code, his three children would be considered half Jewish and could conceivably end in concentration camps with their mother.

Fermi began looking for ways to get his family out.

A golden opportunity came in August 1938. Fermi received a telegram advising him that he had been awarded the Nobel Prize for physics, for work with graphite, a substance that was later to play a role in his famous first atomic pile in Chicago. The telegram invited him to travel to Stockholm on December 10 to receive the award in person.

Fermi asked the president of the University of Rome to request the necessary travel permission for him. The president made the request but Mussolini turned it down.

Desperate, Fermi then asked for a personal interview with the dictator. It was granted. He told Mussolini that the world's attention would be fastened on Stockholm on the day of the awards, and it would be a fine reflection on Rome if an Italian scientist were to share the limelight with other prizewinners. Somehow, Fermi also managed to convey the impression that, in his acceptance speech, he would praise Mussolini for his effective government and support of science.

Mussolini, who may have been more gullible than most, fell for it. He granted Fermi and his family permission to go to Stockholm for the one-day award ceremony.

Fermi and his wife and sons were careful to behave as though they really did plan on only a one-day stay. They took only two suitcases on the trip with them, and they made train reservations for a return trip from Stockholm the day after the awards. Of course, they had no intention of returning to Rome.

In his acceptance speech, Fermi didn't praise Mussolini, but he didn't criticize him, either. Fermi had left family and friends behind in Italy and had no wish to bring reprisals down upon them. After the awards, he and his family went to London and then to the United States, and in 1940 he was recruited into the Manhattan Project—the huge, secret, multifaceted effort that was to produce the world's first nuclear weapon.

The story of Enrico Fermi's escape from Mussolini fascinated me when I first heard it. For one thing, I liked it because it was potentially good publicity for the University of Chicago—a story that could get a lot of media attention and serve my professional purpose of shining a spotlight on the university's scientific team. For another thing, I liked it because I simply could never resist a good story. So I wrote a draft of it, which I passed along to Fermi.

He phoned me and said he would like to ask that I not release the story. I expressed disappointment, but he would not withdraw his plea. He said he would feel uncomfortable if the story were to become public while he was alive. He did not explain his reasons, and to this day I'm not sure just what it was about the story that troubled him. But he left no doubt that he would be very unhappy if I were to ignore his request.

I went along with him, of course. A few days after that conversation, he phoned me again and asked in his heavy Italian accent, "What about that story? What do you intend to do with it?"

"I've destroyed it, Dr. Fermi."

"Thank you."

We never talked about it again.

It was painful to bury a good story like that, of course. But in time I came to feel that I was repaid many times over for respecting a client's wishes.

One repayment was simply the fact that Dr. Fermi learned he could trust me. This trust became part of a mutually respectful and fond relationship—and that is the most rewarding kind of relationship a PR professional can have.

But there were also tangible benefits—gains that I would not have made if I had refused to honor Fermi's wish. When I destroyed that story, he seemed to decide that he owed me a favor in return. Indeed, he did me a whole series of favors.

Until that time, for instance, he had been shy with the press. Some highly respected science writers from major publications such as the *New York Times* had repeatedly asked for one-on-one interviews with the famous Dr. Fermi. I very much wanted to arrange such interviews, but Fermi had always ducked them. Now, however, he became warmly receptive when I suggested personal interviews. I didn't abuse his good nature by sending a constant stream of hacks shuffling though his office. The science journalists I sent to see him were relatively few in number and were the cream of the crop. And with Fermi's help I was able to generate a good number of high-quality articles in the very best places.

Fermi died of cancer on September 30, 1955. The actor Jimmy Dean died in an automobile accident the same day. Dean's death made lurid newspaper headlines and spawned uncountable TV commentaries and gushy magazine pieces. The death of Enrico Fermi, the father of the atomic age and regarded by his colleagues as one of the great scientists of all time, went virtually unremarked. That saddened and and puzzled me. Perhaps this neglect was what made me continue to sit on the story of Fermi's escape. I think I may have felt unwilling to reveal his secret story to a world that seemed to care so little about him.

But all that is in the past. I've presented Fermi's story here because it helps me illustrate an important lesson in public relations. As a PR professional you will inevitably be privy to confidential information. You will be told stories, facts, and opinions off the record. You must honor those confidences despite all pressures to the contrary.

And there *will* be pressures. Among the factors tempting you to betray confidences will be two powerful motives—your wish to secure good coverage for your clients, and your wish to win friends among the media. Any time you find yourself sitting on a good story or a juicy piece of news, these two motives will needle and nag at you mercilessly. It is essential that you get the motives under proper control. They are both excellent motives— indeed, no PR professional could operate without them—but they mustn't be allowed to run 'away with the show.

Always remember that your first loyalty is to your client—that is, the people associated with the client organization. In my case, I owed allegiance first to Enrico Fermi. No matter how much I was tempted to release his story—and there were times when I was sorely tempted, since it could have helped me score a major PR coup—I was required to remember that Fermi's wishes came first.

It hurt at the time, and it cost me some short-term opportunities. But in the long run, it was a winning strategy.

As a PR professional, you must be prepared to lend your skills to clients, after-hours purposes as well as to the needs of the office.
                    —A story of divorce and remarriage

Robert Maynard Hutchins became chancellor of the University of Chicago at the age of twenty-nine, and throughout his tenure there lived in the glare of public scrutiny. The media reported copiously—and generally favorably—on the educational innovations he instituted at Chicago. He liked that part of the publicity. But his private life was also considered newsworthy. He didn't like that, but there was little he could do about it.

Byoir handled his educational publicity, and we liked that part of it as well as he did. But in 1949 he came to us and asked our help with a private problem. We would have preferred not to get involved in his personal life, but there was no graceful way for us to turn him away.

This story illustrates the peculiar nature of the public-relations profession. As a PR practitioner you will often find yourself getting tangled up in your clients' private—as well as their professional—lives. It is all but inevitable, occurring most often as a result of your publicity efforts. You work to make XYZ Corporation and its president known to the public. But if the president becomes drunk and abusive one night in a cabaret, or is discovered to belong to some fringe group of political fanatics, then a part of his private life has abruptly become your concern. You may dislike the situation wholeheartedly, but you cannot avoid it. Life in the office and life after hours don't always stay separate—not with the media watching.

Chancellor Hutchins's problem was that he was planning to marry his secretary, a second marriage for each of them. The American public in the late 1940s was a good deal more prudish and shockable than today, and Hutchins had an uneasy feeling that his planned marriage would stimulate a lot of nasty, gossipy stories in the papers, and so he wanted Byoir's help.

Hutchins had married his first wife, Maude, back in the 1920s. The marriage unraveled in the 1930s, and finally, in 1949, they were divorced. Divorce was not accepted as casually then as now, and the breakup received more attention from the press than Hutchins liked, but in time the story faded away. A few months later, however, he decided to marry Vesta Orlich, his secretary. The two had been carrying on a longtime affair but had kept it under wraps to avoid media attention. But Hutchins and Orlich finally decided to make their relationship official and public.

Hutchins called Byoir's Chicago office and asked for a private meeting with the office head, George Dye, and me. He ex-

plained his fears, and George and I understood immediately that
our client's private life had become our business.

We managed to solve his problem for him. I recalled hearing
or reading that Hutchins's father was a church minister, so I
suggested that the elder Hutchins be asked to perform the
wedding ceremony, introducing an extra note of solemnity and
dignity that might help mute the gossip.

I also urged that the ceremony be performed on a Friday
evening after seven o'clock. This would put the news into Saturday's papers, which were then, as now, the week's thinnest and
least thoroughly read. Many editors would lack space to print
the story and where it did appear, many readers would skip past
it.

Hutchins accepted both pieces of advice. At Byoir we debated
keeping quiet about the wedding but decided we had to issue
some kind of release. An aura of secrecy would only enhance
the attractiveness of the event to gossip columnists—exactly the
effect we didn't want. So we issued a short, dry, three-paragraph
announcement, and, as we had hoped, it was widely ignored.
Considering the fact that Chancellor Hutchins was a public
figure of world renown, his wedding was surprisingly quiet and
private. He called from his honeymoon resort to thank us.

That part of the story ended happily. But there was a less
happy postscript. The chancellor's private life overflowed into
his public life again, and this second time we were unable to
help him.

It happened about a year after his wedding to Vesta Orlich.
His ex-wife, Maude, turned up in Chicago on a publicity tour to
promote a book she had written. Called *Diary of Love*, it was
officially described as a novel, but Maude and her publisher were
careful to let on that it was in the nature of a *roman à clef*, based
on real events and people. And one of the main characters was
clearly recognizable as Robert Maynard Hutchins.

It was quite a sexy book for its time. The chancellor was
severely embarrassed, but worse was to come. At a Chicago
press conference set up by her publisher, Maude said, "If you
think *this* book is bold, wait till you read the next one I'm
writing!"

We were powerless to counteract this kind of promotion. The publisher and Maude had a juicy topic, knew it, and were prepared to push it hard. The press loved it, of course.

There are times when even a strong PR agency such as Byoir is helpless in the face of events, and this was one of them. There was no way to suppress so delicious a scandal. Hutchins's private life had finally overwhelmed him.

A few months after Maude took Chicago by storm, Hutchins left the university for a more private position with the Ford Foundation in Pasadena, California.

Top executives expect personal services, like placing wedding announcements in the papers. Don't take such requests casually. They are more important than you may think.

—A story of Metropolitan Life
and the CEO's daughter

During my thirty-seven years at Byoir I must have taken part in hundreds of presentations, trying to sell our services to prospective clients. Not once in all that time did the subject of trivial or personal services come up. No executive ever asked how efficient we were at getting wedding announcements into the papers or finding scarce tickets to Broadway shows and sports events. Nobody ever said out loud that such services were part of the package we were selling.

But they were part of the package, all right.

I came to realize quite early in my career that personal services are far more important than anybody will admit. True, not all executives require them, and some are even embarrassed by the idea. But there are other top people who expect such services as a matter of royal prerogative. So when you're asked to provide such a service, don't ever make the mistake of taking the request casually. It may seem silly or petty, but it is a fact of PR life—taking personal-service requests lightly has been known to cost agencies their clients and people their jobs.

I always listen with the utmost seriousness when the top man says he wants something, even when it sounds minor. As long as the request doesn't violate my personal code (I won't pimp for clients, for instance, nor will I do anything else illegal), I do my best to fulfill it. Even if it is impossible.

Late in the 1970s, on a Tuesday morning, I received a phone call from Dick Claeys, public-relations director of the Metropolitan Life Insurance Company, a client of ours. Dick said he had just come from the office of Met Life's chairman and CEO, John Creedon, whose daughter was getting married that Saturday. Creedon wanted a story on the wedding to appear in the *New York Times* on Sunday.

"Impossible," I said immediately.

"Literally impossible?" Dick asked. I could almost hear his face falling.

"Literally impossible," I said. I explained that wedding stories and bridal photos for the Sunday *Times* had to be placed at least two weeks ahead of time even to be considered. Even then the odds were tough to beat. Every father east of the Alleghenies wants his daughter's picture in the Sunday *Times* when she gets married, and so does every mother, and large numbers of grandparents, aunts, and uncles. If the *Times* printed every wedding and engagement story submitted, the Sunday edition would be about ten pounds heavier.

"Oh, boy," said Dick gloomily. "John Creedon isn't a man who takes no for an answer easily. Can't you at least try, Bob?"

"Sure, I can try. But I'll tell you frankly, Dick, the odds are a hundred to one against you, probably worse."

He said he would send a copy of Creedon's daughter's story to my office immediately. It got there in fifteen minutes. Such was the level of his anxiety.

Meanwhile I had placed a call to a good friend who was a senior editor at the *Times* and who also happened to be involved in the Sunday society pages. I took him to lunch at Sardi's and over coffee I told him about Dick Claeys's problem.

"That's a problem, right enough," my friend said. "We're just about locked up for Sunday."

"I figured as much. But Dick is about to have a blue fit. I told him I'd at least make an effort."

"Give him some advice from me. If his boss has any more daughters, he should make sure he's out of town the week they get married."

"I'm sure Dick wishes he was out of town *this* week."

"Do you have a copy of the story?"

I pulled it out and gave it to him. He made no commitment, and I asked for none. When I got back to my office, I called Dick Claeys and told him I'd given his problem my best shot, but I saw little realistic hope of a good result.

To my astonishment, my friend from the *Times* did what I hadn't dared hope for. John Creedon's daughter's wedding story ran in that Sunday's *Times*.

Dick Claeys phoned me Monday to thank me. "It was a nice relaxing Sunday," he said.

"Did the chairman call you to thank you?" I asked.

"Oh, no." Dick sighed. "He took it for granted, I guess. But I'm sure he would have called if the story *didn't* get printed."

And then there's the old theater-ticket scramble.
—a story of Midland-Ross, four tickets,
and a bad ending

In early November 1981, the head of our financial news department received a call from a man named Jerry Isham, PR director of a Byoir client named Midland-Ross, a diversified

Cleveland-based manufacturer. He was conveying a request from the company's chairman and CEO, Harry Bolwell.

Bolwell was scheduled to attend a meeting in New York the Tuesday before Thanksgiving. That evening he wanted to take three guests to see the smash Broadway musical *Cats*. Jerry Isham asked our people to get four tickets.

We had a woman in our New York office who was experienced in handling ticket requests, but unfortunately she was away at that time, so the task was turned over to someone less experienced. She got in touch with our usual ticket broker and was told that *Cats* was sold out for the entire Thanksgiving week, that the broker would try to find four tickets, but that she should not hold her breath till they were in hand. What's more, the broker said the tickets would run us at least 60 bucks apiece.

We told Jerry Isham we were working on his request.

When Harry Bolwell got to his Manhattan hotel on the Monday evening before Thanksgiving, he found neither tickets nor messages. He was miffed, to say the least.

I had played no role in the episode up to this point—in fact, I knew nothing about it. When I learned the details later, however, I was shocked. If we couldn't find those four tickets, we should at least have sent an explanation by way of a note or a phone call just to show we cared. Instead, we gave the appearance of ignoring our client.

I pointed out in the last story that it can be a bad mistake to take executives' personal requests too casually. This story will illustrate the truth of that statement.

The situation, already bad enough on Monday night, with Bolwell angry over the missing tickets and the lack of communication, was to get much worse.

It was reported to me the following morning, Tuesday, Bolwell turned up for the meeting that had brought him to New York. It was a board of directors meeting of a company for which he was an outside director. He arrived a little early, and the company's CEO was in the middle of a long-distance phone call. The CEO's secretary courteously invited Bolwell to wait in her office.

As they chatted about this and that, Bolwell told her how he had wanted to take some guests to *Cats* that night but had been frustrated by the scarcity of tickets.

She asked, "Would you like me to try?"

"Why—sure, but I don't want you to spend a lot of time on it."

"It won't take much time. There are a couple of quick phone calls I can make. Maybe I'll get lucky."

New York ticket hunting is an art. Some people are better at it than others. Some have secret sources, which they guard jealously. Practitioners of this art are extraordinarily proud of their successes.

Later that morning, during the directors' meeting, the CEO's secretary walked in smiling and handed Harry Bolwell a note.

She had found him four good orchestra seats for only fifty dollars each.

When I found out from Isham about this embarrassing episode, I called Bolwell to apologize for our seeming neglect. He was polite but not forgiving.

Of course, I have no way of knowing whether there was a connection here, but a month or so later, Jerry Isham called and told me gravely that he had been instructed to write us a letter advising us that our contract with Midland-Ross would not be renewed at the first of the year.

There was no doubt in our minds as to why this happened.

CHAPTER 2

HELPING CLIENTS IN DIFFICULTY

The need for good PR is never greater than when things go wrong. And they surely will go wrong. You can depend on it.

Be sure everybody has the facts and has them right.
A story of Woolworth and President Kennedy

ON FEBRUARY 1, 1960, four black college students sat down at a lunch counter in a Woolworth store in Greensboro, North Carolina. In keeping with a tradition rooted deeply in southern society, the counter had always been reserved for whites. The black students' audacious act catapulted Woolworth to the leading edge of one of the most wrenching social upheavals this country has ever known.

Robert C. Kirkwood, Woolworth's chairman, was profoundly unhappy with his position on that leading edge. All he and his senior managers really wanted to do was conduct their law-abiding business quietly, make money for their stockholders, and stay out of trouble. The company had always maintained a low profile in terms of PR.

It had always been the policy of Woolworth to be a good citizen in the communities where its stores were located, and this had meant observing established social customs. But now, suddenly, it appeared that this peaceful, neighborly policy would no longer do.

In the year after the black students' act of defiance, as the phrase "sit-in" worked its way into the language, Woolworth found itself at the center of an enormous controversy. From black activists at one pole to white supremacists at the other, dozens of vociferous groups bombarded the hapless company with angry mail, fist-shaking speeches, and shrill phone calls. There were boycotts, picketings, and other coercive assaults. The company's 1960 sales revenues dropped by a stunning 35 per cent.

45

Desperate, Kirkwood hired the Byoir organization to seek ways out of this seemingly escape-proof public-relations trap, and, as account executive, I was put in charge of the effort.

I saw many good PR lessons illustrated during my years with Kirkwood and his people. The Woolworth experience was so rich in lessons, in fact, that I will return to it more than once later in the book. This first lesson has to do with the importance of seeing that everybody has all the relevant facts. If you feel somebody doesn't have the facts, find a way to provide them—no matter how much trouble you must go to.

In the case of Woolworth, the person I had to get the facts to was President John F. Kennedy.

JFK involved himself in the sit-in and boycott disputes in mid-1963. As the unrest spread from Woolworth to other big store chains—Walgreen, McCrory, Kresge—he sought to get everybody moving forward from the screaming and name-calling phase of the debate toward a calmer, more productive consideration of the very complicated problems to be overcome. To that end, he invited the chief executive officers of concerned companies to a meeting in the White House. Among these CEOs, of course, was Bob Kirkwood.

I had told Kirkwood that I thought the meeting could be useful. But then an unexpected and worrisome problem loomed up.

On a Tuesday two days before the Washington meeting, I happened to be sitting in the office of Edward Harrigan, Woolworth's public-affairs chief, when the phone rang. The caller was a Justice Department official who was preparing an analysis of the sit-in movement for JFK's meeting, and I was able to listen in because the phone was equipped with a speaker device.

As the official talked, Harrigan and I stared at each other with mounting dismay. It was obvious that the Justice man was not in possession of all the facts. What particularly worried me—no, I'll put it more strongly, scared me—was that the man wanted to assign Woolworth the job of bellwether.

The tangled, prickly, and painful problems of lunch-counter segregation would vanish, he believed, if Woolworth would only take the lead and decree all its counters henceforth color blind.

White segregationists might rant and bluster for a while, he conceded, but eventually they would accept the inevitable. And finally (so went his rose-tinted scenario) other big chains and smaller restaurants, observing the peaceable scene at Woolworth, would conclude that they, too, could desegregate safely, and everybody would live happily ever after.

When the Justice man finished spinning this fairy tale, Harrigan and I tried to show him all the things that were wrong with it. The main problem was that it would never work—not in real life. The second problem was that it would not only fail, but fail violently. If Woolworth were to try to go it alone in this way, abruptly desegregating its lunch counters after a century of racial separation, riots and bombings and arson were virtually guaranteed. The third problem—for Harrigan and me, though maybe not for the Justice man—was that so spectacular a fiasco would be a public-relations disaster for Woolworth.

But the Justice official was sure he was right. He intended to write his views into a report he was preparing for the president.

It was a PR nightmare. I imagined a chain of unfortunate events. The president gives a televised speech in which he publicly asks Woolworth to play bellwether. Woolworth refuses. The company's good reasons are drowned out in a deafening new chorus of screaming and name calling, and the whole painful issue grows immeasurably more tangled.

Somehow, I thought, I had to give JFK the facts. The facts as I understood them came from three years of immersion in the issue, not just from one quick study. I knew almost for certain that the president would embarrass himself if he based his speech on the Justice man's analysis. He would sound naive to those who really understood the complicated forces involved and gain the respect of neither the blacks nor the whites.

Back in my office that Tuesday afternoon, as I wondered what to do, I suddenly thought of a man named Tom Walsh, who lived in my hometown. Tom was the chief administrative lieutenant of Joseph Kennedy, JFK's father. I knew Tom, and that evening I phoned him at home and asked what commuter train he would be taking in the morning. On Wednesday morning I met him on the station platform, and, on the way into New York City, I told him about the problem and my fear that the president was about to embarrass himself.

Tom saw instantly that something would have to be done. There wasn't much time—the President's meeting was scheduled for the following day, Thursday, at four in the afternoon. By sheer good luck, Tom was scheduled to confer with JFK in the Oval Office that evening, Wednesday, at about six o'clock. He would be leaving his New York office for the trip to Washington about noon. If I could write out my analysis of the sit-in situation and get it to him before he left, he said, he would personally deliver it to the president.

I hurried to my office, dictated my analysis as lucidly as I knew how, and managed to get it to Tom before eleven o'clock.

The outcome was everything I had hoped for. JFK was a lightning-fast reader. When Tom Walsh handed him my analysis that Wednesday evening, he absorbed it rapidly and was evidently impressed by the array of facts he had not been aware of.

On Thursday he gave a speech in which he said, among other things, that Woolworth could *not* go it alone.

Bob Kirkwood and the other participants at the meeting were delighted with the speech. The press and TV journalists praised the speech for its sure grasp of a staggeringly complex issue. The speech also drew praise from many of the black leaders I had come to know, such as Roy Wilkins, head of the National Association for the Advancement of Colored People.

On Friday I received a phone call from Tom Walsh, who had just got back from Washington. He was at LaGuardia Airport, and wanted to visit me later in the day. He arrived at my office with a package under his arm.

He reported that JFK was very pleased with the reception of his speech. "He called me into the Oval Office this morning," Tom said, "and asked me. 'Who is this fellow Bob Wood?' "

Tom gave JFK a few details of my background and association with the sit-in issue. The president then said he would like to do something to show his appreciation. Did Tom have any suggestions? Tom said he thought I would welcome an autographed photo. The president promptly pulled a picture of himself and his wife, Jackie, from his desk drawer and wrote on it: "To our Bob Wood with best regards, John F. Kennedy."

Handing the picture over to Tom, JFK said, "Don't just send this to Bob Wood by mail or messenger. I'd like you to deliver it in person."

And Tom handed the package to me.

Woolworth's lunch counters were eventually desegregated without serious violence. So were those of other major store chains, and in the end so were smaller restaurants, diners, and taverns through most of the South. I will return to tell more of this complicated and fascinating story later in the book.

The JFK episode illustrates the importance of making sure people have the facts in any difficult, emotion-charged situation. When facts aren't well understood, emotions will rule—with possibly disastrous results.

As a public-relations professional, you will sometimes find it necessary to make a client cool his temper.
    —A story of Macmillan and a vengeful mood

A bitter antagonism arose in 1974 between the Macmillan Publishing Company and the *New York Times*. Macmillan's executives and shareholders may have been right in feeling they had been maltreated, but I felt they were wrong in their wish to lash out in vengeance at the *Times*. I struggled again and again to restrain them, for I knew it would only make a bad situation worse, and for a time I succeeded. But in the end I lost—and in my opinion, so did everybody else.

It all began on a fateful Friday in October when abruptly, with scant warning, Macmillan fired some 135 editorial staff members and other employees at its New York headquarters.

There were even some senior employees who, having spent much of the day giving subordinates the ax, were themselves handed walking papers late in the afternoon.

An upheaval of that magnitude in an old, major publishing company could hardly be expected to go unreported in the news media. Not surprisingly, there was heavy coverage, particularly in the *New York Times*, and on the whole it was more sympathetic to the fired employees than to the company. Over the next several days, dozens of employees picketed outside Macmillan's offices on Third Avenue, generating still more bad publicity, particularly on TV.

On the Monday after that bloody Friday, I was called to those Third Avenue offices by Macmillan's chairman and CEO, Raymond Hagel. I took a couple of Byoir's top professionals with me, including Muriel Fox Aronson. With Hagel, among others, was Belle Linden, an attorney and close adviser. It was said that Hagel never made a major decision without consulting her.

Hagel wanted to hire the Byoir organization to calm the growing storm over those mass firings. He explained that the firings had been undertaken for good reasons, largely as a result of pressure from shareholders to cut costs and streamline a company grown rickety with age. He felt the company's side of the story had been poorly told in the press and on TV, and he wanted help.

We took on the job. At first things went surprisingly well. We developed a series of stories about Macmillan's major contributions to book publishing over the years. There was no shortage of fine material to work with. Macmillan was the original publisher of *Gone With the Wind*, for example—by several different measures the most successful first novel ever published. Alongside these stories, of course, we also put out what we felt were good, lucid explanations of the thinking behind the firings. Within a few days the media coverage became markedly more positive, and the pickets went away.

Then trouble loomed up.

Marilyn Bender, a respected financial reporter, phoned Macmillan and said she was assigned to write an in-depth study of the company for the Sunday business section of the *Times*.

The immediate reaction of Ray Hagel and other top management people at Macmillan was to turn down her request for interviews. They were in a vengeful mood and wanted to lash out at the *Times* for its previous unfriendly attitude. Moreover, they were worried about the story Marilyn Bender might write, fearing it would merely be a rehash of the many one-sided stories about the firings that had already appeared in the *Times* and elsewhere.

Muriel Aronson and I hurried over to Hagel's office to try to change his mind. We explained to him, Bob Barton, the president, and Bella Linden that Marilyn Bender would write her story with or without Macmillan's cooperation. If she had to do it without, then the story would inevitably be biased against the company's point of view. She would undoubtedly interview some of the fired employees and probably some Wall Street analysts, whose views of the company tended to be pessimistic. Wouldn't it be better, Muriel and I said, to give Bender open access to Macmillan executives and let her hear *their* side of the story?

Ray, Bob, and Bella took our advice. When Bender's long story finally appeared, it was about as friendly as we could have hoped for. There was a good deal of criticism in it, but that was somewhat balanced by quotes from Hagel and others. While it could not be called favorable, it impressed me as at least fair.

After reading it that Sunday, I relaxed. The battle was won, I thought.

But I was wrong. The battle had only just begun.

New trouble arrived on Monday. Ray Hagel and other executives were besieged by phone calls from perplexed and irate stockholders, who were upset by a boxed statistical summary called "Macmillan at a Glance," which had appeared with the Bender story. This summary gave details of the company's recent earnings, stock price, and so on. What upset the shareholders was that these figures were wildly at variance with the numbers they had been working with.

Somebody at the *Times* had made a careless mistake. The published figures were those of a different company.

Muriel, who had been spending much of her time at the Macmillan offices, phoned me that Monday morning and suggested I get over there fast. I did. I found Hagel and his people livid with rage. Not only were they angry over the messed-up statistical box, but also over the Bender story itself. Several executives were claiming distortions and outright misquotations.

Once again they were in a mood to lash out at the *Times*. And once again I found myself in the position of cooling overheated tempers.

They wanted blood and wanted it immediately. They wanted me to get on the phone then and there and demand that the *Times* publish corrections, retractions, and apologies the very next day, Tuesday. I was all but certain this could not happen. By long tradition, the *Times* corrected errors in Sunday stories only on Sundays. But in the overheated atmosphere of the Macmillan offices that Monday, it was hard to get anybody to listen.

Then Bella Linden came up with an idea that made me struggle all the harder to cool everybody down. She said she had a close friend who was also a friend of *Times* publisher Arthur Ochs ("Punch") Sulzberger. She proposed to get to Sulzberger through her friend and win the Tuesday corrections by demanding them directly from the publisher.

"Don't!" I said immediately. "It would be a mistake."

"A mistake?"

"Yes, and maybe a bad one."

I explained why. Even if Bella could get Punch Sulzberger to listen sympathetically to her demands, no good result was likely to come of the conversation. Sulzberger would simply call the Sunday business editor, Tom Mullaney, and tell him to straighten out the problem. Mullaney and his colleagues would undoubtedly be irritated by a Macmillan executive's going over their heads in this way.

The last thing we wanted in this tense situation, I pointed out earnestly, was a group of sullen, uncooperative editors. Wouldn't it be better to go to them directly rather than calling the big boss down on them? And wouldn't it be better to go to them with a reasonable attitude rather than a thirst for blood?

It was a battle against tall odds, but I finally managed to get Ray and Bella and their colleagues calmed down. They agreed that I should call Tom Mullaney, whom I knew well, and discuss the problem with him.

I placed my call at about half past one. I was told Tom was still at lunch. I left my name and a Macmillan phone number, and I added that I was calling on a matter of the utmost urgency.

Urgency? Indeed. While we sat around waiting for Tom Mullaney to return my call, I could feel the tension and anger rising again like an inexorable flood. After about a half-hour, I could no longer stem the tide. Bella Linden was instructed to call Sulzberger directly, and she asked me to go with her and stand by while she made the call from Ray Hagel's office. Reluctantly, still arguing but with diminishing hope, I complied.

I didn't know Sulzberger's direct-dial phone number, but I knew the main *Times* switchboard number by heart. I supplied it, and dialed it. My heart was sinking. A potentially damaging mistake was about to be made, and there was no longer anything I could do to block it. The tide of hot tempers had risen beyond my power to control it.

Unaccountably, the *Times* switchboard didn't answer. We let the phone ring more than a dozen times. Nobody ever responded.

Puzzled, I grabbed a phone book. Was it possible I had remembered the number wrong? It hardly seemed likely. I'd been dialing that number for years. Could it be that the high-voltage emotions of the morning had confused my memory?

I flipped through the phone book, perplexed and uneasy. And at that moment a secretary came in and said Tom Mullaney had returned my call on another line.

To this day I don't know why we got no answer when we dialed the *Times* switchboard. But we were saved by that odd, inexplicable circumstance. Tom Mullaney was gracious and understanding when I spoke to him, as I had known he would be. Subsequently, in two meetings at the *Times* between his people and the Macmillan group, reasonable compromises were worked out. And finally, on Sunday, the *Times* published not only a correct statistical box but also a letter signed by Hagel in which he aired most of Macmillan's main complaints over the Bender story. Both the box and the letter were placed in prominent positions.

This good outcome could not have happened unless Muriel and I had made the Macmillan people cool their tempers. I was feeling especially pleased when I finished reading that Sunday's *Times*. I had won a lot of battles.

Unfortunately, I was to lose the war.

I called Muriel at home that Sunday afternoon. We agreed that Tom Mullaney and his colleagues, though always firm and sometimes contentious in protecting their turf, had treated us honorably throughout. I suggested that Muriel write a letter of thanks to them, for Ray Hagel's signature, which she thought would be an excellent idea. Such a letter would not only be a pleasant ending for a difficult episode, but could generate a lot of goodwill for the future.

The next morning, Muriel phoned me from the Macmillan offices. She said the Macmillan people had flatly rejected the idea of a letter of thanks, because they might want to sue the *Times* at some point in the future, and if they did so, such a letter could weaken their case.

Their tempers were still not cooled.

It was too bad. The letter Muriel and I wanted to write could have made a lot of difference. Difficult years lay ahead for Macmillan—years of uncertainty and upheaval, marked by abrupt changes of top editors and other newsworthy events. The *Times* would always report dutifully on those events. But from 1974 on, most every *Times* story on Macmillan seemed to be tinged with frost.

If there is a genuine problem with a client's product, look the consumers straight in the eye, acknowledge the problem in plain English, and tell them what they can do about it.
                         —A story of exploding glass bottles

The Washington-based Consumer Product Safety Commission made an announcement in the middle 1970s that worried a lot of business people. The commission said it was going to conduct a one-month study to determine the ten most dangerous products in common use in American homes and announce the dread list to the public when the study was complete.

But the agency added that it already knew which product would occupy the number-one spot on this list—the ubiquitous glass beer or soda bottle.

This statement shocked, angered—and baffled—one of Byoir's clients, a trade association called the Glass Container Manufacturers Institute. They were aware, of course, that a broken glass bottle can be dangerous if carelessly handled. But the *most* dangerous of all products in the home? "Most" in what sense? In number of accidents? In severity? In the percentage requiring hospitalization?

Some in the glass-manufacturing industry wanted to issue a press release immediately, angrily denying the charge and complaining that its terms were too vague to make sense. But we at Byoir counseled a cooler course. First we said, Let's go to the safety commission and ask them politely to explain their charge more fully. How was it arrived at? On what data was it based?

We had had experience with this kind of situation before and we knew that when a product is accused of having some flaw or fault, the worst possible response may be an immediate denial. This only creates the impression that you are trying to wriggle off the hook, giving ammunition to the more shrill breeds of consumer advocate.

In any case, the public isn't likely to believe an unsupported plea of innocence from a business firm or group. This was particularly true in the 1960s and 1970s. If the public had to choose between a government agency's assertion that a product was flawed and a business group's denial—in a situation where neither had any hard evidence to offer—the business group almost always lost.

So our advice to the glass manufacturers: Let's assemble all the facts first. Let's see what kind of data the consumer agency has. Then let's study the data and see if we can produce convincing evidence to the contrary, rather than simply issuing an unsupported denial.

So the glass institute sent engineers to Washington. And very quickly we learned the basis of the consumer agency's charge.

The agency, it turned out, had fixed its attention on the fact that filled glass bottles may explode. What wasn't emphasized in the agency's research—perhaps the commission's staff members weren't even aware of it—was that such explosions occur only when filled bottles are put in a freezer. These explosions are dangerous, of course, particularly to the eyes.

So *that* was it. That was why the Consumer Product Safety Commission proposed to put glass bottles at the top of its blacklist. Now we understood.

And with understanding came a plan of action. No angry denials, no pleas of innocence, no wriggling off hooks. I recommended to Richard Cheney, the glass institute's executive director, that we immediately open a campaign in which we acknowledged forthrightly that glass bottles do explode and do cause injuries. But the main thrust of the campaign was to be educational, explaining that explosions happen only when filled bottles get frozen. The lesson, therefore, was clear and simple. *Never put a bottle in the freezer.*

Cheney agreed to go ahead with this campaign and we got to work instantly. We had just one short month before the Consumer Product Safety Commission published its feared list.

Our campaign was massive, with messages on TV and radio, in newspapers and magazines, in feature stories, short films, interviews. The media were receptive because this was a genuine public-service project—an educational campaign to keep people from being hurt.

We explained in as many ways as we could think of that any water-based liquid, including beer and soda, will expand in volume when it freezes. The pressure of this expansion can rend thick metal tanks and pipes—an ordinary glass bottle is no match for it. Evidently many people hadn't known this or hadn't stopped to think of the potential danger, but now the press, TV, and radio were disseminating this information to millions of households.

We made a collection of the most effective TV presentations, press pieces, and other results of our campaign. We took the collection to Washington and showed it to the panel of experts who were putting together the Consumer Product Safety Commission's blacklist. What we were saying to the panel, in effect, was that glass bottles were dangerous only to the uneducated—and the glass institute was providing the needed education at its own expense.

When the list of ten dangerous products was finally announced at the end of that month on a CBS thirty-minute TV show, glass bottles weren't on the list at all.

If the press and broadcasters are beating on you relentlessly, try a gamble. Set up a direct, face-to-face meeting between your top people and your very worst critic in the media.
                    —A story of Kodak in a desperate hour

Byoir received a call one day from Tom Robertson, the public-relations chief of Eastman Kodak. He said Kodak was in trouble and needed help.

Trouble was hardly the word for it. Kodak was in the middle of a public-relations disaster.

It had started in the middle 1960s. An activist group in Kodak's hometown of Rochester, New York, began to complain that the huge photographic and instrumentation company was shortchanging minorities, particularly blacks, in its hiring and promotion policies. At first, the group, led by a black minister, Rev. Franklin Florence, was only local in the scope of its activities, running demonstrations, distributing leaflets, and so on. Press and TV coverage was mostly confined to the Rochester area.

Kodak wasn't worried. The company felt that its record on minorities was excellent and could withstand objective scrutiny. This was, in fact, the truth. If the national media wanted horror stories about discriminatory hiring and promotion practices, there were plenty of companies that needed examination more than Kodak. And so the national press and the TV and radio networks pretty much ignored Rev. Florence's complaints.

But then a Kodak assistant vice president I'll refer to as Jeffrey Nugent committed a blunder that thrust the hapless company naked onto the national stage. In the interest of good community relations, Kodak had assigned Nugent the job of meeting members of Rev. Florence's group from time to time and listening to their grievances. Kodak felt that giving the group an official company ear to talk to might ease some of their frustrations and lead, eventually, to agreements. The Florence group's grievances were not clearly articulated and the company hoped that Nugent could pin them down to specifics. Then the demands could be addressed one by one.

For several weeks nothing much happened in Nugent's meetings with the group. Even the local media coverage of the issue fell off.

Then came a Saturday evening that Kodak's chairman and president will probably never forget.

The chairman and CEO, William S. Vaughn, and the president and COO, Louis Eiler, were in their homes, getting ready for dinner and watching the local TV news. To their amazement, the newscaster read a bulletin that Kodak and the Florence group had at long last reached an agreement.

This was news to Vaughn and Eiler. They hadn't authorized any agreement or even heard about one.

What came next sent their blood pressure up more than a few points. The newscaster outlined some of the purported agreement's main understandings. These, as reported, were astoundingly generous and far reaching—far more than Vaughn or Eiler would have dared to authorize if they had been consulted. Some of the reported understandings sounded incredibly expensive, guaranteed to raise a howl from the stockholders. Others promised to plunge the company up to its ears in the corrosive issue of reverse discrimination—guaranteed to stir up trouble with white employees.

Kodak's policy for years had been to approach race-related problems with deliberation and care to avoid explosions or backlashes. The policy had worked. Real progress had been made and was continuing, but the purported new agreement blew that policy to smithereens.

Vaughn immediately got on the phone to Eiler and asked what the hell was going on. Eiler said he had no idea. They then called Jeffrey Nugent and asked him to meet them right away.

Nugent hastened to the meeting and told Vaughn and Eiler that he hadn't signed a formal agreement with the Florence group. However, he said, he did approve a press release in which the terms of a possible agreement were set forth.

Vaughn and Eiler were horrified. The more they thought about this situation, the worse its ramifications looked. They told Nugent, who by this time may have wished he had never heard of Rev. Florence's group, that he had no authority to approve such a press release. But the damage was done.

Vaughn and Eiler may have had nightmares that night about the trouble they were in. But however bad the nightmares were, they couldn't have been any worse than the reality as it developed over the next few weeks.

That Monday morning, the distraught Vaughn and Eiler summoned Tom Robertson, Kodak's vice president in charge of PR. They explained the problem to him and instructed him to write a press release flatly denying the Saturday evening news reports and saying that no agreement of any kind had been reached between Kodak and the Florence group. Reports of understandings had no validity. The company had not authorized any statement of terms to be made on its behalf and wished to be disassociated from the entire erroneous story.

With profound misgivings but also with the realization that there was no alternative, Tom Robertson wrote and distributed the release.

The media pounced on it like a pack of hungry dogs on a bone. And this time it was a national story. The coverage was massive.

The gist of the story, as the media told it, was that Kodak had reneged on an agreement. Amidst all the torrential outpouring of words on the Rochester episode—the news stories, the pious editorials, the solemn interviews on TV—Kodak's version of the events was almost completely lost. The actual facts—that there had never been an agreement, that the whole thing arose from an unauthorized and erroneous employee statement—were hardly ever mentioned.

There is an old journalist's adage: "Never kill a good story by checking it too hard." In the Kodak case, the media showed remarkable adherence to this ancient apothegm.

Rev. Florence knew a good opportunity when he saw one. He quickly brought to Rochester a professional activist from Chicago, Saul Alinsky, an expert in milking situations like this. Alinsky saw to it that the story stayed hot, and helped insure that Kodak's side of the story was drowned out amid the thunderous preachments, tub thumping, and name calling. Nearly all accounts of the episode favored Rev. Florence's side, and the *New York Times* was particularly unkind. Kodak was made to sound like a company that not only lacked commitment to minority advancement but was actively hostile to it.

Letters by the thousands poured into Rochester from all over the United States and Canada, scolding Kodak for backing out of its agreement with the Florence group. Kodak despaired of responding to such a huge volume of mail from people whose minds were obviously made up, so most of the letters simply piled up unanswered. Many of the letters, as well as a lot of raised-fist speeches by Rev. Florence's and Saul Alinsky's people, threatened a nationwide boycott of Kodak's products.

It was in this desperate hour that Tom Robertson called us at

Byoir. He had heard about our work for Woolworth in somewhat similar circumstances and wondered if we could be as useful to them. George Hammond, our chairman, and I went up to Rochester, and established a formal counselor-client relationship that same day.

One of my first acts for our new client was to figure out a way to answer that colossal mound of letters. Skimming through them, I determined that they fell into three categories, each of which could be satisfied by one letter in response. I wrote the letters and instructed some clerical people on how to decide which letter went to whom. That took care of that.

Simultaneously, we went after the media. We prepared feature stories, short films, still photos, and other material dealing with Kodak's record in hiring and promoting minority employees. As I've said, this record was objectively good; there was no arguing with it. We had stories and pictures of black employees in desirable jobs, and of course we had abundant statistical material for reporters who wanted it. Results began to show up in just a few weeks. The media, including some leading black publications, started to speak of Kodak in more friendly tones and to tell its story more fairly.

But there were still some reporters who seemed determined not to kill a good story by looking at facts. Among them was the man who covered the Rochester events for the *New York Times*. He continued to write of Kodak's reneging on its agreement with Rev. Florence's group, and his stories were relentlessly unfriendly to the company. This troubled me a good deal, for the *New York Times* is enormously influential, with other publications and broadcasting journalists tending to follow its lead. But I couldn't figure out how to change the *Times*'s mind.

Meanwhile, we were getting hundreds of letters in response to our replies to that original mountain of mail. Many of these letters were charmingly contrite and apologetic. The writers acknowledged that they had been too quick to make judgments with insufficient evidence. Many said they hadn't been aware of the real facts concerning Kodak's alleged "reneging" on an agreement; nor had they known of the company's objectively laudable record on race-related matters.

They hadn't known because their newspapers, magazines, and TV and radio news programs hadn't told them. But now our message was getting across.

But there was still that thorn in Kodak's side—the *New York Times*. What could I do about that?

The idea I came up with was, I believe, the single most useful move I made in that whole difficult campaign. My idea was to set up a direct, face-to-face meeting between Kodak's CEO and the top editorial people at the *Times*.

I had seen this work in other difficult situations. When an influential newspaper or TV news show is relentlessly critical of your client or your company, a meeting of top people may be the one thing that can dislodge the ice jam. But such a move carries risk as well as promise. If the top people don't get along, or if your side states its case poorly, then you can end up in even worse trouble than you were to start with.

But I felt it was a risk worth taking. If I couldn't get the *Times* to stop bullying Kodak, the campaign couldn't be counted a complete success. Though most publications and broadcasters were swinging over to Kodak's side, or at least to a neutral stance, there were still some that appeared to be taking their cue from the big New York newspaper.

The chairman and CEO of Kodak, Bill Vaughn, was a personable man, intelligent, candid and likable. I felt that if anybody could put our case across at the *Times*, he could. I asked Tom Robertson if he thought Vaughn would be willing to meet the *Times*'s top editorial group. Tom said he wouldn't even need to ask. He knew Vaughn would do it.

So I phoned my good friend Tom Mullaney, the *Times*'s business and financial editor, and told him frankly what the problem was and why I wanted to set up a Kodak–*Times* summit meeting. I asked what the procedure should be. He suggested that I write a letter to Punch Sulzberger, the newspaper's publisher. "But don't send it to him," Tom said. "Send it to me and let me see what I can work out."

I followed these instructions. A couple of days later Tom called me to say that Sulzberger would like Bill Vaughn to join him and seven or eight top editors for lunch.

Bill Vaughn pulled it off. He told me later, only half joking, that he never had a chance to eat his lunch; he was too busy answering questions. The editors questioned him closely, sometimes sharply but fairly, as did Sulzberger, a publisher who took a direct and lively interest in news reporting. Many of Vaughn's replies seemed to surprise some of the editors, just as those letter-writers had been surprised when the facts were finally presented to them. Vaughn didn't need to oversell his case or even exercise his considerable personal charm. All he had to do was lay out those facts quietly and let the editors examine the evidence for themselves. Kodak's case was unassailable. There were no holes in it. The publisher and his editors were impressed.

From that day on, the *Times* stories out of Rochester underwent a dramatic change. I don't think I've ever seen a 180-degree turnabout executed more abruptly. The stories now were fair and factual, and Kodak was portrayed for what it was—a company trying to be a good citizen in an imperfect world.

As soon as the *Times* stopped picking on Kodak, so did most of the other publications and broadcasters that had been following along. Kodak's nightmare was over.

A postscript: Jeffrey Nugent, the man whose blunder started all this, wasn't fired. That was undoubtedly good thinking on Kodak's part. To fire him might only have reopened wounds that were healing and perhaps landed Kodak in a new mess. Instead, Nugent's duties were changed and his title was eliminated. He was no longer sent out to do community-relations work.

It is useful to have a good preexisting knowledge of a client's business before going to work for that client. But other factors may count more.
—A story of Northeast Utilities and a frank answer

Northeast Utilities was in trouble. This big holding company, whose subsidiaries provided electric power to millions of customers in Connecticut and western Massachusetts, was one of the nation's leading utilities in nuclear power generation. This, of course, brought it into sharp confrontation with antinuclear groups.

But that was only one of its problems. By using nuclear power rather than costly foreign oil, Northeast had always been able to keep its rates lower than those of most other utilities on the Atlantic seaboard. But now the Connecticut and Massachusetts state legislatures were seeking to widen the gap still further. Northeast needed rate increases to keep up with inflation, but it couldn't get those increases.

Everybody was sniping at the company—not just nuclear power foes but consumer-advocacy groups, environmentalists, political leaders, senior citizens groups, and a motley array of others. Nothing Northeast did seemed right. Nobody was listening to its pleas and explanations.

And so in 1979, Northeast decided to go outside for public-relations help. It asked a New York PR specialist, Tom Leighton, to help in screening applicants for the assignment. Leighton contacted twenty agencies and asked them to provide details about their accomplishments, experience, clients, methods of staffing, and manner of charging. He also had personal meetings with key people at each agency.

After four or five weeks, we were told we were among the three finalists and were asked to make a full-dress presentation at Northeast's Connecticut headquarters. There was one further request—to bring along the person who would be assigned as account executive if Byoir were selected.

I went up to Connecticut with George Hammond, then Byoir's chairman, and the prospective account executive. We made our pitch, then went back to New York.

Northeast's chairman and CEO, Lee Sillen, phoned me at nine o'clock the next morning. "Bob," he said, "I've got some good news and some bad news. Which would you like first?"

I gulped and said, "The good news."

He said, "Okay. The good news is that we've chosen Byoir for our three-year program."

"Why, that's wonderful!" I said. "What could possibly be the bed news?"

"Well, the bad news is this, Bob. We weren't happy with the account executive you brought up here."

That was a blow, but not a serious one. I said, "We can fix that." I thought for a couple of seconds. Two good candidates came to mind. "We'll send two other people up there to see you," I said.

Lee said that would be fine. He requested that we send the two separately for one-on-one meetings with himself and other top management people.

One of the candidates I sent was Milton Bellis, a man with solid, varied PR experience. After meeting some other executives, Milt was ushered into Lee Sillen's office.

They exchanged a few pleasantries, and then Lee asked, "How much do you know about the electric utilities industry?"

Milt paused, then decided on an honest, straightforward answer. "Very little," he said.

Lee sighed and said there didn't seem to be much point in continuing the interview.

But Milton Bellis was a man who kept his wits about him. He knew that it isn't strictly necessary to have a thorough, preexisting knowledge of a given company's business in order to do a good PR job. It helps, but it isn't half as essential as some other factors—like a knowledge of the news media. Milt knew this, and I knew it (otherwise I would never have sent him in as a candidate), but Lee Sillen obviously didn't know it.

So instead of jumping up and leaving, Milt decided to try to prolong the conversation and perhaps lead it back to some of his other qualifications. He made a comment about the pressures Lee Sillen must be feeling, trying to run a company that was being criticized from all sides, and he added that he thought it remarkable that people under such constant pressure could stay physically and mentally fit.

I don't know exactly how Milt took the conversation in this direction without sounding obsequious, but he was a man of easy and natural demeanor, and the outcome attests that he pulled it off well. The conversation took on a new life, and Milt and Lee talked for half an hour about sailing, tennis, gardening—and public relations.

Lee phoned me the next morning. "We like your man, Milt," he said. "He's our choice."

Milt did a fine job for Northeast, too. He determined quickly, and the rest of us at Byoir agreed, that Northeast's major problem all along had been that it kept talking about its own needs while seeming to ignore those of its customers and other publics. We worked to change that rather aloof, uncaring image. By the time our program was complete, criticism of the company had died to a barely audible murmur, and the needed rate increases were coming through at last.

Despite the fact that our account executive had no preexisting knowledge of the client's business, the campaign won us a Silver Anvil public-relations award.

If the public won't believe you or your client, maybe they'll believe an authoritative bystander.
　　　　　　　　　　　—A story of Picker X-Ray and
　　　　　　　　　　　　　　　　　a worried community

Picker X-Ray was a family-owned company that became a subsidiary of CIT Financial, a Byoir client, in 1959. We helped

Picker establish good relationships with the national news media—relationships that were virtually nonexistent before—and earned the gratitude of Harvey Picker, the chairman and CEO. Then, in the early 1960s, Picker X-Ray ran into a public-relations problem so intractable that for a time we didn't know how to solve it.

The company, as its name implied, made X-ray equipment for medical and industrial uses. It was also moving aggressively into related fields involving radioactive isotopes and other new technologies. To spearhead its efforts in these new areas of science, Harvey Picker wanted to establish an atomic research center.

The company found a suitable site near its plant in the eastern part of Cleveland. But as soon as the neighborhood residents found out what Picker proposed to build there, they protested.

The phrase "atomic research center" was unfortunate. I don't know who first used it to describe the new facility—somebody at Picker, a news reporter, or one of the local residents—but when it got into the media, it had the effect of a lighted match held to gunpowder.

The neighborhood exploded.

Some citizens took to the streets, shouting their fears of lethal radiation and other nuclear nightmares, marching around the property with picket signs. They wrote letters to the local press and broadcasters, gathered signatures on petitions, and even threatened legal action if Picker didn't take its abominable lab somewhere else.

Surprised and very upset over this unexpected outburst, Harvey Picker called me and asked what we at Byoir could do. At first I had no suggestions to offer.

In our advance publicity we had taken great pains to stress the peaceful nature of the research to be conducted at the proposed center. Picker was not in the weapons business, or even in the nuclear-power business. It was interested only in the uses of radiation in medicine, in industrial diagnostic and quality-control applications, and other nonmilitary uses. Moreover, the research would not pose any hazards to the surrounding community. The levels of radiation in Picker's kind of equipment were far too low to be dangerous to the public. The center's only local impact would be the creation of jobs.

But people believe what they want to believe. No doubt some of the protesters had seen too many science-fiction movies about deadly rays, meltdowns, nuclear explosions, and so on and the neighborhood was in a panic. Nobody listened to what we and Picker were trying to say.

I realized that we needed somebody else to come into this—somebody new, a disinterested outsider with no ax to grind.

I didn't know who this bystander might be until Harvey Picker mentioned Paul Aebersol of the Atomic Energy Commission. I gathered that Harvey and Commissioner Aebersol liked and admired each other. The commissioner was enthusiastic about the proposed research center, it appeared. Harvey mentioned that Commissioner Aebersol was scheduled to give a speech in New York soon, and he added, "I'll be there."

I thought, Aha! I asked if I could meet Aebersol.

"I'll see if he can join us for lunch," Harvey said.

The commissioner and I got along well at lunch, and we met a couple more times over the next few weeks, as the situation in Cleveland grew steadily worse. Commissioner Aebersol sympathized. I knew he would help if I could only find a way to utilize him, and finally I did.

I found a syndicated science writer who was receptive to the idea of interviewing the commissioner. I set up a breakfast meeting, and briefed the commissioner with great care beforehand. I asked him to get onto the subject of Picker's research center and stress its peaceful aims and lack of hazard to the community around it.

The science writer's soothing story was carried nationally. A Cleveland newsman read it, interviewed Commissioner Aebersol by phone, and wrote his own good story on the Picker center.

That did it. The protests cooled, then stopped.

When the new research center was completed, Harvey Picker was happy to welcome Commissioner Aebersol as guest speaker at the opening ceremonies.

There are times to confront an opponent and times to avoid him. The choice should never be made in anger or fear, but on the basis of reason.
—A story of A&P, Rev. Jesse Jackson, and
Operation Breadbasket

This is the story of a large company under siege. The opponent was angry and implacable. There were many times during the long struggle when we were tempted to lash out in anger over what we considered unfair tactics, and there were other times when we began to feel we could never win and were tempted to back down. Luckily, we did neither.

We kept our cool, and in looking back over that long, hard fight, I believe our own enforced coolness was the single most important factor in our final victory. We kept our opponent off balance by sometimes hiding from him and sometimes stepping out to confront him. He never knew which it was going to be. We kept him in a continual state of surprise and puzzlement. But we never allowed ourselves to be surprised by our own responses. We sat on our emotions and developed our responses logically, by thinking them out in advance.

The besieged company was A&P. The attacker was Operation Breadbasket, the economic arm of Martin Luther King's organization, the Southern Christian Leadership Conference.

Launched in Atlanta in 1962, Operation Breadbasket was a pressure group that sought economic gains for blacks. Its specific goals were improved job opportunities, more purchases of products manufactured by black-owned companies, more deposits in black-owned banks, and more advertising in black-owned publications and broadcasting stations. The operation's main weapon was economic boycott.

This powerful battle group scored many victories in the 1960s, constantly sharpening its tactics, beefing up its muscle, and attracting charismatic leaders like Rev. Jesse Jackson. There were many business people who had an almost superstitious dread of Operation Breadbasket, for they felt it was unbeatable. But when the group decided to take on A&P's New York division in the early 1970s, Operation Breadbasket finally met its match.

There had been a preliminary skirmish in Chicago in the late 1960s that had added to the pressure group's reputation for invincibility. In 1967, a local unit of Operation Breadbasket, led by Jesse Jackson, had gone after A&P's Chicago division, demanding more promotions of blacks to responsible positions in A&P stores, more buying of black-manufactured products, more deposits of A&P money in black banks, and more A&P ad dollars for the black press and broadcasters. The Chicago division, contemplating the threat of a widespread boycott of its stores, knuckled under. There was wide disagreement on the justice of the demands, but the issues were highly emotional and not easy to resolve in reasonable debate. Though the cost of settling the dispute was high, the Chicago management felt a boycott would be worse.

Encouraged by that victory, the black group then set its sights on A&P's big New York division in the early 1970s.

The group's first move was to request a meeting with William Kane, A&P's president and chief operating officer, but Kane, after some thought, turned them down. If he were to meet the group in his capacity as president, he felt, it would seem as though he were negotiating for A&P nationally and he had no intention of being snookered into such a position. These negotiations were supposedly about the New York division, and Kane wanted that to be very clearly understood.

A&P therefore offered to set up meetings for the black group with two divisional vice presidents. Operation Breadbasket flatly rejected the offer, calling it an insult.

Positions were hardening. A storm was gathering. Operation Breadbasket's area chairman, Rev. William Jones, called a meeting in Brooklyn and was granted authority to act as he saw fit. He told the press and broadcasters that if A&P remained stubborn, he would have no choice but to begin applying pressure. When A&P refused to budge, Rev. Jones called a boycott of all A&P stores in the New York metropolitan area.

The boycott wasn't effective. One reason was A&P's own policy of trying to be helpful in poor neighborhoods—a policy that had been applauded by civic leaders in the past. While many grocery stores—big chain-owned supermarkets and small Mom-and-Pop stores alike—had fled poor neighborhoods around New York, A&P had staunchly remained, providing both shopping convenience and jobs. The result was that, in many neighborhoods, the A&P was the only food store within walking and bag-carrying distance. And so Rev. Jones's call for a boycott of these stores went largely unheeded.

Rev. Jones then decided on a direct frontal assault of the A&P corporate headquarters. He and two dozen other clergymen, both black and white, turned up one day at the Graybar Building in mid-Manhattan. They took elevators to the twenty-second floor, where A&P had its executive offices, and demanded to see the president, Bill Kane. Kane was out of town on a trip and the chairman and CEO, Mel Alldredge, who was in his office, quickly and quietly vanished before the visitors could find him.

The enraged clergyman then moved into Bill Kane's office, sat down, and announced they were going to stay until they got satisfaction.

A&P had been a Byoir client for several years. Some colleagues and I now hurried to the Graybar Building to assess the situation.

One of our first moves was to suggest that the clergymen be isolated from A&P employees. The employees were promptly moved to the other side of the building, giving the clergy group access to A&P people only when we chose to allow it.

The press, radio and TV reporters, and cameramen were there in force. So were the police. But we earnestly asked the police to take no action. This was logic talking, not emotion. The clergymen were disruptive but were not doing anything physically violent. If the police were to arrest them with dozens of press and broadcasting people looking on, we might well end up with a PR problem bigger than we could handle.

The journalists crowded into Kane's office and interviewed the uninvited visitors and, naturally, A&P was not spoken of kindly. The clergymen hurled accusations of wrongdoing, richly buttered with fiction. One often-repeated piece of fiction that had been around for years and was always dusted off anew whenever people were attacking A&P had to do with the company's pricing policies. It was alleged that A&P stores in poor black and Hispanic neighborhoods charged higher prices than A&P stores in more affluent white suburbs.

The allegation was completely false. But I knew the charge would appear in that night's TV news and tomorrow morning's newspapers unless we did something fast.

Up till then we had been ignoring our opponents, avoiding confrontations. Now I felt the time was right to switch to a directly confrontational stance. I suggested that an articulate A&P spokesman go out to the elevator lobby, where journalists were congregating, and refute the pricing charge and other fictions that were being tossed around. I suggested that the spokesman be executive vice president Bill Corbus, an imposing man, former All-American football star from Stamford, and down-to-earth speaker. I felt that if anybody could make the media listen, he could.

Moreover, I knew that he would be dealing from strength. The case he would present was unassailable. The plain fact, which any reporter could check out for himself or herself, was that A&P's prices were *not* higher in poor neighborhoods. Other unfounded charges being hurled by the clergyman were just as easy to refute.

Other stories in this book deal with the often-difficult question of whether to remain silent in a dispute or get into a public argument. The answer I always come up with is this: If the dispute involves emotional or subjective matters on which reasonable people may differ, you and your client may be better off keeping your mouths shut. But if the quarrel is about factual matters and if you have the facts nailed down, speak out.

Bill Corbus spoke out. Backing him up was another knowledgeable executive, Fred Campbell, the corporate secretary. They were convincing. Our side of the story was well told in the media over the next few days.

Equally encouraging was the fact that A&P then began to

receive phone calls from customers of its stores in both poor and affluent areas. These customers had read and heard the news, were aware of the Breadbasket group's use of economic clout, and wanted to assure A&P that they would continue to buy their groceries in A&P stores. They begged the company not to close down any stores.

In the midst of all this, of course, we at Byoir were feeding the media good, solid, factual material about A&P's hiring and promotion policies. We felt the company's record in hiring minority employees, helping them learn new skills, and boosting them up the job ladder was excellent. We were successful in getting this part of the story into a wide assortment of press and broadcasting outlets, including black newspapers, magazines, and radio stations.

The clergymen in Bill Kane's office read the papers and heard the broadcasts along with everybody else. It must have become apparent to them that they were not winning the tumultuous public applause they had hoped for. After camping in the office one night and staying a total of thirty-five hours, they stood up, dusted off their rumpled clothes, and left.

A few days later, Jesse Jackson came to town.

Jackson by this time was national chairman of Operation Breadbasket. He vowed to remain in New York until he met with Bill Kane. We continued to urge Kane not to expose himself to any such confrontation. After a few days, Jackson and a group of demonstrators turned up at the Graybar Building and started making a noisy disturbance in the ground-floor lobby.

We were in a quandary. As in the case of the clergymen in Kane's office, we were reluctant to ask for police intervention, afraid of making martyrs of Jackson and his followers. The picture could be made to look bad—giant A&P bullying a few harmless demonstrators—and as much as some of us may have wished to respond belligerently, we restrained ourselves.

On the other hand, Jackson's demonstration was noisier than the clergymen's relatively quiet sit-in. It was more public, and there was a chance it could grow into violence. What should we do?

We found an effective solution. To the Jackson group's evident surprise, the police came and arrested them for trespassing and disorderly conduct. But we were very careful to see that all the media got the facts straight. The complaint was signed by the superintendent of the Graybar Building, not by A&P.

So far we had kept the media informed on our side of the controversy—or at least neutral—throughout this whole distressing affair. We were determined to keep it that way. We continued to generate a steady stream of story material. We set up interviews with A&P people, including black store managers and other blacks in well-paid jobs. We made executives available to responsible journalists who were known to us.

But Bill Kane never made himself available to Jesse Jackson. Jackson eventually left town quietly.

Moreover, the store boycott was turning into an out-and-out failure. The public simply wasn't buying the Breadbasket group's charges. As a matter of fact—this was frosting on our cake—the A&P stores in New York's poorest neighborhoods actually *increased* their sales volume over the period of the struggle.

But the Breadbasket group was implacable. They refused to give up. Two months after Jesse Jackson quit the fray, a new standard-bearer turned up. This was Rev. Ralph Abernathy, who had succeeded Martin Luther King, Jr. as president of the Southern Christian Leadership Conference.

Abernathy was tough, persistent, a natural-born leader. We again prepared for trouble.

With a shouting group of forty-four civil-rights demonstrators, Abernathy turned up at the Graybar Building one morning and presented the by-now familiar demand—to see Bill Kane. The answer was the just-as-familiar no. Abernathy then announced that the Breadbasket group would expand its boycott to all A&P stores in the nation. No longer was this just a struggle about A&P New York division, he thundered. Now it was national.

We had seen to it, of course, that the failure of the New York boycott had been well reported in all the media. There were probably not many of Abernathy's hearers who got excited over his new threat.

Abernathy stayed at the Graybar Building for six hours, trying to get something going. He spent much of his time in the ground-floor lobby, where a crowd of journalists and TV camera crews milled about. He kept demanding face-to-face confrontations with A&P's national management. We continued to offer no response.

We were now back in our nonconfrontational stance.

Frustrated, Abernathy decided to board an elevator. "I'm going up to see Mr. Kane!" he shouted.

But A&P had planned ahead. The elevator was set to bypass the twenty-second floor. No matter what Abernathy did, he couldn't get it to stop there. Finally he rode it up to the twenty-third floor and walked down the fire stairs. But the door to the twenty-second floor was bolted from the inside.

Rev. Abernathy went back to the lobby. His demonstrators got noisier. Late in the afternoon, the building superintendent once again signed a complaint, and the Abernathy group departed in police vans.

We were careful once again to stress the fact that A&P had not asked for Abernathy's arrest.

The media were still reporting fairly. All along, this New York story had been reported nationally because of its widespread ramifications. Rev. Abernathy's threat of a national A&P boycott made it all the more interesting in distant towns and cities, particularly those served by A&P supermarkets. But since the petering out of the New York boycott had been widely reported, the new threat failed to make big headlines or generate excited stories.

As it turned out, the national boycott was no more successful than the New York one. It succeeded sporadically in some cities but in a few months was pretty well abandoned.

Operation Breadbasket gave up on A&P. Though there were isolated threats and fist-shaking speeches from time to time, no more troops came to New York. There were no more adventures at the Graybar Building. It was over.

Left to itself, A&P continued to improve the lot of its minority employees. We continued to see to it that these accomplishments were made known to the press and broadcasters.

Our client had won the game.

The media and public are sometimes fair, sometimes not. You never know in advance which it will be.
          —A story of Hallmark and a hotel disaster

Late on the afternoon of Friday, July 17, 1981, disaster struck in Kansas City, Missouri. A tea dance was in progress at the year-old Hyatt Regency Hotel. This was a free public affair, designed in part to help promote the Crown Center, a brilliantly successful urban-renewal project of which the Hyatt was flagship. Hundreds of people were dancing and milling about on the ground floor of the hotel's dizzyingly high-ceilinged lobby. Up above, scores of others stood on two high suspended walkways.

Suddenly the upper walkway's supports gave way. It fell with its burden of screaming people onto the lower walkway. That walkway's supports gave way, too, and both crashed into the dense crowd of people on the lobby floor. More than a hundred people were killed instantly, and nearly two hundred others were hurt, some critically. It was the worst disaster in Kansas City's history and one of the worst hotel disasters ever.

It was the lead story in most TV news broadcasts that night, and the next morning it was on the front pages of virtually all big metropolitan newspapers. It was of special concern to me, for I knew something that the media did not seem to know in those first hours after the tragedy—the hotel was owned by a subsidiary of Hallmark Cards, one of Byoir's oldest clients.

Donald Hall, the CEO, said later that the disaster gave him some of the darkest hours of his life. What made the tragedy almost unbearably poignant for him was that some Hallmark employees and their families were among the victims.

The next afternoon, I called Hallmark's public-relations director, Bryan Putman, and asked if there was anything I could do. He said, no, not at the moment. Don Hall wasn't taking any calls from the media and probably wouldn't for several days.

Bryan said he would call me when the initial surge of painful emotions subsided a bit.

He called a few days later to tell me that Don Hall wanted to set up a meeting to assess the public-relations damage to Hallmark and Crown Center. He wanted me there. I said I was on my way.

It was typical of Don Hall that he was worried as much about his city as about his company. He had always been a Kansas City booster, as had his father, who had Hallmark pay the entire bill for our services in repairing Kansas City's PR damage after that 1950s flood. Later we were hired by Kansas City itself for ongoing PR counsel in the city's effort to change its image from cow town to a bustling, modern metropolis. Don Hall had always been in the forefront of that effort. He and his father conceived and developed Crown Center, a gleaming complex of office buildings, stores, and restaurants, dominated by the forty-story Hyatt Regency.

Before the meeting in Kansas City, I asked our regional offices to give me reports on what their local media were saying about the catastrophe. At that point, just a few days after the event, it was impossible to judge which way public and press opinion would swing. Who would get the blame? It was impossible to guess. Public and media opinion are mercurial and unpredictable.

Byoir regional people reported that no heavy share of blame was being hung on Hallmark—at least not so far. I took this encouraging news to the meeting and though Don Hall was pleased to hear it, he was tense and worried. He was expecting lawsuits, intended to settle them fast, but had no way of estimating the cost. He had spent much time in the past few days offering condolences and help to the families of employees who had lost someone in the disaster or were worrying about a family member in the hospital.

At one point during those early days I received a call from a *New York Times* reporter who was covering the disaster's aftermath. He said he had learned that Hallmark and Kansas City were longtime clients of ours. (At the time we had worked thirty years for Hallmark and fifteen for the city.) The reporter wanted my opinion: Would the Hyatt tragedy hurt the city's efforts to attract visitors, conventions, and corporate offices?

I replied optimistically, saying, "The impact will be temporary. No city is immune to disasters, whether they're natural or manmade." I offered several recent examples, including the outbreak of Legionnaires' disease in Philadelphia and the collapse of a sports arena's snow-laden roof in Hartford, Connecticut. Neither tragedy had brought economic punishment to the city involved, I pointed out.

My words were faithfully reported in the *Times*. But I wondered if I was being overoptimistic.

Investigations of the disaster got under way. Everybody involved was pointing at somebody else. Hallmark continued to be left pretty much out of it. Some blame seemed to be falling on the Hyatt Hotels Corporation, which had been operating the Hyatt Regency, but there were no serious repercussions yet. Several engineering and construction firms were prominently mentioned as the investigations continued, and the public appeared to feel that the heaviest culpability would eventually be found to rest on one or more of these companies or some of their employees.

We had several more meetings at Hallmark. I assigned a Byoir staffer to work in Kansas City full time, dealing with the daily PR problems that kept cropping up as a result of the investigations, the lawsuits, and related matters. These were mostly minor problems, I'm happy to say, but in case a major problem did suddenly arise, I was glad to have somebody on the spot. We worked hard to keep the media and the public informed on Hallmark's civic activities, its sympathetic response to the tragedy, and so on. And we drew up contingency plans in case the media suddenly focused on Hallmark as a scapegoat.

But it never happened.

Why not? It's impossible to say for sure. I like to think our public-relations work had something to do with the outcome— perhaps a great deal to do with it. I'm not referring just to our work specifically dealing with the disaster and its aftermath, but to everything we had done during the three decades we'd had Hallmark as a client.

I remarked in an earlier story that Hallmark was the kind of client any PR counselor could wish to have. It hadn't been difficult for us to help establish it as a company with an unusually warm heart. People *liked* Hallmark. It was this as much as anything, I think, that saved the company from public criticism after the Hyatt disaster.

Kansas City also recovered well. There was no falloff of visitors, conventions, or corporate activity.

The collapse of those walkways was a nightmare, particularly to those directly involved. But the effects of the disaster could have spread much farther and wider and longer than they did.

Some public-relations problems are so huge and complicated that you have to attack them from a dozen angles at once.
—A story of Woolworth in the years of the sit-in

There are public-relations people both inside and outside Byoir who believe the most challenging problem in all PR history was the nightmare Woolworth went through as a result of those sit-ins during the early to middle 1960s. I'm not sure I'd call it *the* most challenging, but it certainly ranks in the top five. It was a period of intense challenge for me personally as well as for Woolworth. There was no precedent.

I'm proud of the outcome. We guided our client through the valley of the shadow, and Woolworth came out the other side with its virtue and earning power intact. Our campaign on Woolworth's behalf has been mentioned many times as a potential candidate for a Silver Anvil or some other PR award, but because of its extreme delicacy, we never submitted it for any nomination.

Our work for the big variety-store chain was a textbook case of how to tackle a complex problem with a many-pronged strategy. It is on that strategy that I'll focus attention in this story.

Black people in southern towns and cities were demanding to be served at Woolworth lunch counters which, by community tradition, had always been reserved for whites. Although other variety-store chains and hundreds of individual restaurants and coffee shops were also targets of sit-in campaigns, Woolworth, because of its size and the universal familiarity of its name, became the main target and, unwillingly, the symbol of white resistance.

I recall reading about the growing mess—the demonstrations, the white-black confrontations, the frequent violence, the store closings—and wondering how Woolworth was going to survive. For months, Woolworth executives tried to make the problem go away by complaining that their company had been singled out unfairly. This wasn't a Woolworth problem, they said, but a problem of the American people.

That cut no ice with anybody, black or white. It was perfectly true, but nobody was listening. The problem continued to get inexorably worse.

Finally, in November 1960, Woolworth decided it needed outside PR help. We and two other agencies were invited to look the situation over and present strategies for pulling the desperate company out of the morass in which it was sinking.

My superiors told me I would be the account executive if Woolworth were to become our client. After some meetings at which Woolworth people showed us the massive scope of their problem, I was told to go into my office, lock the door, and draft a strategy.

It took me two days. The Woolworth people liked it, and we were hired. In the turbulent years that followed, my strategy was the basic guiding document of our campaign. We added to it and modified it as conditions changed and new elements of the hydra-headed problem asserted themselves. Here were some of our main moves:

• We saw to it that every one of the thousands of letters Woolworth had received was answered. The regional office in Boston had collected a staggering total of 45,000 letters, the majority of them threatening a boycott if Woolworth didn't promptly desegregate all its lunch counters. The Atlanta office had taken in some 15,000 letters, most of them threatening a boycott if the company *did* desegregate its counters. That was a stark illustration of the kind of tightrope Woolworth was being required to walk. A blunder in either direction, a slip of the tongue, an apparent lean toward one side or the other, could bring instant disaster.

I felt it was important to answer all those letters quickly rather than just let them keep piling up. The huge number of them had buffaloed Woolworth's people. I made it my first major task to get those mountains of mail cleared away. I read a sampling of the letters and determined that virtually all of them could be satisfied with one of five replies. I wrote the five replies, in courteous, friendly, and personal-sounding plain English. Woolworth then assigned teams of people to read their way through the mail and send the appropriate replies. This was a technique I was to apply in other situations later—the Kodak episode, for instance.

The mail readers worked down to bare tabletops in five weeks. Surprisingly, thousands of people sent courteous replies to *our* replies.

• We worked to make the media stop using Woolworth as a symbol.

Time and again, I found myself reading newspaper and wire-service stories that began like this: "F.W. Woolworth and six other store chains were picketed by student demonstrators today . . ." That lead became depressingly familiar. I not only read it; I heard it on radio and TV news reports.

It seemed to me that this wasn't malicious on the journalists' part, at least not in most cases. It was plain laziness. The name Woolworth had become a journalistic cliché, a buzzword that quickly and conveniently conveyed a whole load of meaning to readers or listeners and thus saved the writer a lot of work. In exactly the same way, years later, the name Watergate (and other names with the suffix *gate*) would become another journalistic work-saver.

Journalists often slip into such cliché-ridden writing without realizing they are doing it. To make them stop, usually all you need do is find some inoffensive way to point out the failing.

So that is what I did. I wrote a letter for the signature of Edward Harrigan, Woolworth's vice president of public relations, asking editors and producers in a pleasant and friendly way to stop singling out Woolworth as a symbol of a massively complicated, nationwide problem.

Journalists as a group are as fair minded as anybody— perhaps more so than most, since they're trained to be impartial. Within a few weeks, most of them stopped using Woolworth's name in this symbolic sense.

• In May 1961, I recommended that it was time to secure the services of a black PR man or woman.

I felt we needed somebody who had good contacts with black leaders. I interviewed several candidates without success. Then, one day, a young black man named Bob Brown came into our New York office on an unrelated matter. The office staff knew of my search, and Bob Brown was sent to see me.

I liked his appearance and demeanor. He had his own small PR firm in North Carolina (where, incidentally, the very first Woolworth lunch counter sit-in had taken place). He also had friendly contacts with people in black organizations such as NAACP and CORE. On my strong recommendation, Woolworth approved our hiring his firm to work alongside us.

• We developed a series of feature stories and other material dealing with black Woolworth employees who had risen to high positions—store managers, advertising executives, buyers, and so on. Bob and his associates then placed these pieces with black editors, broadcast journalists, and others, while the rest of us took care of the general press, radio, and TV.

The media were receptive. The fact was that Woolworth's record in treatment of blacks and other minority groups was excellent. Few other large organizations in the country—or in the world, for that matter—could top it. And there was one other fact we could point to in furtherance of our case—since the start of the sit-ins, not one arrest had been initiated by Woolworth.

• We assigned Bob the task of setting up hospitality suites at leading black conventions and other gatherings where there were large groups of blacks or a special interest in black affairs. On these occasions he would tell the Woolworth story using slides, press handouts, informal talks, and other means.

Among the conventions Bob graced with his friendly presence were those of the NAACP, the Urban League, the National Association of Negro Business and Professional Women, the National Bar Association, the National Newspaper Publishers Association—and even an undertakers' group. Bob and his associates went to literally dozens of conventions over a four-year period. We considered this conventioneering to be one of the most effective components of our grand strategy.

• Events played into our hands when Robert Kirkwood, Woolworth's chairman and CEO, was elected to the board of directors of the United Negro College Fund. Naturally we made full use of this unexpected windfall.

Woolworth had been a generous supporter of this fund for many years—a fact that wasn't widely known. We now made sure it became widely known. We distributed stories on Kirkwood's election and related subjects to the black and general media. Coverage was gratifyingly heavy.

• We set up personal meetings between Woolworth executives—Kirkwood, for one—and black leaders such as Roy Wilkins of the NAACP and James Farmer of CORE. These meetings were private; we made no attempt to milk them for publicity purposes. Their sole purpose was to convince the black leaders that Woolworth was acting out of a sincere wish to cool off the crisis and get its lunch counters desegregated without violence.

The black leaders understood, of course, that to desegregate all counters abruptly would bring on a white backlash and a whirlwind of violence. Nonetheless, Woolworth was able to point proudly to the fact that it had managed to desegregate in more than 100 southern communities in the first year since the sit-ins began. There had been some violence, but it was diminishing.

Our hope was that Wilkins, Farmer, and their colleagues would go away from these meetings in a mood to calm their followers down. We wanted them to say, "Take it easy. It's happening. Give it time." And that is what most of them did say, more and more often as time went on.

• We worked out a special way of desegregating. We refined it as we went along, and it got better and better. In the end, Woolworth was able to desegregate most lunch counters with virtually no violence and only a minimum of demonstrating, shouting, name calling, and other angry reactions.

We recommended, first, that the local Woolworth store manager make himself or herself a visible participant in the public debate in any town where desegregation was contemplated. This often meant joining or helping form a special committee—comprising blacks and whites—charged with handling the problem.

We recommended further that a public announcement of desegregation plans be made three months before any action was taken. This allowed the initial angry explosion to die down. It gave people time to cool off in debate.

Then, we urged that on desegregation day only two blacks

should show up to occupy seats at the disputed lunch counter. Just two—and they should be girls no more than twelve years old. This, we said, should continue daily for the first month.

This, too, had a violence-damping effect. Though sometimes the two girls were jeered at and left in tears, they were never physically molested, and in most towns they were simply allowed to sit and eat in peace. The outcome would almost certainly have been otherwise if those first lunch customers had been half a dozen swaggering young men. That could have led to riots.

And how did it all work? Beautifully.

The success of the strategy was illustrated dramatically in the spring of 1963, about two and a half years after we had gone to work for Woolworth.

At a Woolworth store in Jackson, Mississippi, two young black women and a young black man, all college students, sat down at a lunch counter that had not yet been subjected to our desegregation process. The counter was reserved for whites. Refused service, they remained seated. A crowd of jeering white teenagers set upon them, beat and kicked them, and doused them with mustard, ketchup, and sugar. Other blacks moved in to help them. Before long, the store manager realized he had a full-scale race riot on his hands. It lasted two and a half hours—plenty of time for reporters, TV crews, and other media folk to join the screaming crowds.

Fortunately, I was in Ed Harrigan's office in New York that afternoon when Roy Wilkins phoned to tell us about this latest eruption. We realized it was a major incident. Hundreds of teenagers and adults were evidently involved. The brawl would almost certainly make newspaper front pages and major TV news programs.

"We'd better put out a statement in a hurry," I said.

I wrote it rapidly. It was just four paragraphs long. It said that Woolworth regretted the incident, that the violence had been instigated by people having no connection with the company, that the store manager had not ordered any arrests, and that he had closed the store as quickly as possible so as to forestall further violence.

This statement was of course aimed at what had been our major strategic goal all along—to disconnect Woolworth from the sit-in scene and discourage use of the company's name as a symbol. The statement was hand-placed by Byoir people with major newspapers, magazines, and wire services and with the radio and TV networks.

The effect was exactly as we had hoped. Virtually all the media quoted from our statement. Woolworth was neither blamed nor referred to in symbolic terms.

But then Bob Kirkwood, the chairman, temporarily lost his cool. I was in Ed Harrigan's office the next morning at about eight o'clock to review the media coverage, when Kirkwood came in directly from the elevator, still wearing his hat and coat. He had seen the previous night's TV news and read the morning papers, and the explosion in Jackson had thrown him into a panic. He said he had decided to desegregate all remaining Woolworth lunch counters immediately.

"No, please don't!" I said urgently. "That won't solve any problems and might make them a whole lot worse. It could cause violence worse than anything we've seen yet. In fact, I'd bet on it."

"But here we are, back in the spotlight again. It's going to go on and on."

"Maybe we're in the spotlight," I said, "but we're not in the pillory. This isn't like 1960. Nobody's throwing stones at us any more. All the media reports I saw and read were fair to Woolworth. Your store in Jackson was just a place where a riot happened to break out—that's the way it's being told."

Kirkwood shrugged gloomily. "That's true. But is the public going to pay attention to that?"

"Let's wait a few days and see. If we get buried with thousands of hysterical letters, like 1960, then obviously we've got more thinking to do. But I don't think we will. Let's sit tight until we find out."

The total of letters that came into Woolworth's New York

headquarters, commenting on the Jackson brawl, was exactly six.

Kirkwood was grateful that I'd restrained him. Our strategy had succeeded completely. Woolworth was no longer the symbol of anything. It was just a chain of stores.

CHAPTER 3

PLANNING AND SETTING OBJECTIVES

Because PR campaigns can be highly complex and confusing, you need to establish well-defined goals and plans to avoid getting lost.

A public-relations effort should have specific objectives, not just a general motivation like "making friends."
—A story of the University of Chicago and the Atomic Energy Commission

ROBERT MAYNARD Hutchins, chancellor of the University of Chicago, had a highly specific reason for retaining Byoir. It was right after the Second World War, and he wanted the university to gain world renown as the chief center for peacetime development of atomic energy.

It seemed to me that the most important word in that statement was "peacetime," and in talks with Hutchins, I became certain that he shared this view. I kept my thoughts sharply focused on this specific objective, and by doing so was able to score a major public-relations success.

My main duty on this account was to interview the famous atomic scientists who had been associated with the university—men like Enrico Fermi, Harold Urey, Leo Szilard, Edward Teller—and generate stories about their peacetime activities.

It was fascinating. These men were the very founders of the atomic age. Their association with the university went back to 1940, the beginning of the Manhattan Project—the American effort to develop the world's first atomic bomb. The man in charge of this huge, secret, and desperate effort was Lieutenant General Lesley Groves. He had approached three universities in the very earliest months of the war—first MIT, then Columbia, finally Chicago. He needed a major university to provide the physical setting and the pool of scientific talent necessary for

91

conducting the first atomic experiments. However, he could offer only high risk—and little compensation.

"I'll have to put it to you frankly," he told the three university heads. "If this project succeeds, the government will get the credit. If it fails, you'll get most of the blame."

MIT and Columbia turned him down. Hutchins of Chicago decided to sign on. He was already looking forward to war's end and the fabulous possibilities of cheap, abundant energy from atomic fission and the promise of radioisotopes.

So Chicago became the center of research. And on December 2, 1942, in a squash court on the university grounds, Enrico Fermi and a team of nervous colleagues achieved the world's first self-sustaining nuclear chain reaction.

That was the dawn of the atomic age.

At least, I always thought it was. But I discovered in 1947 that not everybody else thought so.

Some time in the early fall of 1947 I conceived the idea of a special celebration at the University of Chicago on December 2. That would be the fifth anniversary of the atomic age's birth. When I mentioned the idea to Hutchins, he was enthusiastic. So were Fermi and the other atomic scientists; they said they would be honored to attend such a celebration. My superiors at Byoir were also pleased with the idea. Such an anniversary party could be counted on to get media attention the world over—exactly the kind of attention our client wanted.

I suggested we invite David Lilienthal, chairman of the newly formed Atomic Energy Commission, to take part in our celebration. Unfortunately, it turned out that the AEC considered the atomic age to have been born on July 16, 1945, the date when the first atom bomb was exploded near Trinity Site, New Mexico.

The Atomic Energy Commission was thinking about holding celebrations of its own at appropriate dates in the future. But Hutchins decided to stick with December 2, and I agreed. The AEC anniversary date was the birthday of a bomb, but Hutchins wanted the university to be known as a *peacetime* atomic center. Fermi and the squash court seemed more appropriate.

I got on the phone to the AEC. "We're going ahead with our

own party," I told an aide. "We'd still like Mr. Lilienthal to join us."

"He won't. You've got the date wrong."

We went ahead. Advance publicity was widespread and positive. Indeed, it became apparent that everyone who was someone in the peacetime atom business would be there.

On December 1, the day before our celebration, David Lilienthal's secretary called and said he would like to attend after all. His presence officially established December 2 as the birth of the atomic age. Not a single person in the world disputed the date.

The affair was a rousing success. December 2 has had an up-and-down history since then. Some years it is virtually ignored, but it gets resurrected from time to time. The last time was at my suggestion, in 1982, when the NBC network ran a fortieth-anniversary TV tribute to Fermi, and John Barbour of the Associated Press wrote a full-page story that was published by hundreds of newspapers throughout the world. Fermi still lives!

It is important not only to have clear PR objectives but also to measure, if possible, how well you have achieved them.
—A story of the American Bankers Association and a tax law

In July 1982, Congress passed one of its periodic tax-reform acts. Proponents of these acts almost always hail them as being aimed at tax "simplification," and such was the advance billing of the 1982 act. Like all the others, however, its actual effect was to make everything substantially more complicated.

Tucked into its pages of virtually unintelligible verbiage was a provision that went nearly unnoticed by the public but that alarmed the American Bankers Association. The provision called for the withholding, at the source, of 10 percent of most interest and dividends paid out by banks, stockbrokers, and others. If you had a bank savings account, in other words, and if this account earned you $1,000 in interest over the course of a year, the new law would have required your bank to withhold $100 and send it to the Internal Revenue Service.

The ABA was greatly disturbed by this provision, which was about to slip quietly into law. For one thing, it would complicate record keeping and add to banks' clerical costs. Worse, the ABA felt, it was almost certain to annoy depositors once they woke up to its existence—and the main target of the depositors' annoyance was probably going to be the nation's banks.

It was time to roll up sleeves and do some hard PR work.

The American Bankers Association had been the Byoir organization's client since 1979. Our account executive for this client was Nina Palmer, one of the ablest PR staffers I've ever worked with. Back in 1979 she had started our work for the ABA by organizing a program to help bankers make a good impression in public. Bankers from all over the country came to New York for our special three-day course—called MediaCom (short for Media and Communication)—in which they learned how to speak well before groups, how to be interviewed by news reporters, and how to handle themselves on radio and TV. We even had a replica of a TV studio built at our New York offices for this training.

The training was to pay off handsomely when we got into the struggle over the 1982 tax act.

When the ABA told us it wanted our help in that struggle, we suggested that the first move should be some research to find out just where we stood. In particular, we said, there were three things we needed to know:

    1. To what extent is the public already aware of the withholding provision of the tax act, and what do people think of it?

2. What percentage of ABA members would support a major effort by the group to get the provision repealed?

3. To what degree are news reporters, talk-show hosts, and other media people interested in the provision?

The answers were about what we expected, only more so. It turned out that the public was almost completely unaware of the withholding rule—few had even heard of it. But when it was explained to them, most were unhappy over it. They felt it represented a further loss of control over their earnings, smacked of big brotherism, and implied that they were tax cheats. Moreover, if imposed, it would have the effect of seeming to cut their interest and dividend income by 10 percent.

As for the second question, an ABA survey of its members found them solidly in favor of an effort to get the withholding rule killed.

Byoir regional offices surveyed their local press corps and broadcasting media to get the answer to the third question. It turned out that reporters had no interest whatever in the withholding rule, saw no news or feature value in the issue, and responded to discussion of it with a yawn.

So that was that. The job ahead was obviously a big one. If the ABA wanted to get people stirred up over the rule with the hope of eventually getting it repealed, it would have to tackle the task alone. Nobody else was around to help.

We moved into the planning stage of the project. Working with the ABA people, Nina Palmer and I and our colleagues established three specific, clearly stated objectives. And at the same time, we also established measurement criteria by which to judge how well we were moving toward our objectives. The three goals and their associated criteria were:

1. To get Americans stirred up about the withholding rule, make them aware of what it would mean to them, and enlist their help in killing it. To test how effectively we were accomplishing this objective, we suggested that the ABA hire a public-opinion polling firm to quiz people on the issue. The criterion was obvious—to effect the greatest pos-

sible improvement in the public awareness of the issue, starting with a score of just about zero as the campaign began.

2. To make it clear to the public that bankers were *not* in favor of the withholding rule—it wasn't their idea, they had nothing to do with its formulation, and if it were imposed, bankers would not deserve even the smallest share of the blame. The criterion of success—how clearly the bankers' position was portrayed in news stories, editorials, cartoons, and other areas of the media. We would ask continually, Are the media saying strongly and unquivocally that bankers and their association are against the administration and Congress on this issue?

3. To get the rule repealed—or at least to come as close as possible, leaving no doubt in anybody's mind that a good fight had been fought. The ultimate signal of success in this case, of course, would be repeal of the rule. But failing that, there were criteria of lesser success. Could we at least get Congress to vote on the issue? How close would the vote be? And when it was all over, even if the troublesome rule remained on the books, what would Mr. and Mrs. Depositor say when their savings bank chopped 10 percent out of their interest earnings? Would they say, "This isn't the bank's fault"?

We plunged into the battle to achieve these three goals. The MediaCom staff's work with bankers in our training course now paid off. Though Byoir and the ABA coordinated the massive effort, provided kits of relevant material, and worked with the national media, the bulk of the work had to be done by the ABA's 14,000 member banks. It was up to bank executives in each town to speak on the issue at their local service clubs, give interviews to their hometown newspapers and radio stations, get themselves on TV talk shows, and make themselves visible in any other ways they could think of. This was a deliberate policy on our part. We figured people would be more willing to listen to a hometown banker than to an amorphous organization far away in Washington.

However, we did encourage the ABA to wage a high-visibility
battle on Capitol Hill to achieve our second goal, making sure
people knew which side of the issue bankers stood on. Byoir saw
to it, of course, that news of this Washington battle was well
reported in the national press and broadcast media.

And then we organized a massive letter-writing campaign. We
wanted citizens of all income levels and social groups to bom-
bard Congress with mail. For those who didn't want to write
letters, postcards and ballot boxes were placed in bank lobbies,
along with material explaining briefly what the withholding rule
was and what it meant to depositors. A bank customer could
express his or her outrage simply by marking a card and dropping
it in the box.

To support the local bankers in their efforts, Nina and other
Byoir people helped the ABA prepare kits of varied material
which were sent to every member bank. The kits contained
sample postcard ballots, sample letters to Congress, a letter for
the bank to send to its stockholders, a speech to be delivered by
a bank executive, a news release, an op-ed article, and other
items that we thought would be useful.

Simultaneously, ABA spokespeople were fanning out across
the country, backing up the local bankers with their own TV and
press interviews. These ABA travelers concentrated particularly
on the hometowns of members of Congress. Between October
1982 and February 1983 they participated in 219 interviews and
other media appearances, all bearing down hard on our issue.

As our huge campaign got rolling, opposition arose from
congressmen, Treasury officials, and others who favored the
withholding rule. We were ready for this. Whenever they stood
up, we shot them down.

When they said the elderly and unemployed would be mostly
exempt from the withholding rule, the ABA immediately issued
a statement saying that was a laugh. To qualify for an exemp-
tion, you had to fill out a multitude of forms and hack your way
through a typical bureaucratic jungle.

When they said the rule would hardly cost the public a nickel,
the ABA released a set of carefully considered estimates putting
the cost to consumers at about $3 billion a year.

When they said the rule would catch a lot of tax cheats, the ABA smilingly pointed to IRS's own figures, which showed that only a small percentage of people ever choose to cheat on this kind of tax. The chances of getting caught are too large to make the risk worthwhile. As the ABA pointed out, the small number of cheats could be reduced still more by a few simple, inexpensive improvements in the system of matching taxpayer identification numbers with bank and stockbroker forms.

We refused to give them an inch. As our campaign rolled on, some of the most powerful opponents got mad. One of these was Senator Bob Dole, who was then chairman of the Senate Banking Committee. He threatened to raise bank taxes if the ABA didn't lay off. Some bankers got nervous about this and seemed to waver in their support for our campaign. They urged that the ABA cave in, or at least backtrack a bit and seek a compromise.

Byoir strongly urged the ABA to stand firm. To compromise now could be to lose everything, we said. If a compromise were to be worked out, banks would be forced into the position of endorsing it and ending with a share of the blame—the very problem they had struggled so valiantly to avoid.

There were some nervous moments, but the ABA listened to our counsel and stood firm. Our position was supported by Joseph Riley, chairman and CEO of a large Washington bank and chairman of the ABA's Communications Committee.

And we won the game. Careful planning and careful measurement of results enabled us to achieve every one of our three goals with room to spare. Here's how it went:

The first goal: To make people aware of the withholding rule and get them stirred up over it. A polling outfit took a sounding of public opinion in October 1982 and again in April 1983. On a scale of one to ten, the score in October was as low as it could get, one. Six months later, in April, it was all the way up to eight. Another measurement of public concern was the 11 million pieces of mail Congress received as a result of our campaign.

The second goal: Getting the bankers' position accurately portrayed in the media. We achieved this handily. By the end of the campaign there had been so many news reports, editorials, TV debates, cartoons, and other media examinations of the issue, all portraying bankers as adversaries of the rule, that it was hard to believe a single journalist in America was unaware of the ABA's position.

The third goal: Getting the rule repealed.

It was repealed in August 1983.

The American Bankers Association got virtually all the credit for this outcome. For once, bankers were the people's heroes.

The bankers even got a pat on the back of sorts from one of their most dedicated adversaries, Senator Dole. Later that summer the Senate was discussing the touchy issue of raising congressional salaries and allowances. The Senators felt they deserved better pay but knew there would be a lot of public carping about the idea. Senator Dole took the floor and made a suggestion. Maybe, he said, the Senate ought to hire the ABA to do its grass-roots PR work.

A message may have several distinct audiences. It helps to identify them clearly.
                    —A story of the Sugar Association and
                                        a dietary assault

There was a sudden upsurge of diet faddism in the middle 1970s. Newspaper food-and-fashion pages, women's magazines, and the airwaves were filled with strange new diets and dietary notions. People were told they could get thin, prevent heart attacks, rejuvenate aging skin, and gain innumerable other health benefits by eating seaweed, avoiding foods grown with chemical fertilizers, and so on. Much of this stuff was of dubious authenticity, some of it was egregious nonsense, and some was plain, old-fashioned quackery.

Some familiar, well-liked foods that had long been staples of American diets came under attack during this peculiar period.

One such food was sugar. People were told to avoid it for all kinds of reasons. Some of those reasons had a documented basis in scientific fact and some didn't. Naturally, the Sugar Association, which had been a Byoir client since 1973, became alarmed. It was in 1976 that its president, Bill Tatem, called me and said he would like to have our help in fighting the surge of misinformation.

The counterattack we planned was one of the most complex campaigns I've ever supervised. I was lucky to have two good professional people working with me. Our account executive and associate account executive assigned to the Sugar Association were, respectively, Jack O'Connell and Dorothy Buckner. Dorothy was an expert in the food field; she knew and was known by home economists, nutritionists, and other professionals around the country. She was also welcome in many newspaper and magazine offices and broadcast studios.

We began by identifying our target audiences. There were six of them, and we kept them clearly in view throughout the campaign:

• The general public—users of sugar in cooking, worriers about weight and health, lovers of ice cream and cookies—a thoroughly mixed-up lot at that moment. This huge general audience would be reached in part through the other five.
• The medical community.
• Nutrition professionals.
• Sugar-using industries—for instance, makers of soda pop, cake mixes, and the like. These industries were our natural allies. Unlike some of our other target audiences, they wouldn't need any great amount of persuasion to swing their weight our way.
• Government agencies and officials concerned with health and nutrition.
• The general media—newspapers, magazines, radio and TV.

We felt this last audience, the media, would be one of the toughest nuts we had to crack. As it happened, *TV Guide* had

commissioned journalist Max Gunther to write an article about
the current diet fads being promoted by the media. He was
shocked by the amount of false information being fed to the
public.

"What often happens," Gunther reported, "is that a TV producer or magazine editor dreams up some silly topic, like 'Eating seaweed cures athlete's foot,' or 'Sugar causes impotence.'
Then he sends a reporter out to gather the 'facts.' The reporter,
needing to earn her salary or freelance fee, isn't going to come
back and tell the editor his story idea is hogwash. If she interviews a nutritionist who says it *is* hogwash, that nutritionist
doesn't get quoted. She goes looking for 'experts' who will agree
with the cockeyed premise. The result is a story that is full of
quackery. There's no law against doing this, no punishment.
There ought to be, but there isn't."

This was the kind of situation we were up against. As just one
example, alarmists were saying repeatedly that Americans were
eating more and more sugar. The cold statistical fact was that
per-capita sugar consumption in this country hadn't changed in
fifty years.

Our objective, we agreed, was to convince our six audiences
that sugar is a safe and beneficial food when used as Americans
have always used it—sensibly. We worked out a strategy for
getting this message across.

One element of our strategy was to acknowledge forthrightly
that sugar in some forms will contribute to dental caries. Remember the rule I formulated in the case of the exploding glass
bottles—if there is a genuine problem with a client's product,
say so in plain English and then tell people what is being done
about it and what they should do about it. Our plan in the case
of sugar called for appropriate counsel from doctors, dentists,
government health officials, and other experts. We also planned
to disseminate information on research being carried out on
tooth cavities.

Another component of our strategy was the decision that, as
far as possible, we would let health experts do our talking for us.
We would find doctors, dentists, and others who were available
for press interviews, speaking engagements, panel discussions,

and so on. In this we took the risk that some of them might dwell too much on sugar's unwanted effects—the cavities, the results of overeating, and other negatives. But we felt this was a relatively small risk and one worth taking. The media and our other audiences, we felt, would listen more willingly to unaffiliated experts than to spokesmen for the Sugar Association.

For the same reason, the Sugar Association agreed with us that it should use no advertising during the campaign. No matter how carefully crafted, ads from the Sugar Association telling people to eat sugar would be seen as self-serving.

This last item of strategy clearly illustrates an advantage that public relations has over advertising. Later in the book we'll look at a few other advantages.

We swung into action, keeping our six audiences firmly fixed in mind. The campaign was so complicated and ranged in so many different directions that I won't attempt to describe it in full detail. Instead, let's just look at some of the most effective aspects:

• We set up an independent advisory council, including six doctors and two dentists, whom Jack O'Connell worked with closely. One of their assignments was to suggest worthwhile research projects for the sugar and sugar-using industries to fund—research on aspects of caries and oral hygiene, for instance. We also asked the advisory council to assemble existing scientific knowledge on sugar. A report on their findings, titled "Sugar in the Diet of Men," was published in a nutritionists' journal. We distributed 25,000 reprints to the general media—a good example of how we carried out our strategic decision to let experts do our talking for us.

• Dorothy Buckner set up two special sessions for a group of newspaper and magazine food editors. At each session a panel of doctors, dieticians, and other experts talked about nutrition and answered the editors' questions. The first session concentrated on sugar and health, while the second examined the problems of food information, misinformation, and quackery.

• There were at the time many nutritionists in universities and elsewhere—for instance, in the American Medical Association— who were expressing growing alarm over the tidal wave of food quackery and bad advice. We made a deliberate effort to support these men and women. In many cases we directly publicized their views and stood behind them as they attacked diet books, magazine articles, TV personalities, and other sources of misleading or fake information.

• We organized two national mailings to doctors, one on heart disease and the other on obesity. The mailings contained the results of scientific research—reports written by scientists, not by us.

• We went after the swarm of diet quacks and faddists who were infesting TV. Being in many cases colorful personalities, these people had found welcomes at many of the most popular talk shows. As Gunther quoted an AMA nutritionist in his *TV Guide* piece, "We scientific types tend to be pretty dull clods. That's why we don't get equal time against the quacks." But as our campaign moved ahead, we began to see to it that the "dull clods" did get equal time, and it turned out that they weren't all that dull, either.

• We circulated "mini-documentary" radio tapes on nutrition and sugar to 200 stations. The tapes covered a variety of topics and of course featured doctors and dentists, not Sugar Association spokespeople.

• We worked to establish the Association's Washington office as a source of reliable nutrition information. We also saw to it that the office was able to steer reporters to good independent sources qualified to talk on various related subjects.

• We made a deliberate effort to improve contacts with federal, state, and city government health officials. We wanted to be sure they received our message loud and clear.

• Dorothy Buckner spent a lot of time traveling about the country, attending conventions and other meetings of dieticians, food technologists, user-industry groups, and others concerned with our problem.

And the results? They were everything Bill Tatem and his Sugar Association members had hoped for. All six of our audiences responded to our message. The amount of inaccurate advice in the media diminished markedly. Doctors said they appreciated the association's frankness about caries and its encouragement of research. Nutritionists adopted "Sugar in the Diet of Man" as a basic teaching text, and it is still in use today. Sugar-using industries helped distribute our literature and originated campaigns of their own. As for our audience of government officials, both the National Academy of Sciences and the Food & Drug Administration issued documents favorable to sugar during or shortly after our campaign. And the public went on eating sugar as before.

We were proud of this campaign. We entered it in nomination for a Silver Anvil—an award given by the Public Relations Society of America that has the status of an Oscar in our profession. It won.

CHAPTER 4

COURTING THE MEDIA

A PR professional must get along well not only with clients but also with a second key group—the print and broadcast people. This takes study, practice, and patience.

Never try to mislead the media, particularly about earnings.
        —A story of Swift & Company and an ill-
                              advised deception

SWIFT & COMPANY, known today as Esmark, used to be one of the nation's (indeed, the world's) biggest meat-packing companies. When the meat-packing industry found itself in a quagmire of financial problems in the mid-1960s, Swift determined that its best route to salvation would be to diversify aggressively.

As part of this game plan, Swift hired outside public-relations counsel for the first time in its history. Byoir won the job in competitive presentations in 1969.

We went to work for a company that was undergoing a drastic metamorphosis. Under Robert W. Reneker, the chairman and CEO, Swift was in the process of cutting losses in its meat and food businesses and moving into more promising fields. In a five-year period, Reneker laid off roughly a third of the company's huge work force and closed 330 of its 700 plants, warehouses, and offices. Simultaneously he was getting the company into the oil, fertilizer, and retail gasoline businesses, among others.

A company undergoing such radical change is bound to stir up interest on Wall Street and in the business press, as Swift certainly did. The name change to Esmark in the early 1970s was widely noted and commented on. There were wide swings in the company's stock price as analysts seesawed from optimism to pessimism over the constantly shifting outlook for Esmark's future.

Things went well for a time. In 1971, the company was able to tell stockholders that its operating profit had grown from 2.3 percent of revenues to 3.6 percent. Bob Reneker, a natural-born optimist and honest man, predicted still greater glories to come—he said that earnings per share would climb from $2.66 in fiscal 1971 to $3.15 in 1972 and $4.00 in fiscal 1973.

They didn't.

Unexpected reverses hit the company. Bob Reneker's financial people began to warn him that 1972's earnings, far from showing the healthy jump he had predicted, could well show a 20 percent drop.

But some of the accountants had a suggestion. They urged that the company change its accounting method from LIFO (last-in-first-out) to FIFO (first-in-first-out). There were several sound financial reasons for doing this, but there was another reason that had more to do with cosmetic effect than finance— the move would make the company's earnings look better.

The change was instituted in the first quarter of 1972. I was visiting the company's offices one day when an executive vice president handed me a copy of a first-quarter earnings story that had just been prepared and asked me to handle its distribution among the usual business-news media.

I read the story, which emphasized good earnings. But buried on the second page was an almost offhand mention of the fact that the company had changed to a new accounting method.

I winced. "Something this significant ought to be up front," I said.

"What for? The big news is the good earnings."

I shook my head. "This could look bad. Business reporters and editors aren't naive. They'll wonder why your accounting change is buried on page two. They'll suspect you're trying to mislead them."

"Nonsense. Most of them won't even read page two."

We argued for a while longer. Finally he insisted that the story be distributed as it stood. I had no choice but to comply with the client's wishes.

We placed the story before noon on the appropriate day, handing it out to major newspapers, magazines, and the wire services. Around two o'clock that afternoon, we got a call from Bob Metz, a *New York Times* financial writer. Metz said he had some questions about the Swift story and I gave him the name and phone number of Swift-Esmark's PR director.

About two hours later, Denis Quinlan, the Byoir account executive at Swift, phoned to tell me what had happened. Metz had kept the PR chief on the phone for about half an hour and most of the conversation had dealt with the accounting change. The PR chief seemed not to enjoy the conversation. He sounded irritable. At one point he said angrily to Metz, "You don't know anything about accounting!"

Metz knew enough about accounting to know when somebody was trying to pull the wool over his eyes. The story next day in the *Times*, prominently placed, was devastating. Metz had seen clearly that the company's earnings, not too bad under the new accounting method, would have been dismal under the old one.

The Swift management was angry, but it was their own fault. Business journalists pride themselves on being able to understand financial reports. They also know that many or most people lack the knowledge or patience to study such reports carefully, and that as a result, a company that wishes to hide the truth about its financial condition can do so by artful manipulation of numbers. Business journalists consider themselves the public's watchdogs in this sense—they look sharply at corporate earnings reports and are delighted when they uncover attempted deceptions. To hope you can put something over on them is foolish indeed.

About a week after that *Times* story hit the streets, the company's PR director called me to say he had received a request for an in-depth management interview by *Forbes* magazine. This made my stomach lurch. *Forbes* for some time had been running unfriendly stories about big business. I wondered what the magazine had in mind for my client. Had *Forbes*'s interest in Swift been sparked by Bob Metz's piece in the *Times*?

I advised the PR director to tread warily, at least putting *Forbes* off until after the company's annual meeting, which was about a month away. Better yet, I said, he should give *Forbes* a flat no.

But the PR director was more optimistic than I was. He felt it was important to counteract that embarrassing *Times* story as quickly as possible.

Bob Reneker wasn't available for the *Forbes* interview in New York. So the PR chief went to the session with Don Kelly, the chief financial officer. Kelly (who would become Esmark's CEO eventually) performed competently at the interview, with the PR director sitting in. Both of them came out of it feeling that the Swift-Esmark story had been put across well, and were confident that the resulting *Forbes* piece would repair the damage done by Bob Metz of the *Times*.

Bob Reneker wasn't so sure. One day when I was visiting the company's headquarters, he called me into his office and asked if there was anything I could do to insure a favorable *Forbes* article. I told him no. The piece, I said, was probably already written, perhaps even set in type and at any rate, attempts to meddle in the writing process seldom work and usually irritate most journalists. Whatever could have been done to insure a favorable story, I said, had been done by Don Kelly and the PR chief during their interview.

Bob Reneker accepted that but still looked worried. And well he might have been.

The *Forbes* piece, when it appeared before the annual meeting, was even more devastating than the *Times* one. It contained snide comments about "gimmicks," advising investors to think long and hard before committing their good money to Esmark stock.

The saddest part of it was that in the course of a long article, *Forbes* had some nice things to say about Bob Reneker and his diversification plans and it wasn't often in those days that *Forbes* went out of its way to praise a corporate chieftain. The clear impression I got was that the piece would have been generally favorable—might even have been downright friendly—if it had not been for that amateurish attempt to gloss over the LIFO-FIFO accounting change.

And the same went for Bob Metz's piece in the *Times*. The company had guaranteed that the press would throw stones at it.

*A sure way to get coverage in the news media is to
have your client come out with a bold prediction.
Editors love predictions. But be aware that they are
tricky. They can serve you or backfire on you—and
you may never be quite sure which.*
                        —A story of radioisotopes and cancer

In 1947 I wrote a story to go under the byline of Chancellor
Robert Maynard Hutchins of the University of Chicago. It was
about radioisotopes, an enormously promising field of research
in which the university was heavily engaged. The story had been
requested for use in the Hearst chain of newspapers.

I knew Hutchins was enthusiastic about the medical promise
of radioisotope research, so I led the story off with a bold
prediction: Within ten years, radioisotopes—a byproduct of the
atomic bomb—would solve the mysteries of cancerous growth.
The only major change Hutchins made in my copy was to reduce
those ten years to seven.

We were both wrong, of course. Forty years later, there is still
no known cure for cancer.

Was I right to field that prediction? The strange fact is, I don't
really know.

Some months after the story appeared, I was taken to task
over it by a cancer specialist at Billings Hospital, which is
associated with the University of Chicago. The doctor told me
that such stories raised false hopes in cancer patients. "Seven
years from now," he said, "I'm going to have patients coming to
me with copies of your article. They'll say, 'Okay, where's this
cure I was promised?' "

He had a point. On the other hand, the story, when published
on a lot of front pages with banner headlines, stirred up interest
in isotopes and other medical research. The university benefited
handsomely from the publicity, and ultimately we were able to
bring a share of good publicity to Billings Hospital as well. The

publicity brought in a number of substantial money contributions to help the research continue.

And though I kept my eyes and ears open seven years later, I wasn't aware of a single man or woman who complained about the failed prediction. The prediction was long forgotten—but the cancer research continued.

Was I right or wrong? You tell me.

No matter what other public-relations objectives a company may have, it is essential to cultivate friends in the media.
— A story of American Can and a bad day in San Francisco

It is preached elsewhere in this book that every public-relations campaign must have specific objectives, not just "making friends" or "getting known." This is not 1930s Hollywood when movie studios would tell press agents, "Let them write anything about our star they want to write, just as long as they spell her name right."

Still, it is important not to lose sight of the fact that making friends and becoming known are part of almost any PR effort, whether or not these are among the stated objectives. In particular, never forget the need to make friends with the press and broadcasting people. Without them on your side, nothing much is possible.

American Can did lose sight of that need for a time. And regretted it keenly.

American Can, or Canco, as everybody called it, became a Byoir client during the Second World War, before I joined the agency. In hiring Byoir, Canco had two specific objectives.

One was to publicize its contribution to the war effort. Canco turned out ration cans and other containers by the millions for use by American troops. These products weren't as warlike as airplanes and tanks, but Canco was anxious not to be thought of as a company that made only civilian products. By identifying itself with the war effort, it made life easier for itself in various ways—for example, in the competition for scarce materials and fuels.

Canco's second objective was to become known as an outfit that treated employees generously. There was fierce competition for workers during the war years, with companies continually raiding each other. By publicizing its benefit programs and other employee attractions, the company sought to gain advantages in that scramble.

These were two good, solid specific objectives. Byoir helped Canco achieve them. The task was made easier by the fact that the goals *were* specific—clearly seen and understood by all concerned.

Unfortunately, in going after these goals, Canco concentrated almost exclusively on narrowly targeted audiences: military and government leaders and its own large family of employees. The PR effort barely extended beyond those groups to the wider public, virtually ignoring the news media.

The result was that not much was known about Canco. It was neither particularly liked nor disliked. Business journalists in the years after the war considered Canco a somewhat aloof company that seldom generated any news, didn't seem to care whether its name appeared in the press, and was probably too boring to harbor any stories worth digging for. When a *Business Week* reporter sought comment from Canco executives on a question about education in 1950, she couldn't even get anybody to return her phone calls. It wasn't that Canco was trying to dodge her question, which was bland and in no way troublesome, but simply that the company couldn't be bothered.

In that same year, 1950, Canco suddenly discovered how few friends it had.

The United States Justice Department's antitrust division hauled Canco into court in a case involving can-closing equipment. It had always been the company's practice to lease this equipment to the food companies and others that bought its cans, and the leasing operation was immensely profitable. But now the antitrust lawyers were saying that Canco, by refusing to sell the equipment and by insisting that its customers lease the machinery only from Canco, was operating an unfair monopoly.

The trial, held in San Francisco, went on for weeks and generated a good deal of news coverage in the business media. It was seen as a case that could set precedents applicable to many other industries, such as computers.

Most of the news coverage was unfriendly or, at best, neutral, to Canco. *Business Week* sent the chief of its West Coast bureau to the trial. He made a few attempts to get statements from Canco people, was rebuffed, and ended by filing a story with a lot of lively quotes from the big company's rivals.

The press, in its cool attitude toward Canco, pretty well expressed the general national mood. The verdict at the end of the long trial went against the big can manufacturer. From then on, Canco was required to sell its can-closing equipment to those who wanted to buy it.

It was an expensive lesson. But Canco's top executives, to their credit, learned the lesson well and took immediate action on it. Soon after the trial they asked the Byoir organization to help their company make more friends in the media. They said they didn't care how much it cost.

We came up with a two-year program that they endorsed with high enthusiasm. Our main suggestion was that we concentrate our efforts, at least to begin with, in geographic regions where canning was an important component of the local economy. This would give us an obvious and useful key with which to open doors in the region's press and broadcasting offices. We proposed to hit the West Coast to start with—California, Oregon, and Washington, three states with multimillion-dollar canning industries. In our second year we would start operations in some Middle-Atlantic states and in the Northeast.

We worked it state by state. The high point of the campaign in each case was a salute to the state's canning industry. This involved a ceremonial lunch at the state capital attended by the governor. (No governor turned our invitation down—attendance was made virtually mandatory by advance publicity in which we told the public how important the state's canning business was.) During the lunch we presented the governor with a special plaque on which was mounted the X-millionth can filled in his state.

We saw to it, of course, that the press and broadcasters were abundantly informed about these events and about canning in general. We had two economists developing statistical and other material on canning and related industries, and we gave this material to editors and reporters for use in their stories. We also made speakers available to present our story to civic and business groups.

And then there was "Canco Charlie." He was a walking, talking robot who would travel around the targeted state in a truck, attended by a three-person operating crew. He would turn up at sporting events, shopping centers, and other places where there were big crowds. One member of the crew was an actor—Canco Charlie's voice—who would talk informally on canning in that particular state.

Canco Charlie was a gimmick, admittedly. A pretty silly gimmick, some said. But he certainly got attention, and he attracted news photographers the way a honey pot attracts flies.

There are other stories in this book about useful gimmicks, and the moral of them all is: Don't be ashamed of a gimmick if it works.

Our campaign made American Can's name and its nickname, Canco, known not only in those early target states but far beyond their borders. The Canco management was delighted. As the company got better known, there were more and more media requests for interviews, comments, and other material. The company's executives grew more responsible as they became aware of the rewards of good media relationships. Never again was there a case like that of the *Business Week* reporter who couldn't get anybody to pay attention to her.

An editor or radio/TV producer will always ask two tough questions about any story you are trying to promote: Why should I do this story? And why should I do it now?
      —A story of Howard Johnson and a *Business Week* cover

Howard Johnson & Co., affectionately known as HoJo, chose Byoir as its public-relations agency in the middle 1960s. On the day we signed the contract, I had a long talk with Burt Sack, the HoJo PR director.

Burt went over his main objectives. It was the company's hope, he said, that our efforts would help HoJo bring more customers to its restaurants and motels, win new friends in the business and investment community, and attract good young employees to form a pool of managerial talent for future expansion.

Burt then leaned back in his chair. "But there's one objective that towers over all the others," he said. "It's this—Mr. Johnson wants to be on the cover of *Business Week*."

He was referring to Howard B. Johnson, the founder's son and now the CEO.

I laughed. "The cover of *Business Week*? That's a lot easier said than done."

"Don't laugh, Bob. This is serious. He really wants it."

I shrugged. "Okay, we'll do our best. It isn't impossible. We have had clients on that cover before. But it doesn't happen every week, Burt."

"I know that. But I've got to warn you. No matter what else you do for us, Mr. Johnson will never be completely satisfied until he sees that cover."

So that was our real assignment. I decided to take the *Business Week* objective seriously along with the other goals, though it wasn't always easy to tell how serious the younger Howard

Johnson was. There was often a twinkle in his eye that kept people off balance.

He needled us now and then about our retainer fee, for example. We had explained in the beginning that we operated much like a law firm. All our day-to-day work on HoJo's behalf would be billed at cost. On top of that we would take a yearly retainer, in Johnson's case $50,000. That fee represented our entire profit.

Howard would say periodically that he didn't understand why he had to pay us so much. He seemed serious sometimes, and at other times to be joking. I was always puzzled.

But I went after *Business Week*. One man I knew well there was Bill Kroger, at that time marketing editor. I took him to lunch in New York one day, told him that HoJo was expanding rapidly and had exciting plans for the future, and suggested that the company and its chief would make a colorful yet solidly informative cover story. Bill listened carefully. Then he said he would like to know more about the company, and he asked me to send him a three-page memo giving some of the history, some financial data, and a selection of other details.

But as he took a sip of coffee and set his cup down slowly, he said, "I've got to tell you, Bob, if you want a shot at the cover of *BW*, you've got a lot of competition. I'm not saying it's hopeless. You do have a good story to tell. But if you really want your man on that cover, or if you want any kind of in-depth treatment by us, then your memo had better tell us two things. First, why should we do a cover story on Howard Johnson? And second, why should we do it now?"

Those were two excellent questions, and it was not the first time I had heard them. Every young reporter/writer newly hired at *BW* got them pounded into him or her repeatedly. The catechism never changed: "Tell the readers up front why they should spend their good time reading what you're about to write. And then tell them why now."

Why at all and why now? What's important about the story, and why is it important *today*? Why wasn't it published last year? Or why couldn't it be postponed till next year?

Every magazine editor, every newspaper feature writer, every

TV news producer deals daily with the two questions Bill Kroger recited to me. Every public-relations professional ought to learn them, too. If you neglect them, your success rate in placing stories and other material in the media is almost guaranteed to be poor.

The two questions are easy to answer most of the time in the case of straight news stories. The story is in this morning's paper because it happened yesterday. It's news. Nothing more need usually be said. But a newspaper, magazine, or TV feature story is different. It isn't hard news, and so it must embody that double explanation to the readers or viewers. Why at all and why now?

I had no trouble with the "why at all" part of it when I wrote that memo for Bill Kroger. HoJo was a large, important company and also an exciting one. The story was dramatic. Any good business feature writer—and Bill Kroger was one of the best— could make a thoroughly gripping piece out of it.

But the "why now" part gave me problems. I forget exactly what I wrote, but it wasn't good enough. When I phoned Bill a couple of days after sending him the memo, his response was disappointing. He agreed that HoJo was an interesting company and certainly prominent enough to deserve a *BW* piece, but he saw no compelling reason to do such a piece right away. He had submitted the story idea at a staff meeting, and the other editors agreed—Howard Johnson might make a good story some day, but there was no hurry. The idea should be shelved until it ripened.

That was in early April. It took me six weeks to figure out why *BW* should do that cover story *now*, but in late May, it hit me. The Fourth of July!

"That's your news peg, Bill," I told him, deliberately using newsmagazine jargon to show I understood his needs. "July Fourth is the start of the summer vacation season. That's when people hit the road. What more natural subject could there be that week than Howard Johnson?"

Bill laughed. "It could even make a cover story," he said.

And it did. Bill phoned me shortly afterward to say the top editors had told him to go ahead with HoJo, aiming for a July Fourth cover.

I called Howard to tell him the good news. He was delighted. "You've earned your retainer at last!" he said, and he never needled us about that again.

We set up interviews for Bill Kroger with Howard and other key executives. The cover photo itself required some fancy footwork. *BW*'s art department wanted a shot of Howard standing in front of a HoJo restaurant, surrounded by cups containing all twenty-eight of the company's famous ice cream flavors. The company was happy to oblige and picked a particularly handsome restaurant at Parsippany, New Jersey, for the photo. But it can be hot in New Jersey in mid-June. Don Molinelli, our account executive for HoJo, found out that the ice cream started to melt eight minutes after being removed from the freezer. So we had to arrange the photography by planning every detail with military precision, then running like mad.

But the results were gratifying. It was an excellent cover, and Bill Kroger's accompanying story was well done. Moreover, it started a minor Howard Johnson media fad. That summer and fall there were major pieces on the company in *Forbes* and *Financial World,* a profile of Howard in the Sunday *New York Times,* and other stories in magazine and newspaper travel sections.

I was happy with these results, and so was Don Molinelli. But we came down from the clouds with a thump one day when we were having a self-congratulatory drink with Burt Sack.

Burt raised his glass in a toast and said, "Well, here's to the *Time* cover we're looking for next."

*Some of the brightest and most successful executives
are strangely unaware of the way the media operate.
If you run into such a man or woman, it will be up to
you to provide the needed education.*
    —A story of Howard Johnson and a surprise
                                    announcement

Howard Johnson was a man of formidable intelligence and
managerial ability. HoJo expanded under his leadership, income
improved continually, and the stockholders were satisfied. But
Howard didn't think much about the operations of the media,
with which we PR people were of course concerned. As a result,
one day, he almost landed us in trouble without meaning to.

It happened at an annual meeting at Braintree, Massachusetts, where HoJo's main plant was located. We at Byoir were
asked to participate in the process of getting the earnings statement distributed to the media. There was mounting interest in
HoJo that year in the investment community, so we expected
that the business press was going to be hungry for the statement
as soon as it was released.

For reasons of security and to forestall insider stock trading,
Howard Johnson never issued earnings figures in advance, even
to the company's own PR people. Only Howard himself and a
few of his top executives knew beforehand what the figures
were. The rest of the world had to wait until Howard stood up
at the meeting and announced them.

So Don Molinelli set up a hot line from Braintree to our New
York offices. As soon as Howard announced the earnings, the
data were to be phoned to us, our financial people would write
the story, and we would then deliver it hastily to Dow Jones,
Reuters, the Associated Press, United Press International, the
Wall Street Journal, the *New York Times*, and other business
publications.

It worked well. The phone call came and we got the story out in time for publication before the New York financial markets opened the next morning.

But Howard Johnson had a surprise in store for us. He finished reading his prepared text and then, speaking without notes, he told the assembled stockholders a remarkable piece of news. He announced that HoJo had entered into an agreement with KLM Airlines to build a motor lodge in Amsterdam, and that other joint ventures of a similar nature were planned elsewhere in Europe.

It was by far the most significant piece of news to come out of that annual meeting. And we had distributed our story without it!

We hustled. If the newspapers and wire services were to publish the incomplete story and then find they'd missed the real news—or, worse, if some were to miss it while their competitors didn't—we stood to lose a lot of confidence among friends in the media. But by scrambling madly and with more than a dash of luck, we managed to catch all of them before they had put the HoJo story to bed.

Don Molinelli chided Howard Johnson gently over the episode after the meeting. "That surprise announcement of yours certainly raised some blood pressures at Byoir," Don said.

Howard laughed. "What's the matter," he asked, "don't you people like a surprise now and then?"

He simply didn't realize what a PR disaster he had almost precipitated. We did our best to educate him about how PR works, and Howard never surprised us again.

Many corporate CEOs, even the best and brightest, require such education. As a PR professional, you will often find yourself in the role of teacher.

CHAPTER 5

DEALING WITH MEDIA HARD CASES

*Things can go wrong with media relationships as with any-
thing else. Sometimes you can do something about this,
sometimes you can't.*

Good public relations nearly always means cooperating with the press. But there are times when you must make an exception.
—A story of Woolworth and *Forbes*

A CHAIRMAN and CEO of Woolworth Bob Kirkwood was succeeded in 1975 by an equally able executive named Les Burcham. We at Byoir wanted to give Burcham a good introduction to those parts of the business world where he wasn't already known, so we set up a series of one-on-one interviews with reporters from major business publications—*Fortune, Business Week,* the *New York Times,* the *Wall Street Journal,* and others. These interviews produced a crop of fine stories.

There was one publication, however, that I wanted to avoid with the greatest care—*Forbes* magazine. At a meeting with Burcham and some of his people, I went on record with the statement that, in my judgment, it would be a mistake to grant one of these personal interviews to a *Forbes* reporter. For reasons that nobody outside the magazine fully understood, *Forbes* had developed a peculiarly sour, unfriendly tone in its articles on major corporations and had published some particularly nasty comments on Woolworth. My advice to Les Burcham (and to all of my clients) was that he should distance himself from *Forbes* as he would from a nest of hornets.

Not often in my public-relations career have I given such advice. In most situations, you figure that a story will be written with or without your cooperation, so you might as well cooperate and get a hearing for your point of view. But it seemed to me this Woolworth-*Forbes* situation was a special case. The stories we were promoting were in large part personality pieces on Les Burcham the man—his life, his career, his business philosophy, and so on. It would hardly be possible for a reporter to write such a story well without an eye-to-eye interview. I figured that if we kept *Forbes* away from Burcham, in all likelihood there would be no story.

Unfortunately, I wasn't successful in my efforts. I received a phone call one day from Burcham's secretary. She said Burcham had agreed to be interviewed by a *Forbes* reporter and wanted me to sit in.

"But I advised against that," I said, trying not to sound too upset.

"I know," the secretary replied. "But Mr. Burcham feels the article can hardly be critical since he only just started the job. He hasn't really done anything yet to be criticized *about*."

It seemed useless to argue. What was done was done. Sighing, I of course agreed to be present at the interview.

The interview took place on a Tuesday morning on the twenty-fourth floor—the executive floor—of the old Woolworth Building, not far from New York's City Hall. The *Forbes* reporter had a photographer with him and they talked with Burcham for twenty or twenty-five minutes. I was feeling uneasy but heard nothing in the questions or answers that aroused any specific alarm.

Then Burcham got onto the subject of Woolworth's subsidiaries. He mentioned with evident pride that virtually everything he was wearing came from a Woolworth or Woolworth-owned store. His suit came from Richman Brothers, his shoes from Kinney, his watch from Woolco, and so on. The reporter was fascinated by this and prodded Les Burcham for more details. Burcham complied willingly, even stating the approximate prices of the items he had mentioned.

Before the interview ended, the reporter asked Les Burcham to stand up so that the photographer could get some full-length shots. Burcham was the soul of cooperation. I watched, still feeling that vague sense of unease.

Two weeks later, the issue of *Forbes* appeared with the Burcham interview. I grabbed a copy from a newsstand on my way to work in the morning, and when I opened it in my office, my heart sank.

Forbes had chosen to illustrate the interview with one of those full-length photographs of Les Burcham. Superimposed on the photo were price tags indicating what he had paid for all those articles of clothing and accessories. The shot looked like a publicity stunt—there was nothing to say that the whole distasteful exercise hadn't been his own idea.

What was more, the accompanying article was every bit as sour and unfriendly as I had feared all along. But after seeing that doctored photo, I felt the article was the least of our problems. I had barely recovered my composure when Les Burcham's secretary called. "Mr. Wood," she said urgently, "Mr. Burcham just came in, and his veins are standing out on his neck. I think you'd better get down here in a hurry."

I found Les Burcham in his office, shaking with rage, with a copy of *Forbes* on his desk. He told me there'd been a cannonade of unhappy phone calls from Woolworth's outside directors and others. They all felt the seemingly posed photo was ridiculous and undignified—not the kind of publicity gag to which the chairman of a major corporation, particularly a brand-new chairman, should have lent his likeness. "I've been made to look like a fool, Bob!" Burcham said angrily. He wanted to call a lawyer right away and slap *Forbes* with a seven-figure lawsuit.

It took me about an hour to get him calmed down. I said I thought it would be a mistake to sue *Forbes*. "You'll only bring this to the attention of a lot of people who would never know about it otherwise," I pointed out. "Just sit quiet. It'll blow over soon enough. You've had fine interviews in a lot of other big magazines and newspapers, and we can get you more. Don't let this one bad outcome stampede you."

Finally he said, "Okay. You're right. But I'll tell you one thing. As long as I'm CEO of Woolworth, nobody from *Forbes* is ever going to be allowed up here on the twenty-fourth floor again."

And he kept his word.

*One of the toughest assignments in public relations is
to prove that something did not happen.*
—A story of Howard Hughes and Clifford Irving

It was perhaps the biggest literary bombshell of the early
1970s. Harold McGraw, CEO of the giant publishing firm
McGraw-Hill, called a news conference in New York to announce the forthcoming publication of a book on Howard Hughes.
McGraw introduced the book's author, a previously obscure
novelist and journalist named Clifford Irving, who asserted that
his book was based on many personal interviews with Howard
Hughes.

This was startling news indeed. Hughes, then living in a hotel
he owned on Paradise Island, off Nassau, had granted no press
interviews, as far as anybody knew, for years. His reclusiveness
was legendary. He had been a patient in a Boston hospital about
a year back, and there were even rumors that he was not only a
recluse, but was dead. Yet here was this little-known author
claiming that he had had long, intimate talks with Hughes. Was it
possible? Newspapers, magazines, and TV pounced on the story
hungrily, as Harold McGraw had undoubtedly foreseen.

We at Byoir, as Hughes's PR representatives since 1946,
were shocked and puzzled. We were being asked to believe that
our famous client had granted a long series of personal interviews without our ever hearing a word about them. The secrecy
would not have been out of character—Hughes often did things
without bothering to tell anybody—but the act of granting all
those interviews would have been a major change in the reclu-
sive man we had come to know. Richard Hannah, who was then
our account executive in charge of all the Hughes operations,
was deeply skeptical, too, but he found it hard to believe that a
veteran publisher like Harold McGraw could be easily hoodwinked. Certainly McGraw must have done some checking on
his own before accepting Clifford Irving's amazing story as genu-

ine. Dick Hannah and I talked by phone and agreed that it was all very perplexing.

Hannah said he would try to get in touch with Hughes himself by phone and an hour later he called me back. He had reached Hughes, who had read the news reports and was very upset. "Hughes told me," Hannah said, "that he never met this man Irving, never talked to him, and until yesterday had never even heard of him."

According to Howard Hughes, in other words, Clifford Irving's story was a lie. The book was a hoax.

Dick Hannah went on to tell me that Hughes wanted us to distribute a statement to the press and TV saying that the yet-to-be-published book was a fraud. We complied.

This immediately landed us in hot water. A lawyer representing McGraw-Hill promptly showed up at our office and handed us a stiffly worded letter stating that McGraw-Hill intended to file a multimillion-dollar lawsuit against both Hughes and Byoir.

Over the next several weeks, the affair developed into a thundering battle in the media. Clifford Irving and McGraw-Hill kept issuing passionate avowals of their book's genuineness, while we at Byoir kept issuing denials. The press and TV did not know who to believe but reported the seesaw battle day after day with undisguised delight. What made the story all the more juicy was that Irving and his Swiss-born wife were a highly attractive couple, and many of their friends were people with an intriguing air of mystery and naughtiness.

Howard Hughes asked us to send him copies of the press and TV reports on the affair. It was an indication of the story's size that we found ourselves sending him several hundred items a day.

When Harold McGraw started talking in earnest about the date when the long-awaited book would be published, we knew we had to intensify our efforts. But it was a tough assignment. How do you prove that a series of alleged interviews did *not* take place?

First, we thought it would be an excellent idea to distribute a current photograph of Howard Hughes to the news media. This would help us demonstrate not only that he wasn't dead, but that we had actually been hearing denials of Irving's claims from Hughes's own mouth. With some trepidation—Hughes hadn't allowed a photographer near him in a long time—we put the idea to him. He saw its worth immediately and agreed to be photographed, specifying only that a certain Los Angeles photographer whom he liked be flown to Paradise Island to do the job.

But a photograph alone wouldn't prove our point. What else could we do?

The ideal solution would have been for Hughes to appear in person at a news conference, prove his identity, and state his case directly to the reporters and TV cameras. However, he rejected all such suggestions. He was too much of a recluse. Prying him out into the public stage was out of the question.

So we came up with another idea. We asked if he would be willing to participate in a press conference by telephone. To our surprise and relief, he welcomed the suggestion.

With the very greatest of care, we hand-picked six newspeople to go to Las Vegas for this unusual conference. All six were well known, and all six had personally known Howard Hughes at various stages of his colorful career. The six represented the *New York Times*, the *Los Angeles Times*, the *Associated Press*, *King Features*, *United Press International*, and the *Hearst Syndicate*.

As I've stated elsewhere in this book, Howard Hughes, once he made up his mind to do something, did it wholeheartedly. He allowed the telephone press conference to continue for two and a half hours, during which he answered the reporters' questions forthrightly. When it was over, the six reporters all stated that they were certain the man they had been talking to was Howard Hughes. Moreover, they said they were just as certain that he had never been interviewed by Clifford Irving.

We thought the issue was resolved. We were wrong.

The next day, Harold McGraw issued a statement in which he cast doubt on our credibility. He said there was no proof that the voice on the telephone belonged to the real Howard Hughes, adding that McGraw-Hill was still solidly behind the Irving book and would continue with the plans to publish it.

Business Week magazine, which is owned by McGraw-Hill,

then weighed in with an article that attacked both Hughes and Byoir. The rest of the media, however, continued to avoid taking sides. Nobody knew who to believe. At Byoir we believed we had made a very good case with the telephone press conference, and I had the feeling that public opinion was slowly leaning our way. Sooner or later, I thought, something would give.

What gave was the resolve of Clifford Irving.

I like to think that our relentless efforts helped convince Irving it was hopeless to continue with the hoax. He must have come to realize that in fighting the Byoir organization, he was up against an opponent that would not back down.

His capitulation came as a surprise to many, including Harold McGraw. Called to testify under oath, Irving admitted that he had never met Howard Hughes and that the book was a hoax. Asked why he had thought he could get away with such a bizarre scheme, he explained that he had been counting on Hughes's legendary reclusiveness. "I never thought he would come forward to protest," Irving said.

Our job was done. There was no longer any doubt in the public's mind that Clifford Irving had never interviewed Howard Hughes.

A postscript: A few days after the truth came out, I had lunch with Bill Kroger of *Business Week*. I told him Howard Hughes had been put to a good deal of trouble and expense by the Irving hoax, and it was quite possible Hughes would sue McGraw-Hill for damages. To forestall such an unhappy outcome, I suggested that Harold McGraw write Hughes a letter apologizing for the unpleasantness.

Kroger phoned me later that same afternoon to say that Harold McGraw was perfectly willing to write such a letter, providing he could be assured that it would get to Hughes. I gave him that assurance.

McGraw wrote the letter. It was delivered to Howard Hughes.

Hughes took one look at the name on the envelope and then tore the letter up without reading it. However, he never did sue McGraw-Hill—nor, as far as I know, did he ever have any communication with the publishing company again.

Doing an unusual favor for a client can sometimes get you in trouble. But that doesn't mean you should stop doing favors.
—A story of RCA and *Business Week*

Many clients like to be coddled. They like to feel they're special. When a client asks you for an unusual favor, you almost have to listen. And as long as the requested favor violates no professional or personal ethical code, you're almost bound to make at least some attempt to fulfill it. For if you habitually turned down clients' requests—particularly requests that the client considered simple—you probably wouldn't last long as a public-relations practitioner.

This is the story of a favor that we at Byoir did for a long-term client in the early 1980s. It created a flap that surprised us.

The client was RCA. The huge company had a new chairman and CEO, Thornton Bradshaw. *Business Week* magazine decided to do a cover story on Bradshaw, and the response at RCA and Byoir was generally optimistic, though a bit concerned. RCA had been having problems with some of its subsidiaries, including NBC, the broadcasting colossus, and Hertz, the car-rental company. There was some fear that *Business Week,* in its article, would concentrate on these problems and produce a generally unfavorable story, perhaps knocking down the stock price and bringing a horde of angry shareholders down on Bradshaw's head. Bradshaw himself was particularly worried about such an outcome.

But we recommended full cooperation with the magazine. Ken Bilby, RCA's highly professional public-affairs chief, arranged the usual round of interviews with various RCA and subsidiary executives, and of course with the chairman himself. The reporter went away, and three weeks later, *Business Week* said the major piece was finished and would appear in the forthcoming issue.

The suspense was too much for Thornton Bradshaw. He asked Ken Bilby to get him an advance look at the cover story. Ken dutifully called *Business Week*, knowing what the answer would be. It was the expected no.

The magazine was usually distributed at about four o'clock every Friday afternoon. Under a policy of many years' standing, rigidly enforced, no early peeks at stories were ever allowed, nor were advance copies of the magazine ever released. A magazine of huge circulation and influence, *Business Week* was capable of affecting the stock prices of companies featured in its pages. The Securities & Exchange Commission, in past years, had several times asked questions about sharp price moves apparently resulting from *BW* stories. There had never been any charges of wrongdoing by *BW* staffers, and *BW* was determined to keep it that way. Hence the unbending rule: No reader should gain access to the magazine before all readers had access.

But the suspense was still killing Thornton Bradshaw. He asked Ken Bilby to go on trying. Bilby, a man of patience if there ever was one, called me. It was now Thursday.

"You know the rule at *BW*," I said. "I doubt there's anything I can do."

"But if Bradshaw has to wait till Saturday morning to read that story, he'll have a fit," Ken said. "As a favor to me, Bob, see what you can do. At least try."

So as a favor to a friend and client, I tried. To my very great surprise, the effort succeeded.

I began by explaining the problem to a member of our business and financial news staff who, I knew, had a close friend at *BW*. He said he would sound the friend out and a short time later he told me an accommodation had been worked out. If Roger Jones, our account executive assigned to RCA, would call at the main *Business Week* reception desk at half past eleven Friday morning, he would find a sealed envelope waiting for him.

Roger Jones followed these instructions, picked up the envelope, and took it immediately to the RCA offices. The envelope, of course, contained that rare jewel, an advance copy of *Business Week*.

Roger, Ken, and the impatient Thornton Bradshaw all read the cover story and relaxed. It neither praised nor damned. It was essentially a straightforward account of RCA's present condition and future prospects. It allowed that Thornton Bradshaw faced some tough problems in the coming months but made no judgment on how well or badly he might do.

The consensus was that the story would have no substantial effect on the stock price. As things turned out, that forecast was to prove correct.

But it wasn't the stock price that brought us a headache.

Roger Jones, pleased that his morning's pickup and delivery service had proceeded so smoothly and ended with such a happy outcome, was hanging around the RCA offices shortly after noon that Friday, thinking about lunch. He was chatting with Henry Bechtold, Ken Bilby's top assistant, when RCA's advertising manager chanced to stroll into Bechtold's office. His eye fell on the advance copy of *BW* on Bechtold's desk.

"My God, is that today's issue?" he asked, staring at the photo of Thornton Bradshaw on the cover.

Bechtold said that it was, indeed, that day's issue, out on the loose several hours early.

"Where did you get it?" the ad chief asked, clearly agitated.

"Roger here brought it in," Henry Bechtold replied.

"How did *you* get it?" the ad man demanded.

Roger said simply that the advance copy had been provided as a favor to Byoir, but he didn't know the details. He was simply the delivery man.

The ad chief then explained why he was so upset. He said that he, like Ken Bilby, had been asked to scrabble up an advance of *BW* for Thornton Bradshaw. The chairman was obviously in a state of fingernail-biting suspense and was trying many channels in his desperate effort to get that coveted early peek. The ad chief's approach was to call a *BW* space salesman who serviced RCA's ad-space account at the magazine. The space salesman told the ad chief that he was sorry, but there was no hope of getting an advance copy.

And now the ad man was swallowing the fact that someone else had succeeded where he had failed.

He went storming into his own office and called the space salesman. "Byoir's man got hold of a copy before noon!" he roared. "It makes me look silly!" He worked himself into such a towering rage that he ended by threatening to have the space salesman removed from the RCA account.

The startled salesman evidently hung up after this conversation and worked up his own good head of steam. It seemed to him he was being badgered without just cause. All he had done, after all, was to abide by his company's rules. He jumped from his chair and strode wrathfully into the office of Lewis Young, *Business Week's* editor-in-chief.

When Young heard the story, *he* flew into a rage. One of his subordinates, it seemed, was guilty of a serious policy violation— the early release of a copy of Young's revered magazine. He wanted to know how, and he wanted to know who was responsible.

I happened to be in Washington, D.C., when this storm was breaking. Young didn't leave many stones unturned in his search for the culprit—even had one of his editors track me down and ask me what I knew about that advance copy. Unwilling to get my own staff member or his *BW* friend in trouble, I said I had no knowledge of who provided the advance copy. Our account executive, Roger Jones, also refused to be interrogated.

Unwilling to be turned off the trail, Young then wrote angrily to the Securities and Exchange Commission, telling them about the incident and urging that the CEOs of RCA and Byoir be questioned. These CEOs, of course, were Thornton Bradshaw and myself. But the Securities and Exchange Commission, checking RCA's steady stock price and finding no evidence of heavy trading volume or anything else unusual, wrote back to say it had no interest in the episode.

In time things simmered down. For a while I was concerned that this odd little episode might have hurt Byoir's relationship with *Business Week*, but fortunately, there was no lasting effect. In fact, a couple of weeks later *BW* invited, separately, the CEOs of two Byoir clients to lunch and eventually published good stories about them.

So we were lucky. The incident of the advance copy could have hurt us with a most prestigious magazine.

But I still feel I was right to try to get that advance copy to Bradshaw. When a valued client comes to you with what he thinks is a simple and reasonable request, what are you going to do?

There are a lot of risks in the public-relations business. You just have to live with them. If I had that RCA-*BW* episode to go through again today, I think I would do what I did the first time—with one change. I would tell my client's people to be more aware of the need for secrecy in such a situation.

There are stories that are so compelling that you don't have to promote them. You may get hold of such a story once or twice in a lifetime.
—A story of a new Bible and a recalcitrant editor

In the spring of 1980, Byoir was asked by the U.S. Catholic Conference, a client, to introduce a new English translation of the Bible. Considered to be a major event, this was the first new Bible to be introduced in English-speaking Catholic churches in over 200 years. Working under Catholic sponsorship, fifty-one scholars had been involved in the translation over a twenty-five-year period. Twelve publishers across the United States were to print it.

This was a story so big that it needed no special hard-sell.

It was so big, in fact, that for once we were able to thumb our noses at media hardcases.

We scheduled the official introduction at a news conference on August 24, 1980, at the National Press Club in Washington. Unfortunately, we couldn't give out advance copies of the new Bible because they weren't yet off the presses. All we could do was hand out mimeographed comparisons of selected old and new passages.

One wire-service religious editor said this wasn't good enough for him. "Unless I get advance copies," he huffed, "I'm not coming to your news conference. What's more, I'm not even going to cover the story."

We laughed. We told him he *had* to cover the story. It would be impermissible to ignore a story of such size.

He covered it, all right. So did every major newspaper, newsmagazine, and radio and TV news show in the country. Oh what a wonderful position to be in!

The media won't always tell your story as promptly as you could wish. An essential item of PR equipment is patience, and there are times when you need a lot of it.

—A story of a star-crossed project

The Oil Shale Corporation, which derived the nickname TOSCO from its initials, was a company that was always up to its ears in controversy. Its purpose was to extract oil from oil shale, of which there is a virtually limitless supply in Colorado and other Rocky Mountain states. TOSCO was continually being jabbed with two sharp questions: Is your process economical? And can you operate without damaging the environment? The company kept answering yes, and those who didn't want to believe the answers kept disbelieving them.

With this much-needled company as our client, we at Byoir were kept busy. Much of the work was frustrating, and the most frustrating project of all involved *Life* magazine.

Life, in the middle 1960s, was enjoying one of its periodic peaks of affluence and influence. The business editor at the time was an able young man named Chris Welles. One day I sent him a backgrounder on TOSCO and the scientific and economic facts of oil shale.

Chris and I were both to wish, in time, that my backgrounder had got lost in the mail.

He did nothing with it immediately, but over the next several months, by serendipity, he came across related material that sparked his interest. He found what he thought was convincing evidence that some major oil companies were worried about competition from oil shale if TOSCO were ever to go into full-scale production. (The company at the time had only a couple of small demonstration plants going.) If the more optimistic projections were to be believed, oil might be derived from shale more cheaply one day than from conventional wells. Some Big Oil interests evidently did believe these projections, or at least were concerned about them. According to Chris Welles's research, these interests had bought up privately owned shale lands so as to prevent TOSCO and other shalers from getting them, while simultaneously lobbying in Washington to block access to government-owned shale lands.

Chris wrote a twenty-four-page story to this effect. That was too long, but he was virtually certain he'd have to rewrite it. That was standard practice at *Time* and *Life*; it was rare that a first version of anything, even a picture caption, got printed without extensive editorial meddling.

The senior editors who read Chris's piece were enthusiastic, but his guess was correct. Everyone had suggestions, some conflicting with others, and Chris rewrote the piece three times.

Meanwhile I had told the people at TOSCO that Chris's story, on which he had interviewed them, was finally in the works at *Life*. They were delighted, of course. So was I. Making *Life* in those days was a real feather in any PR man's cap.

After his third rewrite, Chris began to detect a certain vague uneasiness in two of his superior editors. They seemed nervous over the story's allegations about Big Oil, the buying-up of shale tracts, and the high-powered lobbying in Washington. To soothe them, Chris rewrote his piece twice more.

After this fifth revision, everybody approved the story and it was tentatively scheduled in a pre-Christmas issue of the magazine.

Chris was relieved. TOSCO and I were happy.

When the story was bounced to a January issue. George

Hunt, *Life*'s managing editor, explained that the piece didn't harmonize with the Christmas holiday season.

Why wasn't this decision made earlier? If you were to ask this question of a *Life* staffer, your answer would be a resigned shrug and the comment, "Such is *Life*."

My client and I waited eagerly for January. We were doomed to more disappointment.

On January 1, 1968, a man named Thomas Griffith was moved over from *Time* to become editor-in-chief of *Life*. As all newly installed editors must, he read through his inventory of inherited stories. Chris Welles's oil shale piece disturbed him. He was particularly worried over some of the story's comments about Gulf Oil.

Chris plowed wearily through a sixth rewrite. It was then that he began to suspect, and then confirmed, that *Life's* advertising department was leaning on the editorial side. The ad people had apparently learned of Chris's story from oil executives, whom Chris had contacted in the course of his research. The ad people feared that the magazine would lose a lot of revenue if the story ran and got Big Oil mad. One estimate was that the magazine stood to lose between $5 million and $20 million a year if the oil companies pulled out.

Whether the ad people had received threats to this effect or were simply generating their own nightmare was not established. It is a really bad idea to try to use advertising as a club to beat the media into submission, and most large companies avoid even the appearance of doing so. So it is likely that *Life*'s ad people were simply suffering from a case of nerves—*Life* had always been a notoriously nervous place. Or perhaps one or two individual oil executives had uttered veiled threats, which their CEOs would have repudiated immediately if the affair had come out into the open. But whatever the hidden background might have been, a pall of fear was emanating from the ad department.

Tom Griffith insisted that the editorial side of the magazine would not allow itself to be pushed around by the business side, and for a while he appeared to stand by that pronouncement. Early in February the story was locked up for publication in the March 1 issue. The ad people bleated but did not interfere.

When page proofs and color engraving proofs arrived in New York, Chris called me to say that it looked as though this long-delayed piece would make it to the newsstands this time.

Once again I called the TOSCO people with the good news.

And once again the story got shot down.

George Hunt, the managing editor, called Chris into his office in the middle of February. Some new questions had arisen, Hunt said. In particular, he and others felt the story should clarify and sharpen certain passages dealing with differences between the oil industry's statements and those of its critics.

The story would be rescheduled for March 15, Hunt said.

Chris went back to his typewriter for a seventh rewrite. When he turned it in to the managing editor, he let some of his exasperation show.

"This has been going on a long time, George," he said. "I'm getting worried. Are you really going to run this story?"

Hunt assured him that all was well.

But two days later, at about six in the evening, Chris was called into Hunt's office to meet with Griffith and some other uncomfortable-looking senior editors. Hunt said, "I'm terribly sorry to have to tell you this, Chris, but we're not going to run the shale story."

Chris was stunned by the bluntness of the statement. "You mean," he said, "you're not going to run it at all? Ever?"

"That's right," said Hunt. "I'm afraid the story is dead."

Tom Griffith then said that no advertising pressure was involved in this decision but that the story left him with too many doubts and worries. He went over some of these doubts and worries—all dealing with points that had been discussed, settled, and resettled many times before.

After Griffith left, Chris turned angrily to George Hunt. "How could this happen?" he asked. "We've been going over and over all these points for months. Everyone seemed satisfied. The story was approved. Just a couple of days ago you assured me it would run. But now you tell me it's dead. What happened?"

"I'm sorry, but it's a difficult situation," Hunt said. "I'm embarrassed about it. Don't make me feel worse than I already do."

Chris, in telling me about this later, recalled that he felt no sympathy for Hunt that evening in the managing editor's office. He kept trying to find out what had happened. Hunt finally said that he was killing the story because Tom Griffith had ordered him to, and for all he knew, Griffith was following orders from somebody still higher up.

The decision was not George Hunt's, but Chris had no way of finding out for sure whose decision it was or what was behind it. Baffled, he said good night to George and left.

After a troubled night's sleep, Chris awoke next morning with a firm resolve. He was not going to put that story away in a file cabinet and let it die in the dark. He had worked on it too hard and too long. It was a good story, he felt—and when I eventually got to read it, I agreed. It took no sides for or against shale, for or against Big Oil but simply reported the existence of a controversy. Certainly it contained passages that Big Oil could object to, but it was hardly an encomium for TOSCO or the oil-shale industry. It was a solid, workmanlike piece of journalism.

Chris thought for a long time about what to do with it. He finally took a step that he knew would cost him his job. He submitted the story on a freelance basis to *Harper's* magazine. He knew that the editor, Willie Morris, was a transplanted Texan who had written extensively on oil.

Life, like any magazine, newspaper, or broadcasting company, had a firm rule against such freelance peddling of staff-written material. Material developed by a salaried staff member on company time, using company facilities, is felt to belong to the company, not the employee. Chris was aware of this. He was also aware that companies quite often are willing to waive the rule. If an employee asks special permission to freelance an otherwise dead piece, the answer may well be yes. But Chris doubted that *Life* would release the shale story to him in that way. And so he submitted it to Willie Morris without either asking permission or letting anybody at *Life* know what he was up to. He explained the circumstances fully to Morris.

Morris read the story and asked Chris to rewrite it.

Ironically, the rewrite Morris wanted would carry the story full circle, back to the very first version Chris had written at *Life* many months ago. Morris didn't want a detached journalistic overview that coolly reported the existence of a controversy. Instead, he wanted the author to pick sides, take a stand.

I was delighted when I heard about this. Chris Welles's inclination all along had been to side with my client's point of view. He had listened with care to TOSCO executives and engineers and had absorbed their thinking—that oil shale, if carefully developed, could become a national resource of the greatest value.

On Morris's instructions, Chris went back to his typewriter for an eighth rewrite.

He knew his superiors at *Life* were going to be furious when they learned of his move. But at least, he knew, nobody would be able to accuse him of doing it for money. *Harper's* was among the lowest-paying of all major newsstand magazines. When Willie Morris accepted Chris's final revision, *Harper's* coughed a check for $500.

The story ran in *Harper's* that August.

Life fired Chris Welles.

My client executives were delighted with the piece when they finally saw it. We got a lot of mileage out of it. We obtained permission from *Harper's* to distribute reprints, and we sent them to newspeople all over the country. The piece was well received everywhere—except at *Life*, of course.

Patience had been rewarded.

Sadly, the oil-shale business came virtually to a standstill in the next decade, largely for political reasons.

As for Chris himself, he went on to write books about Wall Street and other business topics. The last time I saw him, he was modestly affluent and content on the editorial staff of *Business Week*. We both agreed that the oil-shale adventure had taught us the value of patience.

*If a news reporter promises to let your client see a
story before broadcast or publication, get the promise
in writing— preferably from the top editor.*
                              —A story of RCA and *Forbes*

Ken Bilby, the RCA public-relations executive, received a
phone call one day from a senior reporter-writer at *Forbes*
magazine. The reporter said his magazine wanted to publish a
covery story on RCA and its chief, General David Sarnoff.

Bilby was not enthusiastic. Nor would any PR man in his right
mind have been. In that era—the early 1960s—*Forbes* had earned
a reputation for publishing distinctly unfriendly articles about
big business. *Forbes* today is like any other business magazine—
critical when it feels it must be but in general sympathy with the
goals and practices of the business world. Back then, however, it
was widely believed that its top management had established a
policy of publishing critical stories in an effort to create more
interest and circulation.

Bilby told the reporter bluntly that he saw no good reason
why he should expose his company and his boss to the roasting
that had become a *Forbes* habit.

But the reporter made a promise. He said that if Bilby would
cooperate, setting up interviews with Sarnoff and other headquarters and subsidiary executives, *Forbes* would submit the
story to RCA for clearance before publication.

Bilby was startled, as any veteran of the PR business would
have been. It isn't often that you hear a promise of pre-publication
or prebroadcast clearance. Indeed, most large magazines,
newspapers, and TV news organizations have a firm rule against
making such promises. And even where no explicit company
policy exists, many individual reporters and freelance writers
have rules of their own. When you promise such clearance, you
give somebody else the right to edit and censor your work.
Moreover, as any veteran journalist knows, you expose yourself

to the risk of endless hassling. Your story (and if you are a freelance, your fee) can be held up indefinitely while people argue over wording, and, to make things worse, the entire project can be killed.

So Ken Bilby was greatly surprised to hear an offer of clearance before publication. He knew that reporters and editors do make such offers on rare occasions, most often when a desperately sought story can't be had any other way, so he told the *Forbes* man he would think over the offer and let him know the outcome.

Bilby talked to Sarnoff and other RCA people, and he consulted us at Byoir. RCA had been our client for a long time, and I liked Ken Bilby personally. I told him I felt uneasy about the situation, for I had had some painful experiences with *Forbes*. Bilby was uneasy, too. But in the end, RCA decided to go ahead with the project, on the understanding that Ken Bilby and his colleagues would see the article before it went to the printer.

Bilby set up the interviews at RCA's New York headquarters, while Byoir staffers around the country made the necessary arrangements with subsidiary executives. All interviewees were told of the clearance agreement, and as a result many talked more candidly and casually than they would otherwise have allowed themselves to do. They assumed they would have a chance to correct inaccuracies, amend wrongly remembered figures, tone down exaggerations, and so on.

The process took a couple of weeks. A photographer came around to get General Sarnoff's picture for the cover. And that was that.

During the next few weeks, the reporter phoned Ken Bilby from time to time, picking up on loose ends. When Bilby asked when he would see the manuscript, the reporter said no firm publication date had been set.

A couple more weeks went by. Then, suddenly, an issue of *Forbes* appeared with General Sarnoff's face on the cover.

The story was inside. It had been published without the promised clearance and without advance warning of any kind. It was full of errors and misquotations. Its tone was the usual *Forbes* tone—nasty.

The people at RCA were outraged. So were we at Byoir. A

good client of ours had been badly used. I felt sympathy for Ken Bilby in particular. He had acted prudently and honorably throughout, and he felt he had been conned by *Forbes*.

Furious, he phoned the reporter and asked him why he had broken his word. The reporter said his editors had overruled him.

Undoubtedly there were some RCA executives, particularly those the story made look bad, who needled Ken Bilby for this sorry episode. He should have been more careful, he should have done this or that. But we at Byoir, who knew Ken and also knew the world of journalism, could not find fault with his actions.

The journalistic world is one in which men and women trust each other's spoken promises to an extent that astonishes people in other fields. Written contracts are rare, even when large amounts of money are involved. An editor may phone a freelance writer and assign him or her to write an article for $5,000 plus expenses. With nothing put in writing, the freelance goes ahead and performs the work, assuming confidently that the editor will pay the promised amount. That is the way it is in the journalism business. One's word is one's unbreakable contract.

Ken Bilby accepted the *Forbes* man's promise of pre-publication clearance on that basis, and although he felt uneasy about it, I did, too. Neither one of us would have dreamed that the promise would be broken so completely. I was genuinely astounded when I saw the general's picture on that magazine cover.

It is always a sad day when an honor system begins to break down. The honor system of the journalistic world cracked a little the day that magazine came off the press. From then on, we at Byoir always insisted that promises to submit material for checks and clearances be in writing. We preferred, in fact, that these written promises come not from a reporter, staff writer, or freelance, but from an editor high up on the masthead—or, in the case of radio and TV, a director or producer.

There are ways to ask for such a written promise without giving offense. All the same, I've always hated to make the request. It implies that the world isn't as nice a place as one could wish.

CHAPTER 6

GOOD SILENCES AND BAD

Good PR usually means communicating, but sometimes it can mean keeping your mouth—and your client's—shut.

In overcoming a negative image, the best approach often is silence.
                         —A story of the Ingram Corporation and a
                                               prison sentence

IN DECEMBER 1980, I received a call from George Moore, retired chairman of Citibank. George is now a financial consultant, and one of his clients had a peculiarly difficult public-relations problem.

The client was Frederick Ingram, known to all as Fritz. He was founder and CEO of the Ingram Corporation, a large, privately owned company with diversified interests throughout the world. Among other businesses, Ingram owned a fleet of oil tankers and barges and was active in city waste-disposal projects. Fritz, a handsome man in his early fifties, was not only an astute businessman but also a jet pilot. He was said to have a personal worth of some $600 million.

Fritz had landed in trouble in the late 1970s. The city of Chicago had invited bids on a multimillion-dollar garbage and sludge-removal contract. Fritz sent an aide to the Windy City to check it out, and after a lot of talking and listening, the aide phoned Fritz to say that if the Ingram Corporation wanted this contract, under-the-table payments to five or six people would be necessary. When Fritz protested, the aide said he was simply passing on what he had been told. This was the way business was done in Chicago. Everybody accepted bribery as a fact of life—just one more cost of dealing with the city.

Fritz finally said all right, if that was the way it was, he would have to go along with it.

The Ingram Corporation won the contract. Six months later, when the *Chicago Sun-Times* published a series of stories about the illegal payoffs, Fritz Ingram was in hot water.

It got hotter. He and one other Ingram executive were indicted, tried, and convicted of illegal business practices. Fritz was sentenced to four years in the Eglin Field Federal Prison in Florida.

George Moore asked, "Will you talk to him?"

"Of course."

"Can you help him?"

"That I can't tell yet."

"He and his company both need a lot of positive stories in the media to counteract this, wouldn't you say?"

"It's possible," I replied, but I was by no means sure.

I was thinking of the ancient apothegm that silence is golden. Public relations has the reputation of being a talky business, but there are times when the best advice you can give a client is to keep his mouth shut.

At the time I talked to George Moore, late in 1980, Fritz Ingram had served some thirteen months of his sentence. President Carter was about to leave office, and there was reason to hope the president would pardon Fritz as one of his last official acts. It was when Fritz got out of prison—perhaps in April 1981—that the danger of bad publicity would be particularly high.

I visited Fritz Ingram at Eglin Field Prison. I found him pretty depressed. A prison sentence is unpleasant for anybody, of course, but he had some extra problems that were peculiar to his position. He was a wealthy man in prison for bribery. The warden and guards of the prison were anxious not to give any appearance of doing him special favors, for they were afraid they, too, could be accused of taking bribes. And so, instead of giving him soft duty assignments such as work in the library, they had given him the job of getting up every morning at half past three and scrubbing pots and pans in the kitchen.

He told me he was hoping President Carter would grant him a pardon effective April 1, a couple of months away. I told him that, in my opinion, it was essential that he avoid reporters and

TV cameras that day and perhaps for years to come. No personal interviews—that was my prescription—as they could hardly turn out any way but badly for him. The reporters would inevitably question him about his time in prison, his views on white-collar crime, and so on. No answers he could give could make him look good, even with the friendliest reporters—and I could guarantee not all of them would be friendly.

"All right," he agreed. "But how do I avoid them on April 1? Suppose there's a whole crowd of them waiting for me when I step out the door?"

I thought for a moment, then asked, "If your pardon reads 'effective April 1,' exactly what does that mean? Can you walk out at six that morning, or noon, or what?"

"As far as I know, I can walk out at one second past midnight."

"We'll check that and find out for sure," I promised.

We did. We found out that his guess was correct. If a pardon says April 1, the prisoner is free to go as soon as it *is* April 1—meaning immediately after midnight.

I told Fritz Ingram what I thought he should do, and I helped arrange for him to do it. As expected, President Carter did sign that pardon before leaving office, and as expected, the document read, "effective April 1." My guess was that newspaper and TV people would start turning up at the prison early that morning with doughnuts and coffee and would camp there until the wealthy white-collar felon came out. I was virtually certain none would show up at midnight, and I was right.

Fritz Ingram walked out of there at 12:01 in the morning. It was lonely and dark—just as we had hoped. A waiting limousine whisked him to a nearby airport where a private plane was waiting. Ingram flew to Tennessee, to a friend's remote mountain retreat. The media never caught a glimpse of him.

I worked with him for a year after that, helping to rebuild his company's damaged image. I continued to keep reporters and TV people away from him personally, certain that no good could come out of one-on-one interviews. It turned out to be a winning strategy. In a short time the prison episode was forgotten, and we at Byoir were able to generate some good stories about the Ingram Corporation. When these stories appeared in print, no mention was made of the CEO's personal difficulties. In time it seemed that many journalists were not even aware Fritz Ingram had been in prison.

Silence had won us the game.

There is an interesting postscript to this story. A few months after his release, Fritz was still bitter about his experience at Eglin and felt he had been a political scapegoat because the Ford administration wanted to embarrass Mayor Daley of Chicago, a Democrat.

Before the year was out Ingram gave up his United States citizenship and became a citizen of Ireland.

But silence is dangerous when it leaves a large and baffled public clamoring for information.
—A story of a Texas wheeler-dealer and CIT
Financial

Billy Sol Estes came from the foothills of west Texas with barely two nickels to make a jingle in his pocket. A young man of unshakable self-confidence and the golden tongue of a natural-born salesman, he rapidly made a name for himself in Texas, parlaying borrowed money into a business empire of astonishing size and complexity. He was in many businesses, but the one for which he became best known was that of supplying farmers with liquid fertilizer and associated services and equipment, especially mobile four-wheeled fertilizer tanks.

The United States Junior Chamber of Commerce named him one of the nation's outstanding young businessmen before he was thirty. CIT Financial, a Byoir client, began providing some of his financing needs in 1957 and by the early 1960s, CIT and Byoir wished we had never heard of him.

Rumors began circulating in west Texas during the late 1950s that there was something odd about certain Billy Sol Estes ventures. In 1961 the *Pecos Independent,* a newspaper in the city where Estes maintained his headquarters, uncovered a startling fact. Estes, through a series of clever financial moves, had managed to borrow many millions of dollars by mortgaging thousands of fertilizer tanks that didn't exist.

The tanks were supposed to be collateral to secure the loans. Now it turned out that the collateral was nothing but Texas air. The companies that had made the loans were in trouble.

The company holding the biggest bag of endangered loans was the Walter Heller Finance Company of Chicago. It's total of loans to various Estes-controlled companies was some $7.5 million. Second came CIT, with $5 million. There were half a dozen others, with loan portfolios ranging down to $1 million.

The exposure of the fraud made the front pages and TV prime-time news all over the country. Estes immediately announced that he would straighten out the tangle and pay all his creditors off. CIT and other major creditors decided to sit tight for a few days and see what happened. I talked the situation over with William L. Wilson, CIT's vice president of public relations. We decided, too, that our best short-term course would be to do and say nothing, for the situation was still too fluid and confusing to allow for an intelligent PR response. Whatever we might say today could make us look like fools tomorrow.

Then the affair suddenly heated up. One of the smaller creditors filed a lawsuit against Estes. Estes responded by announcing that he would hold a press conference in Dallas and explain everything. To our dismay at CIT and Byoir, rumors began circulating that he would place blame on a CIT employee who had figured out the scheme of borrowing against nonexistent fertilizer tanks.

I flew to Dallas immediately.

When I arrived, I learned to my relief that Estes, on his lawyers' advice, had decided to cancel the press conference and make no further public comments on the case. It seemed to me that this was a wise policy for Estes. But I was now beginning to feel a strong and growing conviction that continued silence wouldn't be a wise policy for CIT.

There was a lot of puzzlement and worry in the air. People were wondering if they had been told the whole story. Were there worse revelations yet to come? These fears and frettings were evident in news accounts of the affair. Particularly worried were people who stood to lose money one way or another as the shock waves rolled outward, and among these were the stock-holders of CIT.

CIT's stock price on the Big Board had been holding fairly steady over the past few turbulent days. It was as though the shareholders and everyone else in Wall Street had decided, as CIT, Bill Wilson, and I had, that it would be best to do nothing for a short time and see what developed. But now I had a definite feeling that this wait-and-see period was about to end. There was a jittery quality in the air that at any moment could ripen into a full-blown panic.

It was time to break the silence.

At the CIT Dallas office I learned that the staff there had no great worries about the company's $5 million in loans. The Dallas people believed they would get most of that money back—from seizures of Estes properties, court-ordered payouts, and other sources, including a couple of employee fidelity bonds. The bonds were expected to figure in the recovery process because two CIT employees had apparently been taking cash payments from Estes and were presumed to have helped him in illegal transactions, thus violating the trust the company had placed in them.

I recommended that we issue a statement immediately, setting forth these facts and asserting that, as a result, the Estes affair was not expected to have any effect on CIT's earnings.

I wrote the statement and cleared it with Walter Lundell, then CIT's chairman and CEO. I placed it with the Dallas bureaus of Associated Press, United Press International and Dow Jones and in various Texas media while our main office was taking care of the big New York business magazines, newspapers, and TV and radio wires.

We were just in time. CIT's stock price had begun to dip on rising volume—a sign of the beginnings of panic. But then it firmed. For weeks afterward it held as steady as a rock. The panic was avoided.

But the stock of the Walter Heller Finance Company, which issued no statement, plunged in two days by a frightening nineteen points.

The people at Heller had made the mistake of keeping silent at the wrong time.

The practice of public relations sometimes becomes mere handholding, but don't feel diminished when that happens. If you can quiet a client who has lost his temper and is about to do something dumb, that is a valuable service.
—A story of Howard Hughes and an unwelcome book

In the early 1950s the novelist Harold Robbins, until then relatively obscure, published a book that brought him instant fame. *The Carpetbaggers* was billed as a novel, but word quickly got around that it was in fact a thinly disguised story of Howard Hughes.

There was a good deal of fictional embellishment in the book, including some torrid sex episodes and accounts of secret wheelings and dealings. The real-life Howard Hughes read some of the reviews, and then read parts of the book, and then flew into a thundering rage. He wanted to sue everybody in sight.

Byoir counseled him to cool it.

Public relations is a strange profession in some ways. Usually you find yourself trying to stir up action—launching promotions, setting up press conferences, seeking coverage for this purpose or that. But there are times when you find yourself in exactly the opposite position, counseling inaction. You will recall other stories in this book about such episodes.

It troubled me the first few times to find myself in this position. I felt uncomfortable telling clients to do nothing. I felt as though I wasn't fully earning my salary. After all, if a client gets himself into a big, public fight, shouldn't his PR people be out there with him, urging him on, handing him ammunition?

No, not always. "Do nothing" is sometimes the most valuable advice you can give.

We told Hughes that to sue Harold Robbins and the book's publisher would be to play right into their hands. They would love it. Such a lawsuit would bring them millions of dollars' worth of publicity.

After a couple of days, Hughes calmed down. In the end he not only abandoned the idea of a lawsuit, but he also refused to even comment to the media about the novel.

The effect was what we had hoped it would be. *The Carpetbaggers* was, to give it its due, a skillfully written and compelling book. It enjoyed a long success and was made into a movie. But in a remarkably short time, people were regarding it simply as a work of fiction. The Hughes connection was almost completely forgotten within a year after publication.

The book is still on library shelves. But I doubt that one reader in a thousand realizes today that the leading character is supposed to be modeled after Howard Hughes.

Beware of the kind of executive who likes to talk about intramural differences and difficulties in public.
—A story of Firestone and a hard-luck tire

Firestone Tire & Rubber selected the Byoir organization as its outside public-relations counsel in 1978, when the company was up to its neck in trouble. Our assignment was to patch up the company's tattered public image. We had just begun to make headway when some ill-chosen words from an executive pulled the rug out from under us.

This is a story with an unhappy ending. I've thought about it often in the years since, and I don't believe there was much we could have done about it. I can't think of anything we left undone or should have done differently. It is a story of public relations rendered helpless by an unexpected turn of events— and it is, in that sense, a story of a PR failure. But I believe it embodies a valuable PR lesson all the same.

The problem that hit us stemmed from an executive's habit of airing private quarrels in public. We were unable to stop him. But there are situations in which an alert PR professional *can* plug such a leak—and when you can, you should. Most companies have enough to do to protect themselves from damage coming from the outside. There is no sense in exposing a company to additional PR damage coming from the inside.

Firestone, in particular, had more than its share of external problems affecting its public image. It didn't need internal ones, too.

The external ones went back to 1972. That was when the company began producing a steel-belted radial tire designated Model 500. Over the next six years, Firestone made and sold some 24 million of those tires at about fifty dollars apiece.

The 500 tire was fatally flawed—some of its components tended to separate at high speeds.

Slowly and quietly at first, then with ever-growing volume, a chorus of public outrage built up. At first there were some private lawsuits by individuals and families alleging that deaths and injuries had resulted from the unsafe tires. Then there were some nosier, less private suits. Then consumer advocacy groups got into the act, followed by a howling pack of print and broadcast journalists. And finally a collection of powerful government agencies took up the cudgels.

There was the National Highway Traffic Safety Administration, which wanted Firestone to recall all the 500-series tires and replace them with a new model at its own expense. There was the House Oversight and Investigations Subcommittee, which determined that the 500 tires had indeed been the cause of many accidents. And the Securities and Exchange Commission decided to use the unhappy Firestone situation as a test case to answer a question that had long been in the minds of equity-market regulators: If a company does something which it knows could stir up civil penalties, should it be required to notify its shareholders? Such a case could arise, for example, when a company knowingly discharges pollutants into air or water, or markets an unsafe product.

There was no doubt Firestone was in a mess. It was to get much, much worse.

The key question in all the investigations was: Did Firestone executives know the 500-series tire was unsafe all along? And if so, did they go on selling it despite their knowledge?

The company and its executives stoutly denied such knowledge. But in mid-1978, a devastating piece of evidence came to light. Investigators found it in a truckload of documents that Firestone had been ordered to turn over to the Traffic Safety Administration. It was a memo, written in September 1973 by Thomas Robertson, Firestone's director of development, and addressed to the top management. The memo warned that the company was manufacturing a radial tire of inferior quality that could suffer a separation of components at high speed.

The memo was released to the media.

And that was when everything hit the fan.

Under intense pressure from all sides, Firestone announced in the summer of 1978 that it would stop producing 500-series tires and would comply with a Traffic Safety Administration order to start a recall and replacement program. Meanwhile, the company's president and chief operating officer, Mario DiFrederico, resigned. He cited personal reasons, but Firestone was now a company of such ill repute that hardly anybody believed him.

It was in July 1978 that Firestone decided it needed some outside public-relations help. Byoir made a presentation and was hired. We started work that September.

One vice president told us off the record that in his opinion, top management had relied too much on lawyers during this difficult period and not enough on public relations. He included the chairman and CEO, Richard Riley, in that criticism. But when we met Riley, he had obviously seen the light. He was counting on PR, he said, to help his company get out of the dreadful mess it was in.

The media had fallen into the habit of highlighting negative news about Firestone while all but ignoring positive news. We took it as our job to change that. We developed a series of stories about the company's continuing efforts to improve the 500 tire before halting production. We handed out statistics showing that buyer complaints about the tire had fallen off markedly in recent years, and many of those complaints were no doubt prompted more by the flood of adverse publicity than by any actual flaw in the tire. Any tire will fail when overstressed, improperly inflated, or mistreated in some other way. We also developed stories about newer products and other positive goings-on at Firestone.

And when the tire recall campaign got going, we were able to make positive news out of that. By the end of 1978, Firestone had fallen some $172 million into the red, largely because of the expense of that campaign. We were able to portray Firestone as a company making an honest effort to do the right thing.

The media response to our efforts was very encouraging. Our biggest disappointment was that the personable Richard Riley made it his policy to avoid one-on-one interviews during the period. The company was being assaulted with a lot of product-liability lawsuits, and Riley was afraid of making some casual remark that might later be turned against his company in court.

But we made progress anyhow. Gradually the media ceased their relentless hammering on Firestone. By the end of 1979, the public viewed Firestone as a company that had problems but was calmly and resolutely working them out.

That was about as good an image as we would have hoped to produce under the circumstances. We were pleased with our progress. But then, suddenly it stopped.

The man who stopped it was a new president, John J. Nevin.

Richard Riley, in his early sixties, was approaching retirement, so Firestone's board elected the fifty-three-year-old Nevin as president in early 1980. He would become CEO in due course, and Riley would gradually lighten his duties and withdraw.

Nevin, a former marketing vice president of Ford and chairman of Zenith, was evidently a man who believed in saying whatever was on his mind. That is certainly an admirable trait in some circumstances. A little more openness would have served Firestone well during the years of its agony over the 500 tire, for instance. But when openness reaches the point of unnecessarily revealing private, internal corporate matters, then it has gone too far.

Not long after Nevin arrived at Firestone's Akron headquarters, he gave an interview to a *Forbes* magazine reporter and was quoted in the resulting article that he found the company swarming with "smart-ass young consultants." They were concerned with everything, he said, except the fact that the company was going broke.

Nevin was also quoted in the article as saying, "They call me an S.O.B., and I'm paid to be an S.O.B. Firestone has been run by administrators, not decision-makers—almost a culture of clones. Some guys just have to go."

That was Nevin's style. Let it all hang out.

Comments such as these were guaranteed to make Nevin some bitter enemies in the company, to spread fear among employees, and to damage the company's public image.

We had accepted all along that Firestone had a lot of external problems that couldn't be hidden. The problem of the unsafe tire, the staggering cost of the recall campaign—there was no sense in trying to sweep these difficulties under the rug. They were external and public. Firestone executives might as well talk about them candidly. With the greatest of care, we had shown through the media that the company was tackling its problems coolly, firmly, and deliberately.

But now came the new president with comments that made Firestone sound like a company disintegrating in panic.

It was bad public-relations judgment. Tensions exist in every company. There are disagreements among members of every staff, no matter how amiably they get along. These tensions are healthy and productive under most circumstance but they are also, in the main, private. There is usually not much to be gained, and a great deal to be lost, by airing them in public. If executives of a company talk continually about their private disagreements and quarrels, the image emerges of a company that doesn't know what it is doing or where it is going.

Firestone survived, but not before it went through the wringer.

The company's common stock, traded on the New York Stock Exchange, had hit prices well over twenty dollars a share up to 1976. But then a long slump began. The stock hit a dismal low of six dollars and a fraction in 1980. It didn't manage to struggle back above twenty dollars until 1983.

Avoid loose talk until the contract is signed.
—A story of John DeLorean and the Chevy Vega

The lesson above applies to any line of work, but I think should be studied with particular care by anybody in the public-relations business. We PR people make our livings in large measure by exploiting accomplishments—most often our clients' or those of our employer, but sometimes accomplishments of our own. Self-promotion is a natural mode of expression for us—"See how great this company is!" So we are often tempted to sound off much too soon. It is wise for anybody, but especially for a public-relations professional, to keep silent about accomplishments until they are in fact accomplished.

A client isn't a client until he or she signs the contract. A job isn't a job until you report for your first day of work and find a desk waiting for you.

Here is a case in point.

One day in the early 1970s, Campbell-Ewald, a Detroit-based ad agency, got in touch with Byoir. We had been doing PR work for the city of Detroit, and that was how our name had come up. The Campbell-Ewald people told us they were the ad agency for GM's Chevrolet Division. Chevy was about to introduce a new model called the Vega, and everybody was excited about it. They wanted it unveiled to the public with more fanfare than had marked Ford's introduction of its enormously successful Mustang a couple of years back.

To help pull off this exciting publicity campaign, we were told, the Chevrolet people had decided to hire an outside PR agency for the first time in Chevy history. It was to be an international effort, encompassing Europe as well as the United States and Canada, with a budget of $2 million.

Wow!

This, we could see, was a biggie. *Two million!* Never before in PR history, as far as we knew, had this much money been allotted for a single promotional campaign.

The Campbell-Ewald people went on to say that they had contacted about fifty PR agencies for screening. The competition was to proceed in two stages. First, we would be asked to fill out a long questionnaire. The three best sets of answers would be selected, and those three agencies would be invited to make formal presentations in Detroit.

We sent in our questionnaire and three weeks later a Campbell-Ewald man, Dave Davis, called to tell us we had survived the first round. We were invited to make a presentation.

We were elated. We could almost taste those two million bucks.

In preparing our presentation, we learned a little about the recent history of Chevy and its Vega. The CEO of the Chevy Division was Ed Cole, but the real genius behind the Vega was the division's general manager, John DeLorean. That name was to become world famous in the 1980s. Back in the 1970s, DeLorean was a spectacular legend—only in Detroit.

John DeLorean was a young engineer with a flair for design who could take any old piece of bent metal and make it look elegant. He also had a finely tuned sense of popular tastes and an intuitive grasp of promotion. He had been assigned as general manager of Pontiac when that was GM's weakest division and within a few years, he had produced a line of cars so appealing that Pontiac outperformed all other GM divisions in sales growth.

One division it outstripped was poor old Chevy. There hadn't been much good news for Chevy in recent years. Its hated rival, Ford, was walking all over it. Ford's brilliant Mustang promotion was a particularly hard blow. Chevy executives had nightmares about Mustangs and shuddered whenever they saw one on the street.

The CEO of Pontiac during DeLorean's heyday there was a man named Bucky Knudsen, who was later to be lured away by Ford. When GM was wondering what to do about its sagging Chevrolet division, Knudsen recommended that his young bailout specialist, John DeLorean, be installed at Chevy as general manager.

DeLorean had now given birth to the Vega. His hopes for it were high. And so Byoir and two other agencies were being invited to compete for a $2 million promotional budget.

We won. We were asked not to say anything to anybody until the official announcement was made. With the greatest difficulty, we kept our mouths shut.

Bob Henkel, an executive vice president, and I met John DeLorean in New York. DeLorean was bubbling with enthusiasm. "I want to outpromote that Mustang and leave it in my dust!" he said. We said we would give the Vega our best shot.

The official announcement for our selection was set for a Monday morning, timed to let *Advertising Age* print the story at the same time as the daily business press. We could hardly wait till Monday. After that, we would be at liberty to blow our horn as loud as we wished.

Jack O'Dwyer, a columnist for the *Chicago Tribune,* broke the story on the preceding Friday morning, three days early. Our guess was that it had been leaked by one of the two unsuccessful PR agencies in our competition.

When GM's top management read the leaked story, they exploded with anger. Until then, they hadn't known anything about Chevy's plan to hire outside PR counsel. Ed Cole and John DeLorean had devised the plan on their own, without asking approval.

A wire-burning phone call shot from GM headquarters to Ed

Cole's office ordering Cole to cancel the plan immediately. No outside PR help was to be used.

And that was how we almost had, and then lost, the biggest one-shot PR budget in history.

As it turned out, the Vega promotion was not half as spectacular as the one we had started to dream up. The Vega didn't out-Mustang the Mustang. That was some small consolation. But what comforts me still more is the knowledge that we kept our mouths shut when we had to. If we had blabbed, we would have ended up very red in the face.

CHAPTER 7

THE CARE AND FEEDING OF IDEAS

Good PR ideas don't pop up every day. When one comes along, you must know how to recognize it and nurture it.

All good ideas involve risk. Never back away from one just because it means taking a chance.
A story of Woolworth and a well-polished image

WOOLWORTH HAD a reputation for being a somewhat stuffy and stiff-collared organization, which was not doing the company any good during the sit-in crisis, and I was always looking for ways to reveal the genuine warmth that I knew existed behind the aristocratic facade.

One day I happened to talk to a charming old gentleman named Mike, who for decades had been shining shoes in the Woolworth executive offices. He told me he had been earning his living that way for a full fifty years. Among other achievements, he had sent two youngsters to college on his earnings.

Aha, I thought.

I recommended a fiftieth anniversary party for Mike in the company's Manhattan offices and it was approved with real enthusiasm. The press and TV people were attracted to the story and I thought we would probably get good coverage. Then, suddenly, I saw a way to *guarantee* good coverage.

The idea was risky. For a few minutes I wandered around the party, alternately playing with the idea and then trying to bury it in some dark place where it wouldn't cause me any trouble. Finally, I decided, *Okay, Wood, out with it.*

I went up to Bob Kirkwood, Woolworth's CEO. "Mr. Kirkwood," I said, "I may get fired for this, but I'd like to make a suggestion."

"What is it?" Kirkwood was not a frosty man, but he did tend at times to have a frosty look.

167

I hesitated, then took the plunge. "I think it would be a nice gesture if you were to shine Mike's shoes," I said.

Kirkwood stared at me, momentarily flabbergasted. But he knew exactly what I was saying. I didn't need to give him reasons. He understood them perfectly. The idea was too good to throw away.

He nodded. "Find the equipment and I'll do it," he said.

The scene appeared in newspaper photographs and on TV programs all over the country. Woolworth's stodgy image was eliminated virtually overnight.

If an idea wants to grow, stand back and let it.
—A story of the Chicago & Northwestern Railroad

I learned this lesson at the very beginning of my civilian public-relations career, in the mid-1940s. If an idea wants to grow, don't stand in its way. And a corollary lesson was that not every public-relations campaign can be completely planned in advance. Sometimes you can get good results simply by starting it up and taking advantage of opportunities as they present themselves.

In 1947, the Chicago & Northwestern Railroad retained Byoir to help promote a hundredth anniversary celebration the following year. I was assigned to another account at the time but sat in on many creative staff meetings involving C&NW. We developed a campaign that included feature stories, historic photos, brochures, and other standard elements. These were good, workmanlike ideas, of course, but they weren't particularly exciting. However, we did generate three ideas that excited the railroad people.

The first was a flop. We approached the composer Meredith Willson and asked him to write a song about the C&NW Railroad. Willson was a young man at the time; his blockbuster hit of later years, "The Music Man," was not yet even a gleam in his eye. But he had some solid musical achievements to his credit. We offered him $500 plus all royalties to write our song and he accepted. We hoped it might come to rival other grand old railroading songs, such as "The Atcheson, Topeka, and Santa Fe" or "The Wabash Cannonball." Unfortunately, it didn't. It never made the top twenty list of hit songs or even, as far as I know, the top hundred. It vanished quickly into obscurity.

Our second idea worked out a bit better. We asked a lot of Chicago business and civic leaders to guess what the city might be like a hundred years in the future—in the year 2048—and buried a time capsule containing this information in a downtown Chicago location. This generated some good local press coverage for a while, but there was only so much mileage we could get out of it.

I remember feeling worried and discontented. The promotion didn't seem to be catching fire, and nobody seemed to have any especially appealing new ideas.

What I wasn't prepared for was something that often happens in the public-relations business. An idea unexpectedly took on a life of its own and ran away with the whole show.

This was the third of the three ideas that we proposed to the C&NW people. Our notion was to stage a parade down Michigan Avenue, Chicago's main drag. The parade would feature old-time railroading equipment and would be keyed to the contribution of railroads to the city's history. Leading the parade would be the C&NW "Pioneer" engine—the first locomotive to travel west of Chicago.

When we first thought of this idea, we saw it as a one-day promotion. It might generate news stories for a few days or perhaps a couple of weeks if we were lucky, but then, it, too, would peter out. What would we do then? What act would we produce to follow it? We didn't know.

What we didn't foresee was that our parade would lead into a grand promotion that would last not just for days, but for years.

As part of our preparations for the parade, a group of railroad and Byoir people went to see Colonel Robert McCormick, the

publisher of the *Chicago Tribune*, to solicit his support for the
parade. McCormick was not only the autocratic chief of the
city's leading newspaper but also a mighty power in local civic
and political affairs. If you had his support in any project, you
had more than half the battle won. If you lacked his support,
you might as well abandon the project.

To everybody's astonishment, the colonel was very enthusiastic over the idea of a railroad-oriented parade. He suggested
carrying the idea much further than we had dared to envision.
He wanted to invite other well-known old railroads that had
served Chicago to participate—the New York Central, the Penn-
sylvania, the Santa Fe, the Burlington & Northern, and others.

He issued the invitations personally. When Colonel McCormick invited you to something in Chicago, it was dangerous to
turn him down. All the railroads accepted.

All kinds of nostalgia-dipped old railroading equipment began
to roll into Chicago. Publicity about this and about the coming
parade was heavy—greatly enhanced, of course, by the editorial
enthusiasm of the *Tribune*. Encouraged by this, Byoir suggested
a modest extension of the original plan. Since all this fascinating
equipment was being gathered in Chicago, we said, why not put
it on display for a few weeks after the parade? Space was
available in some city parkland.

Everybody thought this was a good idea. The parade and the
exhibit drew unexpectedly huge crowds—not just railroad buffs,
but people who were interested in Chicago history, people fascinated by the Wild West, and untold others.

Our idea was still growing far beyond our original notion. Nor
was even this the end.

The chiefs of the railroads, pleased and surprised by all this
public interest, got together and started to talk about a railroad
fair that would last for at least two years.

At this point there were some voices starting to say, "No,
enough!" The idea had already ballooned far beyond its original
scope. Some felt that to let it balloon still further into a two-year
fair would be to milk it too hard.

But others, including me, held the opposite view. This idea
had a life of its own. It wanted to keep on growing. Instead of

standing in its way, we felt we should go along for the ride and see what happened.

Many good things happened. The two-year fair, which ran in 1949 and 1950, drew heavy crowds and generated continuous news coverage, more than we had ever dreamed possible when we first began talking with C&NW back in 1947.

The C&NW exhibit at the fair featured a thirty-foot foam-rubber statue of Paul Bunyan, the mythical woodsman of the upper Midwest. The statue was wired so that the arms, eyes, head, and lips moved. Most of the time we had an actor hidden near the statue, and he would tell stories in such a way that Bunyan appeared to be doing the talking. That was popular with the crowds, but when I visited the exhibit one day, I was hit by an idea that produced considerably more news coverage.

I suggested that we invite celebrities to sit on Paul Bunyan's lap and talk to him. A silly notion? Maybe. But it was also a lot of fun. Dozens of actors, actresses, senators, governors, and local bigwigs were happy to let themselves be photographed in earnest conversation with the giant woodsman. The good results enhanced my enthusiasm for public relations.

There was one more happy result from all this. The two-year fair not only enabled us to generate good publicity for our original client, the Chicago & Northwestern Railroad, but also to bring another Byoir client in on the action—Pullman-Standard, a major manufacturer of railroad cars.

When there is nothing else left to try, even a seem-
ingly silly idea is better than nothing.
   —A story of Pullman-Standard and an upside-
                                    down freight car

When the two-year railroad fair got rolling, we suggested that another of our railroading clients, Pullman-Standard, also participate.

Pullman-Standard was a maker of railroad passenger and freight cars. Executives of the company liked the idea of participating in the fair, and after considerable discussion, they decided that their exhibit should feature an upside-down freight car. By displaying it upside-down, they could give fairgoers a good view of the trucks, wheels, bearings, brakes, and other components of a well-built piece of rolling stock. They felt this exhibit would attract a lot of attention.

They were wrong.

Fairgoers avoided that upside-down freight car in droves. Part of the problem may have been that the exhibit was in an out-of-the-way location, but whatever the reason, only hard-core railroad buffs were attracted to it. The Pullman-Standard people were upset and depressed.

A Byoir staff meeting was called to discuss the problem. I had a suggestion to offer. In a department store recently, I had seen an odd promotion that intrigued me. People were invited to stand in front of a TV camera and see themselves instantly displayed on a screen—a real novelty in 1949—and the promotion was attracting many excited people. I now suggested that the same kind of see-yourself-on-TV promotion be set up at the end of the Pullman-Standard exhibit, so people would have to walk past that upside-down freight car and look at it whether they wanted to or not.

Over the next several days, this idea was batted back and forth between us and the Pullman-Standard people. Many were doubtful about its usefulness. As I recall, the debates tended to go like this:

"The idea sounds pretty silly."

"Sure, but what have we got to lose?"

"Nothing, granted. But what does a see-yourself-on-TV promotion have to do with railroad cars?"

"Well . . . nothing. But at least it might bring people into the exhibit."

"If it flops, it could make us look pretty dumb."

"We already have a flop. How could it get any worse?"

Finally the decision was made to go ahead with the TV promotion.

It was wildly successful.

To this day I don't fully understand why. I know only that the experience taught me a valuable lesson, which I have never forgotten—never reject an idea, even a seemingly silly one, without at least giving it a fair hearing. Particularly when all else has failed and no other ideas are around, even a goofy idea may be better than nothing.

Within two weeks, that Pullman-Standard exhibit became the third most popular at the fair. It was so successful that it was maintained throughout the fair's second year.

Try to postpone judgments until you have examined things for yourself.
—A story of S. C. Johnson and a dark-horse movie

When a New York World's Fair was announced for the middle 1960s, to last two years and to be located near LaGuardia Airport, the possibility of enormous crowds attracted many large companies as prospective exhibitors. General Motors, IBM, RCA, and other industrial giants announced plans to sponsor exhibits, many of which were expected to cost tens of millions of dollars.

Several Byoir clients said they planned to participate in the fair, and we anticipated a busy couple of years. Some of our clients' exhibits were quite grandiose. But there was one client with a modest little idea—so modest that it almost died of neglect a couple of times.

The client was S. C. Johnson & Son, maker of Johnson's Wax and an assortment of other consumer products. The Johnson people told us that their contribution to the fair would be to commission a short movie and build a special theater to show it in. They said they had acquired the services of Francis Thompson, an independent producer and director, and told him to produce a twenty-minute movie about the joy of living.

This news didn't exactly produce an outburst of exuberance in the Byoir offices.

A twenty-minute movie on the joy of living? When we thought of some of the spectacular exhibits it would have to compete with—multimillion-dollar extravangazas, fantasies, and spectacles, our hearts sank. Some of our creative people wanted to warn Johnson that the idea was a loser. Why would fairgoers want to sit in a movie theater with so much else to attract them? The idea, some of our people thought, would be unappealing even if we were talking about an exciting movie. But a movie on the joy of living? It sounded dull—probably a lot of pictures of kids running around in fields of daisies.

The Johnson people were undoubtedly aware of our doubts, though we didn't harp on them. Still, the project went ahead anyway. Francis Thompson produced his film, and about a month before the fair was scheduled to open, we asked him to show it to our account team and the heads of our specialized departments—magazines, radio-TV, lifestyles, and so on.

The eighteen-minute film, titled *To Be Alive,* required three projectors and three screens and Johnson built a special round theater called the Golden Rondelle to accommodate it. The effect was a feeling being surrounded by the film—being actually *in* it rather than only watching it. When Francis Thompson came up to our offices to show it to us, he had to improvise a setup of three small screens.

We didn't expect to be much impressed. To our surprise and delight, we were.

The film was genuinely moving. Thompson had compiled scenes of people enjoying life all over the world; his theme was that people everywhere get pleasure from essentially the same things. A simple idea? Yes, of course it was simple, but sometimes the very simplest ideas are the most powerful. This odd little film brought a lump to the throat.

Our earlier skepticism changed to high enthusiasm. We had been taught a lesson about the foolishness of passing judgment on what you *think* you are going to see and hear.

We saw the lesson repeated many times.

One memorable instance was in the Golden Rondelle theater itself, out at the fairgrounds. When we at Byoir saw how good the film was, we asked Francis Thompson if he would help us set up a preview. He agreed, and we contacted all the major New York film critics. As we had expected, they listened politely when we told them about the little movie we wanted them to see. Their level of enthusiasm was about the same as ours when *we* first were told about the film.

Still, virtually all the critics agreed to turn up at the round theater. Many, we knew, were doing it just as a favor to us.

The audience assembled at the theater five days before the opening of the fair. Francis Thompson introduced *To Be Alive,* the projectors began to roll, and the critics sat glumly through the opening minutes. They undoubtedly were pleased to note that the only reference to S.C. Johnson & Son was a single brief showing of the corporate logo. Then the film proper began, and the air suddenly became charged with a palpable electric tension. The jaded viewers, all of whom during their careers had sat through many thousands of hours of movies—good, bad, and mediocre—seemed to stiffen suddenly into attitudes of alert attention. I felt the hair prickling at the back of my neck.

When the film ended, there was a brief, total silence. And then came the most extraordinary reaction I believe I've ever witnessed after any film of any kind. The critics arose from their seats in a body and gave *To Be Alive* a standing ovation. It seemed to go on and on. I didn't time it; it may not even have lasted a full minute. But in its intensity it seemed to span an eternity.

The reviews those critics wrote in their newspapers and magazines during the following days and weeks were outright raves. We had hoped for good reviews, but these were far better than anything we had dreamed of.

We continued to promote *To Be Alive* after the fair opened, of course. The success of this little movie was astonishing. The Golden Rondelle was filled to capacity for every showing of the film, from the day the fair opened until it closed at the end of the following summer. Francis Thompson's simple eighteen-minute essay became one of the main attractions at the fair. Word-of-mouth recommendations promoted it as strongly as our efforts at Byoir did. People interviewed at the fair sometimes said the Johnson exhibit was the major attraction that had drawn them to the fair from hundreds or even thousands of miles away—"My neighbor said that if I only see one thing, that's the one." The film's success seemed all the more remarkable when we reflected on our client's relatively modest investment—a fraction of what some other exhibitors had spent on grandiose buildings and extravangazas.

After the fair closed, Johnson dismantled the theater and rebuilt it at the corporate headquarters in Racine, Wisconsin. *To Be Alive* was obviously too good to put in a can and shelve. The company continued to show the film on a regular schedule at Racine, and it still rolls today, many years after its humble birth.

And the little movie collected one more honor along the way—an Oscar in the category of short documentary films. It was the first time such an award had been given to a film sponsored by a company not associated with show business.

And that is the story of my favorite ugly duckling.

Don't worry too much about losing control of an idea. Other people may enlarge it well beyond its original size and power—if you let them.
        —A story of Servomation and the Olympics

The Servomation Corporation is one of the two biggest institutional feeding companies in the United States. It serves food—sometimes cafeteria-style, sometimes through vending machines—in schools, colleges, factories, and other places where lots of people eat meals. In addition, it owns or franchises some 300 Red Barn restaurants in twenty-seven states. Servomation became a Byoir client in 1970.

I was having lunch with the very competent chairman and CEO of Servomation, Allen Lucht, one day in 1971 when he remarked that he would like to see a slight change in the direction of our public-relations effort. Until then, we had concentrated mainly on publicizing the quality of the food, the low prices, and other features that would attract new customers. Lucht was pleased that Servomation had grown steadily during its time as our client, but now he wondered if we could think of a way to connect the company in people's minds with the idea of public service.

Public service? It's fine when it's well handled. IBM, for instance, does a spectacularly good job with it. But it can backfire on you when it has a faked or rigged-up look, which it very often does. The American public is deeply skeptical of fakery and cannot easily be fooled. "What public service?" people ask scoffingly. "So you're giving out doughnuts to orphans. What you're in it for is cheap publicity and a tax deduction."

So Byoir moved carefully. We held one long meeting and kicked some ideas around, but rejected them all and scheduled another meeting a few days later to try again.

Then an idea hit my head like an apple from a tree. And what a lovely, big, red apple it was!

I was invited to a meeting of the 1972 Olympic Committee, which at that time—mid-1971—was making plans for the summer games the following year in West Germany. The most important topic of discussion at this meeting was the committee's pressing need for money. The main source of money for American Olympic teams had always been private contributions, and that was still true in 1972. But because of worldwide inflation in the early 1970s, the need was now more desperate than ever.

I went home that night and thought about the Olympics. The next day I talked to my colleagues at Byoir, and then to Allen Lucht.

We put together a plan. Boys and girls aged twelve and younger would be invited to solicit Olympic donations house to house. The campaign would be conducted in the twenty-seven states where Red barn restaurants were located, and the restaurants would become the campaign headquarters. To become a fund raiser, a youngster had to register at a Red Barn and receive a special collection container. Prizes would be awarded to the most successful young house callers—local and state-level prizes and a grand prize for the two top youngsters nationally. The grand prize was to be a free trip to the summer Olympics at Servomation's expense.

We set about the task of publicizing this campaign. The kick-off, a press conference at New York's Tavern on the Green, was a big success and the Olympic Committee cooperated happily. We assembled a lot of former Olympic medalists—so many, in fact, that we were able to boast that there had never been a bigger collection of Olympic gold winners anywhere outside the games themselves.

That brought us a wave of national publicity and we supplemented it with state and local publicity centering around those 300 Red Barn restaurants. The restaurant managers were almost all pleased with the campaign. We furnished them with press kits, which they in turn gave out to local reporters and broadcasters. The campaign rolled faster and faster as hundreds of youngsters signed up as house-to-house canvassers.

And then my idea began to grow in size and power. People outside the Byoir organization latched onto little pieces of it and added their own thinking. No longer "my" idea, it belonged to more and more people as it went from mind to mind.

I could have reacted with annoyance—I've known some people who would have. "I'm losing control of my own idea!" they would cry, and they would rein the idea in and slap controls on it to preserve their proprietorship.

But I felt that would be a mistake. If people were adding alien elements to my idea, distorting it, or turning it aside from its original purpose, then I would have been unhappy and probably would have tried to reestablish personal control. But in this case quite the opposite was happening—the idea was being made to move more surely toward its original goal. Because of the addition of other people's thinking, it was putting on muscle day by day.

So I didn't object. I just watched. And enjoyed.

In many communities, without any special invitation from us at Byoir, the Boy and Girl Scouts and other youngsters' organizations got themselves involved. In some cases they virtually took over control of the local fund drives. That didn't bother me at all.

Nor was I upset when politicians began to get into the act. In some towns, kids were awarded prizes in special town-hall ceremonies, usually with the mayor officiating. I hadn't asked for that, but it was fine by me.

The idea snowballed. State governments began awarding state-level prizes, and sometimes the governors gave them out. Naturally, we made sure that the name of Servomation didn't get lost in the festivities.

Finally we hit the jackpot. We arranged for the two national winners, a boy and a girl, to be invited to the White House in Washington. Vice President Agnew congratulated them personally and praised their efforts. This event got wide coverage in the press and broadcast media, including network TV.

When we flew the two lucky youngsters to the site of the original Olympic Games in Greece and on to the games in West Germany, unsolicited publicity continued to enlarge our already well-grown idea. Politicians and others kept getting into our act and we didn't stand in anybody's way.

There were two excellent results. The first was that the nickels, dimes, and quarters collected by the young house callers amounted to an impressive $93,000 for the United States Olympic team. At a ceremony that we *did* arrange, Allen Lucht gave a check for this amount to William Simon, the Olympic Committee's chairman.

And the campaign generated enormously valuable publicity for Servomation—exactly what Allen Lucht had asked for, publicity in linking his company's name with public service.

I would have been foolish to hobble my idea simply for the sake of keeping personal control. By letting other people take over pieces and add their own ideas, I saw the idea grow far bigger than I had imagined.

Sometimes a good picture can be worth a thousand press releases.
—A story of Hughes Aircraft and 480 telephones

Hughes Aircraft developed and built a communications satellite named *Early Bird,* which was launched in 1973 and placed in a geosynchronous orbit—it orbited above the equator and precisely matched the earth's speed of rotation, appearing to hover always in the same spot in the sky.

Our problem was how to publicize it.

Bob Meyer, the Byoir associate account executive assigned to Hughes, had an idea that he explained to Bill Utley, the account executive and Meyer's immediate boss. The *Early Bird* had 240 communications channels, Meyer said. Therefore, a good way to publicize it would be to photograph a full-size model of it linked with 240 telephones.

Bill agreed that this was a fine idea, but he wondered how Bob planned to get hold of 240 telephones. Easy, Bob responded. He thought he could get them from Parker Sullivan, the president of General Telephone (which today calls itself GTE). Bob knew Sullivan from a somewhat silly episode three years back. Bob had gotten married, he told Bill, and when his new bride moved out of her old apartment, she received a final bill from General Telephone for one cent. This struck Bob as so dumb that he wrote a derisive letter to General Telephone's president. Parker Sullivan sent back a courteous reply, and the affair ended good humoredly.

Bob Meyer now phoned Sullivan, explained his idea about a picture of 240 telephones, and pointed out that it could mean good publicity for General Telephone as well as for Hughes. Sullivan agreed, offering not only to supply 240 telephones in all shapes and colors, but to have them delivered to wherever the photo was to be shot.

Bill Utley and Bob Meyer then tried the idea on Jim Beam, Hughes Aircraft's very professional vice president for public relations.

Jim Beam said, "Fine idea! There's just one thing. The Early Bird's 240 channels are all two-way channels. That means 480 people can hold conversations simultaneously. You get what I'm saying?"

"Oh, damn!" said Bob Meyer. "You're saying we need 480 telephones."

"That's what I'm saying," agreed Jim Beam.

Bob Meyer was embarrassed at the thought of going back to the accommodating Parker Sullivan and asking him to double the favor. But Bob finally managed to gather up his courage and phoned Sullivan to explain what he needed.

"No problem," said Sullivan without a moment's hesitation. "You want 480 telephones? You've got them."

So that was how we borrowed all those phones. Working with our own award-winning industrial photographer, Hank McAllister, the Byoir team set the phones up on tables in a huge, empty, barnlike building on Hughes Aircraft's property. They hired two professional models to pose as phone operators and shot pictures for two long days. Then they invited *Life* magazine to come and look at the display. Intrigued, *Life* sent one of its ace photographers, who rigged up the phones with strings of lights leading to the satellite overhead. He shot pictures for an entire night.

On the third morning, as the exhausted photographers and PR team arrived at the display for some last-minute work, one of the phones inexplicably started ringing. Nobody knew which one it was. It wouldn't stop. Exasperated, Bob Meyer crawled and weaved his way through the display until he finally located the culprit. It turned out that a Hughes engineer had wired a bell circuit as a practical joke.

Bob Meyer wasn't sure he saw the humor of it. But he cheered up considerably as the results of his grand visual idea began to make themselves known. Hank McAllister's expert photos were printed in newspapers and magazines around the world, and *Life* ran a stunning full-page photograph in full color.

Howard Hughes himself at that time—the early 1970s—was already a real recluse. It wasn't often that he bestirred himself to issue plaudits, but he did in this case. Through Bill Gay, his chief liaison man in dealing with us, he congratulated the Byoir team on a good idea brilliantly executed.

CHAPTER 8

INFLUENCING PUBLIC OPINION AND LEGISLATION

The most intimidating of all PR campaigns.

Perhaps the most challenging task in public relations is that of turning public opinion around from one view to its opposite. It seems almost impossible sometimes, but it can be done, given time and a multi-pronged attack.
—A story of CIT Financial and a great battle

THIS IS a story about one of the most extensive public-relations campaigns I have ever been associated with. In the course of this massive campaign, we at Byoir used, I believe, every PR technique any of us had ever heard of, plus a few that we made up on the spot.

The purpose of this extraordinary effort was to make a 180-degree change in American public opinion, not just in a single city or state—difficult enough in most cases—but throughout the entire nation. When I heard the first conversations about it and learned of its grandiose goals, I was seized with the most serious of misgivings. How can you hope to shift opinion throughout this huge country? How can anybody even dream of trying? I thought, This is hubris! This is the ultimate in optimism!

But public relations, well and steadfastly applied, can pull off just such a gigantic result.

The campaign involved a Federal Reserve Board rule called Regulation W, which imposed severe restrictions on consumer installment credit. Congress first gave the Fed the power to restrict consumer credit during the Second World War, when there was widespread fear of runaway inflation. Regulation W was rescinded after the war but kept popping up again during the postwar boom years and during the Korean War, whenever economists and others got worried about new inflation.

Under its terms, consumers were required to make a down payment of at least one third the purchase price when buying almost everything except homes and to repay the balance in a maximum of fifteen months. The regulation covered big-ticket items such as cars and major appliances. And so these items were placed out of the reach of many—perhaps most—Americans.

Regulation W had last been imposed during the Korean War and rescinded in 1952. Then, in early 1953, people started to talk about reinstating it permanently. That was when Byoir got into the act.

The main proponents of Regulation W were some governors and staff members of the Federal Reserve Board. They very quickly drummed up a lot of support in Congress, the media, and elsewhere. There were a lot of news stories about families sinking into unmanageable debt, and the regulation was applauded as a way to save consumers from themselves and from unscrupulous car and appliance dealers. In addition, economists had more arcane worries about the effects of rising consumer debt on the economy. These worries were shared by some noted business leaders and were reported in the financial press and on radio and TV.

When the Fed finally went before Congress and formally asked for authority to reinstate controls, Regulation W became a very hot issue. Politicians vied with each other in supporting it, while editors scrambled for ever more harrowing stories about debt-ridden wretches being turned out of their homes, drowning in drink, and shooting themselves. The tide of public opinion was strong and unequivocal—something must be done about the evils of debt.

The opponents of Regulation W were strangely silent, perhaps intimidated by the huge weight of public opinion against them. In this silence, just one company dared to raise its voice. This was CIT Financial.

CIT, through a subsidiary, derived some 70 percent of its income from auto loans at that time. The company was understandably worried about a law that would, in effect, make it impossible for most people to qualify for such loans.

Arthur Dietz, CIT's chairman and CEO, pointed out that Regulation W had originally been intended to fill a need during wartime emergency conditions but had no place in a peacetime economy. It was an unwarranted intrusion on people's right to make their own choices. Was it proper, he asked, for the United States government to deny lower-income citizens the right to buy cars, appliances, or furniture?

This was what Arthur Dietz felt and said. But nobody was listening.

What was needed, he thought, was a major PR campaign to turn public opinion around. Ideally, he felt, such a campaign should be undertaken by a business association, not by one lone company. But nobody seemed willing to pick up the ball. And so, reluctantly, Dietz decided that if the job was going to be done at all, CIT would have to do it alone.

Well, not quite alone. Byoir was brought in to help.

CIT's public-relations chief, William L. Wilson, was a true pro, as able as they come. But his staff was too small for the monumental campaign Arthur Dietz envisioned. So he and Dietz invited a number of big New York PR agencies to say what they would do if hired for this task. Byoir's presentation won and I was assigned as account executive.

Our first move was to prepare a statement for Dietz to read at the CIT shareholders' meeting in April 1953. This statement was not only the opening shot of the campaign; it became a basic positioning document for the entire program. The opening paragraphs said:

Installment credit, or mass financing, is the fundamental support of the American system of mass production and mass distribution. However, the fulfillment of the public need that is made possible through installment buying is not the full measure of the benefit of mass financing.

If markets were restricted only to customers who could pay cash for goods, the economies of mass production would largely disappear, and prices for automobiles, refrigerators, kitchen ranges, and the like would be out of reach for most American families.

We developed dozens of feature stories that made these points in various ways and from various angles. Simultaneously, we worked up other stories that probed other parts of the issue. For example, we countered a widely held but largely unexplored belief that consumer debt had risen or was rising to dangerously high levels by pointing out that, on the contrary, debt, when measured in comparison to personal income and personal wealth, was in fact quite modest.

These stories appeared in all the expected places—newspapers, business magazines, TV financial reports. But we didn't stop there by any means. This was an all-out effort.

We arranged radio and TV interviews, debates, and panel discussions. We sent CIT executives around the country to speak to various groups, and we set up forums and panels for them to participate in, and naturally we saw to it that these events were abundantly reported in the appropriate local media. We sent out truckloads of press releases, transcripts of speeches, photos and charts, and other material. The printing and mailing costs were staggering, but we were determined to get our story told in every corner of the United States.

We paid special attention to women's magazines, women's newspaper pages, and the hostesses and commentators on TV talk shows with large female audiences. We furnished special features for their use and were rewarded with excellent coverage. Some editors and commentators presented our story virtually untouched; some quarreled with it or presented opposing points of view, but virtually all brought the CIT argument out into the open where it could get a fair hearing. That was what we wanted.

While these efforts were thundering along, I had another tactical gambit going in New York. CIT had a private dining facility at its Park Avenue headquarters, a relaxing and pleasant place. Over a period of five or six months, the head of our magazine department, Patricia Lochridge, helped me bring some of the nation's most influential business editors and journalists to these rooms for lunch and a private chat with Arthur Dietz. The guests were people such as Barney Kilgore, editor of the *Wall Street Journal*, Merrill Rukeyser, syndicated columnist, and the top business columnists and writers of King Features Syndicate, the Associated Press, and United Press International.

These quiet little lunches produced astonishing results. Arthur Dietz was a highly persuasive man in such eyeball-to-eyeball situations, and he sent most of his luncheon guests away feeling that the points he made were valid or at least worth offering for their readers' consideration. Articles and columns growing out of these Park Avenue lunches apeared throughout the country, and since they were written by widely respected people, the views presented were picked up by other journalists and commentators in a kind of intellectual osmosis.

Patricia and I were delighted, of course. Assessing the campaign later, we felt that those lunches were perhaps the most effective single move in the whole great effort.

But there was much more. Among other things, we arranged some major speaking engagements for Arthur Dietz. This entailed a good deal more work than it usually does, for Arthur Dietz, persuasive and almost hypnotic in face-to-face encounters, was not a good public speaker when we first began to work with him. He tended to stiffen up. Instead of speaking *to* his audiences and drawing them into his arguments, as he did with such remarkable effect across the lunch table, he would simply stand there and read his speech in a flat voice.

Before I could send him out to speak, I had to make him into an effective speaker. And so a quick training program became a part of our massive campaign. Dietz agreed to undergo several hours of coaching by our specialist, Muriel Fox Aronson. The results were amazing. Dietz was a fast learner and was, in addition, strongly motivated to put his points across effectively. His poor speaking manner was not the result of any deep or difficult problem but stemmed largely from an array of minor mannerisms which were quickly trained away.

I won't say he became a brilliant speaker, but he did become a very good one. The final speech of the series we set up for him was a triumph. It was in San Francisco, at a luncheon gathering of the august Commonwealth Club of California. Dietz stood up and grabbed his audience as powerfully as he had grabbed those journalists at our Park Avenue lunches. When he finished speaking, he got a standing ovation.

That San Francisco speech may have been the last nail in the coffin of Regulation W. Press coverage of the speech was heavy, nationwide, and almost without exception, favorable.

The press, radio, and TV were now solidly on CIT's side. In less than a year of ferociously hard work, we had turned them around completely.

And where once the pro-regulation side had been doing all the talking, now it was their turn to be silent. The Fed's governors and staff members were no longer pressing for authorization to reimpose Regulation W, undoubtedly because they realized the timing was no longer right. Public opinion had turned against them. Politicians were also silent. They could read the voters' mood just as well as the Fed could. The American people had decided they wanted no federal government restrictions on their right to buy goods on credit.

The issue was dead. It never reached the floor of Congress.

Good public relations sometimes seems magical, but you should never hold out a promise of magical results. If an offered assignment sounds impossible, turn it down.

—A story of Aristotle Onassis and a New Hampshire oil refinery

On a Tuesday afternoon in the mid-1970s I received a phone call from Paris, from a man named Johnny Meyer. He had once worked as an administrative aide to Howard Hughes, and I had come to know him during the years when the Byoir organization served as Hughes's PR counsel. Johnny Meyer was now working for the famous Greek oil and shipping tycoon, Aristotle Onassis, who was having a public-relations problem in New Hampshire.

A couple of months back, Johnny told me, Onassis had announced that he planned to build a large oil refinery in New Hampshire. The initial reaction to this announcement had been highly positive. The governor, the two United States senators, the state legislature, the local newspapers, and the general public all seemed to feel, on balance, that the refinery would bring welcome benefits to the state. It would create jobs, boost the economy, reduce the state's dependence on oil from distant refineries, and so on.

But then some strong objections arose from a group of wealthy people, many of them retired New Yorkers, who lived near where the proposed refinery was to be built. Their objections were the standard ones of people in such circumstances—the refinery would destroy the area's pleasant rural character, overstrain the capacity of local highways, and take more from the state than it could repay in taxes and other benefits.

This well-heeled opposition group included some highly professional PR and ad retirees, who knew how to put their point of view across. They appeared to be succeeding, and public opinion was decidedly swinging their way. Even the two United States senators had begun muttering about changing their minds.

It seemed to be an emergency. Johnny Meyer asked if the Byoir organization could turn things around. I replied that we could not perform miracles, but it was certainly possible we could help, and I would be willing to study the situation in more detail. Johnny then asked me to call the man in charge of Onassis's North American operations immediately.

The man was in New York, and I called and made an appointment to meet him on the following morning, Wednesday.

In our hour-long talk, he gave me more details of the PR battle being fought, and it was plain that he had a tough problem. The Onassis organization was up against skilled public-relations opponents, and I had to admire the effectiveness of their work. It seemed to me all but certain that the Onassis side would lose the battle unless a powerful new factor was introduced into the picture.

That factor, the Onassis people hoped, would be the Byoir organization. "Can you help us?" the North American chief asked me.

I shrugged. "As I told Johnny Meyer, we can't perform miracles. But we *are* good at what we do. Give me a little more information. I'll need to know the deadline, for one thing. When is the state legislature scheduled to vote on the refinery?"

"Saturday."

I sat straight up in my chair. "You mean three days from now?"

"Yes."

I slumped back into my chair, completely deflated. The man looked puzzled. I explained that this deadline would leave us just two working days, Thursday and Friday, to try to produce a useful effect. That simply wasn't enough time. No matter how good you are, you can't turn an entire state's public opinion around in two days.

To my great regret, I said, the Byoir organization would have to turn the job down.

The legislature's vote that Saturday was overwhelmingly against the proposed refinery. Several other northeastern governors promptly phoned the Onassis group to say they would offer a more hospitable reception to a refinery, but Onassis eventually decided to abandon the whole effort.

It was too bad. I honestly believe we could have won the New Hampshire battle if we had been given three or four weeks. I also believe we could have won any of those other northeastern states if we had been brought in on the debate at the beginning.

But to take on a two-day turnaround miracle would have been foolhardy. It would have been like accepting a dare to walk across Niagara Falls on a tightrope. The chances of winning would be slight, and the costs of losing would be huge.

I thrive on tough assignments and honest challenges, as any PR professional should. But I never offer to perform magic.

Sometimes a good public-relations result can be achieved by assembling a task force.
—A story of Borg-Warner and a California vote

Borg-Warner, a longtime Byoir client, ran into a serious problem in 1976. Californians were about to vote on a public referendum called Proposition 15 which, if it were to become law, would virtually close down all nuclear generating plants in that huge state. Borg-Warner had a substantial investment in the nuclear power industry—its Energy Equipment Division was (and still is) a supplier of pumps, valves, and seals for nuclear plants.

The company felt the state's antinuclear forces were exploiting public ignorance in the drive to get Proposition 15 voted into law. Byoir was asked to step in immediately and get the propositon defeated.

We looked around the state. What we saw intimidated us.

Hardly anything ever happens on a small scale in California. The antinuclear forces were banded into a very large, articulate, well-funded, active organization. Moreover, they had picked up support from sundry environmentalist groups and other concerned citizens. As Borg-Warner pointed out, few of them appeared to have a clear idea of what a nuclear generating plant is, how it works, what benefits it produces, and what its hazards are. Many in the antinuclear camp were simply people who had a fear-filled emotional response to the word "nuclear."

By contrast, those opposing Proposition 15 had no large, active organization to push their point of view. They were largely isolated voices like Borg-Warner's.

But it appeared that the great majority of business people in the state were in favor of nuclear power. To them, it was an economic issue, not an emotional one. They understood that fossil fuels were going to grow inexorably more scarce and expensive as time went by, and no other substitute technology offered as great a promise of cheap, abundant electric power as nuclear generation.

We wondered if we could fuse these business men and women into a task force.

A task force can be made to work well if you can identify and approach the prospective members—that is often a problem. There are other stories in this book about situations in which we were asked to mold public opinion, but only in a few cases were we able to assemble a task force. The problem is to find a large pool of people who will be mainly on your side and to enlist them fast. Speed was essential in the Proposition 15 case because there were only a few months to go before the vote.

The California business community was just such a pool of people. They were visible, easily identifiable, approachable. We went out to sign them up.

We approached the pool initially through two organizations—the Los Angeles Chamber of Commerce and the California Merchants and Manufacturers Association. Through them we got in touch with some companies, mainly large ones, that were willing to lend us executives to work full time on the campaign until the day of the vote. We rounded up thirty-four of these people, and this cadre of executive talent was put under the direction of a Borg-Warner man.

Working with Byoir's Los Angeles office, the cadre initiated a program of public education through the press and broadcast media. Simultaneously the group raised funds and recruited local precinct workers, so that the task force continually expanded.

We also conducted a massive mail campaign. Once again, this was relatively easy to do because our targets were visible and readily tracked down. We prepared a letter that was sent to the president of every California company we could find that had 250 or more employees—1,350 such companies, and I doubt we missed many.

The letter, of course, urged support of Borg-Warner's position—in favor of nuclear power, against Propositon 15. After the letter went out, our thirty-four executives went out to visit the recipients in person. They called on 1,015 of them, taking a carefully prepared kit containing sample letters that the company president could send to employees, shareholders, business colleagues, and friends.

This expanded the task force still more. Many of the company chiefs and other executives thus contacted were delighted to join in our campaign. Many had arrived independently at a judgment in line with Borg-Warner's but had felt frustrated by the lack of an organization through which to express their views. We were presenting them with just such an organization, and new executive recruits signed up eagerly.

We tried to get some feedback on the results, and the statistics were highly encouraging. At least 100 companies published articles in house organs and newsletters urging the defeat of Proposition 15. The total number of personal letters sent out by executives as a result of our people's visits was 502,000. Simultaneously, our own people and the task force cadre were distributing some 230,000 pieces of literature and 6,000 bumper stickers. And of course we continued working hard with the media—at least eight good, strong editorials were published in major newspapers supporting our side.

The upshot: Propositon 15 was soundly defeated.

The vote was two to one against it. And in southern California, it was even more lopsided: 73 percent to 27 percent, or three to one. The antinuclear forces had been the most active in the southern part of the state, and it was there that our task force concentrated its hardest efforts.

It was a good campaign. It illustrated a particular approach to public relations that can be made to work marvelously well—when the circumstances are right.

When you need to explain and/or dramatize a difficult concept, ask if a scale model will do the trick.
    —A story of CIT Financial and a highway bill

CIT financial and its determined chairman, Arthur Dietz, frequently seemed to be taking on the role of a business association. Only a few years after Dietz and his company, with Byoir, did battle against a consumer credit law called Regulation W, Dietz mounted his association horse again.

This time, in the middle 1950s, he went out riding in support of a highway bill that had become roadblocked in Washington. As CIT's longtime public-relations counsel, Byoir was called on to help in this campaign, too. It was a difficult campaign because it dealt with large, complicated concepts that were hard to explain and dramatize to the media. The media, in turn, had trouble communicating these ideas to the public. People's eyes would glaze over; they would turn the page or change TV channels. But then I was hit by an idea—a scale model.

The National Highway Act authorized spending $33 billion to extend and modernize the nation's highways. President Eisenhower had pushed it, Congress had passed it, but then it had become bogged down, the money to implement it held up by fancy financial footwork on the part of some of its opponents. Since nobody in Washington was writing the checks, no actual work was being done out on the roads.

Into this vacuum leapt a powerful, well-funded, highly organized lobbying group that wanted to see the money spent on urban mass transit instead of highways. This group had as its nucleus a consortium of companies that stood to make money from mass transit—rail and subway outfits, bus manufacturers and operators, and so on. Their campaign was proving successful. Through skilled public relations they were winning the media, the public, and Congress to their point of view.

Enter Arthur Dietz and CIT Financial. As the nation's biggest independent provider of automobile loans, and a leader in the leasing of highway construction equipment, CIT had a big stake in the legislation to improve highways.

Dietz wanted an association to take on the fight, but he couldn't find one that felt it had the power. The lack of opposition served to encourage the mass transit lobby to still greater efforts. Finally, Dietz called me into his office along with Bill Wilson, CIT's vice president in charge of public relations.

"There's a good chance that Congress wil divert all or most of that $33 billion to mass transit," Dietz told us. "I'm not against mass transit, but I hate to see the Highway Act coming apart. I think that money should be spent as originally intended."

He then announced that since nobody else seemed willing to take up the sword, CIT would do it alone. "Maybe others will join us," he said. "But it looks like it's up to us to get it going."

"When do you want us to start?" I asked.

"Today," Dietz said.

So Bill and I went to work. In one of our initial discussions we recalled that Arthur Dietz was president of an outfit called the Highways for Survival Committee. It was not large, wealthy, or very active, nor was it the kind of association Dietz had been looking for—one that could wage the fight on its own. But at least, Bill and I saw, it had an appropriate name that we could use. With us doing the work and CIT providing the budget, the Highways for Survival Committee could be our flagship. Dietz agreed. We used the committee's name instead of CIT's in most of our publicity.

We swung vigorously into the campaign, setting up interviews and radio and TV appearances for Dietz. At my sugestion, he emphasized repeatedly that he was not an opponent of mass transit—which could help ease steadily worsening congestion in many cities—but he pointed out that our nation desperately needed an efficient highway system to sustain its economic growth. This had been the president's original reason for pushing the Highway Act and Congress's for passing it into law. It would be a mistake, Dietz said, to forget that thinking now and divert the money to a different use, laudable though that alternate use might be.

While Dietz was making these points, we recruited many business people and others to help tell our story, particularly on the local level. Every city in the country had some kind of debate going—highway proponents on one side, mass transit boosters on the other, politicians and commuters and media people in the middle. We provided speeches, background material, media contacts, and other help to the local highway partisans in these debates.

After only a few weeks, we began to get indications that our campaign was having an effect and gaining momentum. Most adult Americans drive cars, after all. While many could see the need for better mass transit systems, they also began to come around to Arthur Dietz's point of view—money for mass transit should come from a separate source rather than being scooped out of a fund that was earmarked for highways. We began to see this point being made more and more often in the press and in TV news reports.

But Bill Wilson and I both felt the need for something more. We wanted something dramatic to give our campaign an extra shot of oomph and shift it into high gear.

It was at this point that I came up with the idea of a scale model.

I said to Bill, "Look, what's this debate about? It really has two levels. On one level it's about mass transit versus highways. But on a more emotional level it's about cities versus all the rest of the landscape. When we say 'highways' people think of an eight-lane turnpike out in the farmlands. They think the highway program is going to benefit a lot of rural and suburban communities, and truckers and other business interests, leaving the cities choking in their own traffic congestion the same as always."

Bill agreed with this analysis. So I concluded, "Okay, then, let's give them dramatic evidence that the highway program won't be the death of cities. Let's show them all the good thinking that's been done about relieving congestion downtown."

"Show them how?"

"A scale model of a typical downtown area. We'll call it Traffic City."

Bill liked the idea. We hired an architect to design the model. At Bill's suggestion, we sent the architect's design sketches to Washington for approval by engineers of the Automotive Safety Foundation, a group with wider interests than its name implied—it had been active in the search for ways to ease downtown congestion. Its engineers suggested some relatively small changes in the design and officially approved Traffic City as a showcase of the latest ideas on midtown planning.

The model was about eight feet wide and four feet deep, with an expressway on which tiny cars moved, and streets and buildings such as you might see in any American city. But the main attraction of the model was its collection of new ideas for resurrecting downtown from death by traffic jam.

The model included pedestrian ramps and underpasses, express lanes for buses, special pickup and discharge locations for bus passengers, and a lot of other features. To show how parking problems could be attacked, there was a standard street-level parking lot that could hold fifty cars. By placing a building over this lot, we could demonstrate that several hundred cars could be parked in the same square of city space.

I knew this model would attract news photographers and TV camera crews. It was a natural. But I thought its newsworthiness might be enhanced if we could find some special way to introduce it to the press and public.

I thought about this for a time. Then an idea came to me, but I rejected it as too grandiose. But it kept drifting back.

Finally, I thought, Okay. If we're going to do this, we might as well do it big.

What I had in mind was an unveiling at the White House. "After all," I explained to Bill Wilson, "this model was built to help promote President Eisenhower's highway modernization program, right? So it isn't all that farfetched to think Ike might want to play a role."

Bill Wilson stared at me. Finally he shrugged. "Well," he said, "what have we got to lose? The worst they can do is say no. Let's give it a whirl."

The head of Byoir's Washington office put the proposal to Ike's press secretary, Jim Haggerty, who said the president couldn't commit himself to attend any unveiling ceremony, but would allow us to conduct the ceremony in the White House annex. Moreover, Ike would ask some of his top transportation aides to put in an appearance.

We milked that for all it was worth. We scheduled the unveiling for three o'clock one afternoon. Before the ceremony, we hosted a lunch, to which we invited several senators, representatives, and other government people who had been active in addressing transportation problems. The lunch and the unveiling were well attended. Pictures of the model and the assembled bigwigs appeared in hundreds of newspapers and newsmagazines around the country. In the process, we got extremely good publicity not only for the highway program, but also for CIT.

Then we sent the model out on a cross-country tour. We had it loaded on a truck, and two articulate people went along to set it up, demonstrate it, and answer questions about it. They visited some twenty-five cities.

In each city, of course, we notified the local press and TV people in advance of the model's arrival. It met an enthusiastic response everywhere it went. In fact not one TV producer turned down our invitation to show it to the viewers.

The coverage of that model and our message was enormous. We could feel the groundswell of public opinion, and with startling suddenness, the mass transit lobby virtually ceased all its efforts, almost as though a faucet had been turned off.

About four months after Arthur Dietz had talked to Bill Wilson and me that day in his office, highway improvement money began to flow out of Washington.

Shortly after Traffic City finished its tour, I received a call from Jim Haggerty. He said Ike had asked him to express his personal appreciation to Bill Wilson and me.

It was a good PR effort, and it demonstrated how useful a scale model can be in certain kinds of difficult PR situations.

When you need dramatic results and need them fast, personal visits and appearances should play a major role in your planning.
      —A story of Service Insurance and a full barrel

Service Insurance, one of CIT Financial's more profitable subsidiaries, wasn't making much profit in New York State—a problem Byoir was asked to solve.

Service sold automobile insurance, often in conjunction with the auto loans made by CIT's credit operation. Impressed by Byoir's success in getting Regulation W defeated, Service's president and CEO, Emil Chervenak, called me to his office one day and said he would like to present us with a somewhat similar challenge on the state level.

The problem had to do with auto insurance rates in New York State. State law defined the maximum rates that could be charged by Service and its competitors. The rates were too low to allow the companies a reasonable profit, and as inflation and other factors drove the companies' costs upward, the fixed rates were becoming an ever more burdensome problem. Some companies, Emil told me, were finding the squeeze intolerable. If something didn't give soon, several companies might simply withdraw from the auto insurance business in the state, with potentially disastrous results for many drivers. Hundreds of thousands of people might find that they couldn't buy auto insurance from anybody, at any price.

Service and others had been lobbying hard in Albany, the state capital, without success. Recently, Emil and two colleagues had paid a call on the state insurance commissioner. The commissioner was sympathetic. He understood the need for higher rates, realized that Service and other companies were facing heavy losses, and was aware of the danger that some companies might quit the business. But he had a problem—the policyholders.

"I know you need higher rates," he said, "and you know it,

but do the policy holders? I doubt it. If I recommend higher rates, I'll be massacred."

Emil suggested that the policyholders might be more reasonable than the commissioner supposed. Maybe they would understand, or could be made to understand.

The commissioner was skeptical. "Before I'd be willing to stick my neck out," he said, "I'd want to see some kind of evidence that I'm not going to get lynched."

"What kind of evidence?"

"Evidence in the media. Tell you what—I'll make you a deal. If you come in here with a barrel of press clippings saying your rate increase is a fair recommendation, I'll take it from there."

So that was Byoir's assignment—filling that barrel. And not just filling it, but filling it fast—in two or three months if possible. Losses were mounting alarmingly, and there was no time to waste.

We began by preparing a package of background material on the issue, including charts and other good visual items that dramatized the problem and could be used by print media or TV. The backgrounder emphasized the potential catastrophe that lay ahead—the possibility that some companies would close down their New York State operations if they didn't get rate relief. Nobody was quite sure what would happen in such an event, but all the likely scenarios were nightmares.

This background package was to be an all-purpose tool for use throughout the campaign. It could be handed out to all the media in a variety of circumstances. But our sharpest and most telling weapon was a strategy of personal visits and appearances.

First, we asked Emil to assign three particularly personable, articulate Service Insurance people to us. We planned to send them out on statewide tours for speeches, interviews, panel discussions, radio and TV appearances, press conferences, and other in-person contacts with the media and the public. Before we sent them out, we put them through a two-day training session at our New York City headquarters. The training was supervised by Muriel Fox Aronson, one of our media experts who was especially good at preparing people for public engagements of this kind.

Next, we assigned four Byoir men and women to another face-to-face effort. Their job was to pay personal visits to editors and editorial writers of every daily newspaper in the state. During these visits they would hand over our backgrounder and other material and would talk about the seriousness of the rate problem. We also sent the backgrounder to all the weekly newspapers in the state.

The emphasis on face-to-face contacts required a lot of planning, a lot of travel, and a lot of other work. It made our campaign more expensive than it might otherwise have been. But it got the kinds of results we wanted—faster, more solid results than would have been likely if we had simply mailed out press releases. Within about two months, it was plain that we had a large majority of the print and broadcast media on our side.

We collected clippings assiduously, of course. When the time came for Emil and his two colleagues to pay their second visit to the state insurance commissioner, I suggested that they take a barrel into the office with them.

Emil agreed that would be good fun. We found a medium-sized barrel and filled it with clippings favorable to the idea of an auto insurance rate increase. Emil and his colleagues triumphantly marched up to the commissioner's desk with it.

The commissioner roared with laughter. And then he kept his word. He recommended the needed rate increase, and not in timid language either. The state legislators, who had been reading the papers, watching TV, and listening to the radio like everybody else, recognized that what the commissioner was asking for was what the public realized was needed. The increase was approved with virtually no opposition.

CHAPTER 9

THE IMPORTANCE OF GOOD BRIEFING

People will perform well for you in interviews and other showcases if you prepare them carefully. If you don't, they can take you by surprise.

Always be sure you know what people are going to say in media interviews.
   —A story of actor Bob Cummings and cigarettes

THIS STORY illustrates the importance of defending yourself against surprise. No such defense is foolproof— life is full of surprises, and the public-relations business is not immune. No matter what you do, you are going to be surprised from time to time by unexpected events, sometimes unpleasant ones. But if you take steps to protect yourself, you can at least reduce the number of unwanted surprises to a minimum.

This is particularly true in a common public-relations situation. A client of yours, or somebody important to a client, is about to be interviewed by the press or on TV. Do you know how the interview will go or what will be said? Of course you don't—not in detail. But don't just *assume* it will go well for your client. Ask yourself, "What can go wrong?" And then brief the prospective interviewee about anything that worries you.

This won't guarantee a good interview, of course. Even with the most careful preparation, things can go disastrously wrong. But good preparation at least improves the odds in your favor.

This is a story about preparations that we didn't make—a lapse we lived to regret.

Sometime before the day in 1971 when cigarette advertising was banned from television, Byoir was retained by the Brown and Williamson Tobacco Company for general public-relations support. At that time B&W sponsored several TV shows, and the company hoped we would boost those shows' popularity. I suggested, among other things, that we generate publicity about the stars of the shows—feature stories, column items, radio and TV appearances, and so on. The B&W people were enthusiastic about this. Since the shows in question were filmed mainly in Hollywood, we put our Los Angeles office to work on the project. Results were excellent, and for a while everybody was happy.

One popular B&W offering—indeed, one of the most popular prime-time TV shows in those years—was the Bob Cummings Show, a dramatic hour in which the versatile actor played various roles. To increase Cummings's exposure, we took aim at one of the very top magazine markets—*TV Guide*, with an enormous circulation second only to *Reader's Digest*.

We sold a top *TV Guide* editor on the idea of a major interview and article on Cummings. Cummings himself was receptive, but he told us he was about to leave for Hawaii, where a segment of his show was to be shot. He would be delighted, he said, if the magazine's writer were to meet him there. This was fine with *TV Guide*, and everything seemed set.

Unfortunately, because Cummings was an affable and intelligent fellow, we made the mistake of simply assuming the interview would go well. We didn't see the need to send anybody from our Los Angeles office out to Hawaii to sit in on the interview. Nor did we see the need to brief Cummings. We relaxed too much.

TV Guide's reporter had two lengthy interviews with the actor. Toward the end of the second interview, the reporter commented that Cummings had not smoked a single cigarette the entire time. The reporter asked, "Why not? Don't you enjoy your sponsor's product?"

This was a question we should have anticipated. If I or any seasoned PR professional had taken the time to talk to Bob Cummings before the interview, we would have noticed that he didn't smoke and would have thought immediately, *Oh-oh, here's potential trouble*. And we would have counseled the actor on ways to answer the expectable question without damage to our client.

But we didn't brief him, and the result was catastrophic.

Replying to the reporter's question, Cummings said he wasn't getting any younger, and, determined to preserve his good health, he was exercising regularly, watching his diet with care, and avoiding anything that might undermine his fitness. So he wasn't smoking cigarettes.

It was a bombshell, and the reporter knew it.

Remember when this happened. Comments on the health hazards of smoking are routine today, but in the era of the Bob Cummings Show, the debate was still wide open. If you had predicted back then that cigarettes would soon be banished from TV, and that eventually health warnings from the United States Surgeon General would be required by law on cigarette packs and in ads, people would have laughed at you.

Bob Cummings's views on his sponsor's product were, of course, mentioned prominently in the *TV Guide* article. No reader was likely to miss the point—an actor collecting a good income for advertising a product to other people shunned the product himself because he considered it hazardous to his health.

The people at B&W were outraged. We at Byoir were sorry we had ever set up the interview.

But we were even sorrier that we hadn't taken the time to brief our man. We never made that mistake again.

If you brief people well, they will often surprise you by how effectively they perform for you.
—A story of Woolworth and Rhonda Fleming

This is a story of a public-relations effort that almost backfired. If it had, the results would have been personally embarrassing to me, since the whole thing was my idea. Luckily, it was saved by a quick-thinking actress.

Did I say luckily? Yes, luck certainly played a role. But Byoir also deserved a little credit, I thought, for we had taken the trouble to brief the actress thoroughly on our public-relations objectives, which were specific and sharply defined. If we had not done that, we might have ended in the soup as we did with Bob Cummings and his comments about cigarettes.

It happened in the middle 1970s. Woolworth had decided to upgrade its image; management wanted to eliminate forever the common conception of Woolworth as a chain of five-and-dime stores where you got cheap merchandise, root beer, and hot dogs. So we developed some fashion shows and attendant publicity in key cities. The fashion shows—of course featuring men's, women's, and children's apparel from Woolworth stores—were really quite appealing, demonstrating that clothes of high quality could be found at low prices. Our campaign drew a lot of attention from the media—and very favorable attention at that.

Then I was struck by an idea. One of the most popular television shows back then was "I've Got a Secret," an oddly intellectual quiz show that lacked the razzle-dazzle and extravagant prizes of other quiz shows but drew huge prime-time audiences. The host and moderator at the time was Garry Moore, and appearing with him was a panel of four celebrities, who would confront a series of guests from assorted walks of life. Each guest had a secret, and the panel tried to discover that secret through astute questioning.

It seemed to me that this show would be a fine vehicle for our campaign to upgrade Woolworth's image. Suppose, I thought, we found a beautiful woman, perhaps a well-known actress, who was willing to appear on this show on our behalf. And suppose her secret was that all the clothes she was wearing that night were purchased at a Woolworth store.

Everybody liked the idea. Byoir's TV department got in touch with the producer of "I've Got a Secret" and tried the idea out on him. He was receptive but not willing to commit himself immediately. So we escorted him to the Woolworth store at Fifth Avenue and Thirty-eighth Street in Manhattan, and invited him to examine the clothing for himself and see what he thought of the quality. He was impressed, and we had him on our side.

Next we needed a glamorous woman, outfitted by Woolworth,

to appear as the show's guest. With the producer's help we found a world-class beauty—the stunning red-haired actress Rhonda Fleming. Amused by our idea at first, she finally agreed with our point—a woman needn't be rich in order to look good. It was a point Rhonda Fleming felt needed to be made, and she was looking forward to making it.

We took her to that same Fifth Avenue Woolworth store. She chose a complete outfit—dress, pantyhose, undergarments, shoes, handbag, scarf. All the while, our people were talking to her about Woolworth's concerns over its image, and by the time she walked into the TV studio and shook hands with Garry Moore, she was very thoroughly briefed. She understood our objectives perfectly, was fully in accord with them, and was prepared to do her best in putting our point across.

She took her place in the guest chair, beautiful as ever, poised, and confident.

She handled the first three panelists easily. They didn't come close to guessing her secret. The fourth panelist was the Broadway actress Kitty Carlisle, one of the show's regulars, who usually displayed a good-humored wit and easy charm but on occasion could be waspish. On this particular night she chose to sting Rhonda Fleming.

Kitty Carlisle's opening comment was that Rhonda usually looked extraordinarily glamorous, but tonight she didn't seem to be up to her usual standards. Did the secret, therefore, have to do with what she was wearing?

I squirmed in my chair. *Oh, boy*, I thought, *this tears it! This is going to be a disaster*! I imagined all the Woolworth executives in front of their TV sets at home, their mouths dropping open in dismay, hands clapping to foreheads.

But Rhonda Fleming came through for us.

She looked at her questioner coolly and said yes, she supposed she was dressed in a less Hollywood style than usual. Was that what Kitty Carlisle meant by her question? Kitty, looking a bit flustered, agreed that she had probably meant something of the sort. Proceeding with her questioning, she quickly elicited Rhonda Fleming's secret—everything Rhonda was wearing and carrying had been purchased at a Woolworth store.

Rhonda then did something we hadn't expected and would never have dared hope for. She stood up in front of the TV camera and showed what she was wearing, including the hem of her slip, remarking that she had been genuinely amazed to find clothing and accessories of such high quality in what she had always thought of as a variety store.

And finally she looked straight at the camera and said, "My entire outfit cost me less than thirty dollars."

It was a triumph of public relations. On the next day, Woolworth stores all over the country and in Canada were mobbed by eager customers.

A good briefing will also prevent an interviewee from freezing.
—A story of Libby-Owens-Ford and a farm expert

Libby-Owens-Ford, one of the nation's biggest glass manufacturers and a Byoir client, launched a campaign in the early fifties to sell more glass to dairy farmers. The typical cow barn was a dark and cheerless place, LOF pointed out, particularly gloomy and cold in winter. And research at several respected agricultural colleges had shown that cows would grow healthier and give more milk if exposed to more sunlight and warmth. So it made sense to install more windows and skylights on barns.

LOF planned to send a farm expert I'll call Ernie Downing on a cross-country tour, to spread this message by interviews with newspapers and farm publications and on TV and radio talk shows. One of the first major cities he hit on this tour was Chicago, where I was then posted. Harry Saladen, the New York-based Byoir account executive for LOF, asked me to set up some press and broadcast interviews.

I got a good reception at the *Chicago Daily News* and from a popular TV talk show, hosted by a genial fellow named Bill Evans, who had a relaxed, just-folks manner that endeared him to many. The Bill Evans Show had a big farm audience and so made good sense for our client.

When Ernie Downing came to town, I escorted him to the *Daily News* interview, which went well. After lunch, we turned up at WBKB-TV for the Bill Evans Show. The session, to be broadcast live, was scheduled for two o'clock.

We got there a bit early so that Ernie could talk to Bill Evans and get some guidance on what kinds of questions to expect. As very often happens, however, Bill wasn't there. I showed Ernie around the studio and introduced him to some of the people I knew. I could see that he was getting nervous and I tried to calm him by telling him what an easygoing guy Bill Evans was.

Bill blew into the studio about two minutes before air time. The producer and his assistants plunked Ernie into the hot seat and wired him for sound and the red on-the-air light flashed on. Bill introduced his guest and then drifted into a folksy mono-logue—a trademark of his show. There were a couple of com-mercials. Then it was time for the questions.

Bill leaned toward his guest and said, "Ernie, I understand you're the farm expert at Libby-Owens-Ford."

Ernie's response was: "That's right, Bill."

There was a long silence. Bill Evans was a good on-the-air interviewer. His questions were designed to lead a guest easily into telling a story or stating a case. But Bill's first question didn't seem to be doing the trick.

Bill tried again. "And I also understand," he said, "that dairy farmers would be better off with more windows and skylights in their cow barns."

Ernie's response: "That's right, Bill."

There was another long, long silence.

Bill tried a third time: "The reason, if I understand it right, is that cows are more contented when they get more sunlight and warmth."

Ernie's response: "That's right, Bill."

There was still another silence that seemed to stretch into the middle of next year. Finally Bill Evans gave it one last try. He said, "And that means the cows are healthier and give more milk, right?"

"That's right, Bill."

More silence.

Exasperated, Bill Evans looked up at me. I was standing behind the camera.

"Bob," he said, before his live TV audience, "can't your client say anything except 'That's right, Bill'?"

Ernie then got his jammed synapses freed and started to talk on his subject. But the interview was irreparably damaged. It limped along for a minute or so and then was cut short.

As Ernie and I walked out to the elevators later, he apologized. "When that red light came on," he said, "I simply froze! I couldn't think!"

I mumbled some soothing noises. Later, I called the LOF account executive in New York to report on this disaster. I strongly urged that if Ernie was to be sent on a protracted tour as LOF's spokesman, he should first get some training. Byoir ran a short training course in New York for just this purpose. It was designed to brief neophyte interviewees on what to expect before a TV camera and in other common PR situations. The account executive agreed to send Ernie to New York.

I next called Bill Evans to apologize for the embarrassment. He was understanding and generous. He had seen interviewees freeze before and expected to see it happen again, he said. But he added that he hoped I would brief my clients' people a bit more thoroughly in the future.

"At least tell them they're expected to take the lead from a leading question," he said. "That's elementary, I should think."

I said, "That's right, Bill."

Actors and actresses are especially likely to surprise you if you don't make careful preparations.
— A story of Hallmark and Richard Burton

Hallmark Cards was a Byoir client for more than thirty-five years. We handled advance publicity for the "Hallmark Hall of Fame," a series of TV dramatic specials usually seen three or four times a year during weekend prime time. The series dated back to the so-called Golden Age of TV drama in the 1950s—and indeed helped establish that Golden Age. Hallmark always put a lot of money and care into these productions, and since there was almost always something genuinely "special" about them, we seldom had any great difficulty in publicizing them.

But the work brought us into contact—sometimes close contact—with leading actors and actresses, an occupational hazard of the PR business. While these folk of stage and screen are like any other people in most respects—there are nice ones and mean ones, smart ones and dumb ones—they do tend to be a bit less predictable than most. This can land you in trouble. Learn to expect it.

In 1974, Hallmark decided to produce a "Hall of Fame" program based on Winston Churchill's book *The Gathering Storm*, about events leading up to the Second World War. The role of the pudgy, cigar-chomping prime minister was offered to Richard Burton, who accepted readily. The filming was to be in London.

As part of our advance publicity, we got in touch with the editor of the *New York Times* Sunday Arts and Leisure Section and suggested an article on Churchill. The article was to be bylined by Burton, but it was understood—as it usually is in such cases—that the actor probably wouldn't write the piece himself, it would be ghostwritten. The *Times* editor was enthusiastic about the idea, giving us a deadline that would allow the piece to appear on the Sunday "The Gathering Storm" was scheduled to be broadcast. The deadline was several months off, and we felt comfortable with it.

Then a surprising turn of events happened. Our associate account executive for Hallmark, Jack Meelan, was in London setting up press interviews and other publicity events for Burton. The actor was businesslike and cooperative through it all. But after one interview, he took Jack aside and said he had been thinking about that article planned for the Sunday *Times*. He said he had known Churchill personally, had become absorbed in the prime minister's life while studying his part for the show, and would like to write the article himself.

Oh, boy.

It is always dicey when a nonwriter says he wants to write something and I discourage it when I can. Warning bells clang in my head. But in this case we went along with Burton. We knew he was literate and articulate, so we had reason to hope for a good outcome. We told him what the *Times*'s deadline was, and he said he'd meet it.

And then we waited.

And waited.

And waited some more. The months went by and there was no sign of the promised article. Jack Meelan was in touch with Burton's London-based secretary, who kept saying she'd needle the actor but kept failing to produce any results.

The article finally arrived at our office on the very day of the deadline. It came by telex from the Grand Hotel in Rome—the printout was six feet long.

When we read it, we were horrified.

"It is to be understood at once," Burton's lead began, "that I write this with a virulent hatred of Winston Churchill and all his kind." The article then went on to compare the bulldog-chinned prime minister with Attila the Hun, Adolf Hitler, and other mass killers.

It was a shock to us. Never once in his contacts with Jack Meelan or other Byoir people had Burton said anything about hating Churchill. What had brought on this sudden, bizarre attack? We couldn't imagine.

We immediately called the *Times*. Under the circumstances, we explained, we couldn't deliver the article.

The Sunday editor retorted that we *must* deliver it. We were committed to do so, he said. When we continued to resist, he started to make threatening noises.

Oh, boy.

I knew I should have listened to those warning bells. How fervently I wished now that we had assigned the article to a reliable freelance writer—or had sounded out Burton more carefully. But it was too late.

How would it look, we wondered, when this crazy article appeared? A world-renowned actor, appearing on the "Hall of Fame" program in the role of Churchill, harbors an intense hatred for Churchill. How would it look? Weird, at best. Just plain bad, at worst.

We finally hit on a plan that we hoped would minimize the damage. We would deliver the byliner to the *Times* as promised, but we would also deliver a letter from Donald Hall, Hallmark's CEO. In this letter, Hall would state in unequivocal language that the opinions expressed in the article were Burton's, that Hallmark did not share them, and that Richard Burton hadn't given the company any advance warning that this was how he felt.

Burton's article ran as scheduled in the *Times* and, as expected, it raised a storm of controversy. *TV Guide* reprinted a shorter version in its own pages, making the controversy national in scope. The following Sunday, the *Times* letters to the editor dealt entirely with readers' responses to the Burton piece, and included in a prominent spot was Donald Hall's letter.

Most of the readers were critical of Burton. They not only disagreed, some of them passionately, with his unkind assessment of Winston Churchill, but they questioned his judgment and good taste in thus castigating the prime minister just before the "Hall of Fame" show. If Burton didn't like Churchill, the readers asked, why did he accept the role? Or if he accepted the role and pocketed Hallmark's money, why didn't he keep his thoughts to himself?

Nobody ever found out exactly what was going through the actor's head. With actors, you often don't.

I held my breath pending the outcome. It could have gone either way for Hallmark. Luckily, it went the way we wanted. The controversy greatly increased the audience for that "Hall of Fame" show—indeed, may have doubled it. And through the whole nerve-wracking episode no smear of blame ever stuck to our client.

CHAPTER 10

FLOUNDERERS AND FRAUDS

Beware the kinds of people who can make your job harder.

Not everybody you meet in the public-relations business is a true PR professional. Watch out for the ringers; they can give you trouble.
          —A story of CIT Financial and a hunt for a
                                              genuine pro

THERE ARE frauds in every business, no doubt, but it may be that a fraud can hoodwink people more easily in the PR business than in many others. This can happen in certain corporate structures, for example, where a PR director may report to senior executives who don't know anything about PR. In such a setting, a man or woman with inadequate credentials can get promoted to or hired for the top public-relations job. The company may pay his or her salary for a long time before learning that it isn't getting its money's worth.

This doesn't happen easily in an organization like Carl Byoir & Associates. A group of PR professionals can usually spot a ringer in short order. We checked credentials and skills at Byoir with the greatest care before hiring anybody, not only looking for a winning personality—often the only criterion in some corporate settings—but also for news media experience and the ability to write good, clear, straightforward English prose. Even when hiring a newcomer without previous PR experience, we still leaned heavily toward men and women who had at least worked on a newspaper or magazine or in a radio or TV newsroom.

When our clients were hiring for their own corporate PR staffs, we urged them to let us help in selecting candidates. We knew from sad experience how easily a fraud can slip by—and we knew this would mean problems for us because we were the ones who would have to work with this person. Most clients welcomed our advice, but a few didn't. This is the strange and sad story of a company that didn't.

The company was CIT Financial. No longer in existence as a separate entity (it was engulfed by RCA and then by Manufacturers Hanover), it was a big power in the consumer and industrial lending field for sixty years. Companies in that turbulent business had always needed good-public relations counsel, and Byoir had represented CIT for thirty-two years.

When CIT's able PR vice president left for another job, the trouble began.

At first things seemed to go well. Byoir was able to prevent a mistake from being made, only to watch helplessly as a second mistake followed.

The first mistake almost happened when the vice president of personnel elected to fill the empty job by using an executive recruiter. The headhunter came up with a man who had recently left the PR staff of a major bank. The people at CIT liked this man and were on the point of hiring him. Before formally offering him the job, however, the personnel chief decided to ask for an opinion from Byoir. He phoned me and asked if I knew anybody at the bank.

"Matter of fact, yes, I do," I replied. I was referring to an old friend who had recently become the bank's top public-relations executive.

"Will you give him a call and ask for a candid opinion of our candidate?"

I was happy to oblige. I phoned my friend and explained that I wanted to check on a candidate's professional PR qualifications.

"What's this candidate's name?" he asked.

I told him.

There was a long silence. Finally he said, "Well, Bob, I'll give it to you straight. When I first came into this job about a year ago, one of the first things I did was look over the staff I'd inherited. There were about forty-five people all told. I wanted to foster the feeling of starting out afresh, so I asked everyone of them to submit a letter of resignation."

He paused. I prodded, asking, "And?"

He answered, "Out of all those resignations, I accepted just a few. Your candidate's was one of them."

That was that.

He then went on to say he knew of a financial PR man who was interested in changing jobs. For purposes of telling this story I'll call the man Fred Williams. "I used to know Fred socially, and we served on a couple of community-service projects together," he told me. "He's personable and seems like a nice guy. But I really don't know anything about his professional PR qualifications."

I thanked him for his help and relayed the information to the CIT people. They took my advice and immediately abandoned all thoughts of hiring the candidate dredged up by the headhunter. They thought Fred Williams sounded like a good possibility and told me they would contact him.

Two weeks later the personnel chief called me and said he and his colleagues were very favorably impressed by Williams. They had had him up to their New York offices twice. His references seemed good. He was evidently quite amiable, and nobody had a mean word to say about him.

But I wondered what he knew about public relations. I kept my mouth shut, however.

Then CIT's personnel chief, to my relief, told me he would like to have an opinion from Byoir, or from somebody whose judgment Byoir trusted. Did I know anybody who might have dealt with Fred Williams?

I said I would scout around. I called the Byoir regional office serving the city where Williams currently worked, where I found a man who said he knew Fred Williams well.

"Oh, sure, Fred and I bump into each other a lot," the man told me. "I hate to tell you this, but if it were up to me, I wouldn't hire him for *any* PR job, let alone PR chief of a big company. I'll grant he's personable. People like him. But he has no media background, he was fired by at least one company I know of, and the people he works for now will be relieved if and when he moves out."

So I had a second bad report on a candidate to carry back

to CIT. This time, however, nobody wanted to believe the report.

The personnel chief told me tartly that mine was the only bad word he had heard about Fred Williams. He said he would pass my report along to his superiors, but he doubted it would have much influence.

He was right. A week later I received a call from Fred Williams himself. He told me he had been hired as CIT's vice president in charge of public relations.

I went to his office to meet him and fill him in on Byoir's past and current work for CIT. As advertised, he was a genial fellow with a ready smile and easy manner—the kind of person you can't help liking. Even if that hadn't been the case, I was still eager to do everything possible to ease his transition into his new job. It had always been a Byoir policy to help the corporate PR staff people we worked with, if they asked for help or we sensed that they needed it. We didn't cluck around them like a bunch of mother hens, but if we saw a man or woman floundering, we did what we could as quietly as we could. After only a short conversation with Fred Williams, I had an uneasy feeling that he was going to need some kind of propping up, though I couldn't immediately judge what kind.

Bill Fox, the Byoir account executive in charge of CIT's affairs, was the first to discover Fred's major inadequacy. Bill spent most of his time in an office at CIT and worked daily with the CIT staff people. He came to me one day and told me Williams couldn't write.

The man, it seemed, could barely put together a plain, declarative English sentence. As for turning out a press release or news story with a logical structure—a piece of writing that strode firmly in a straight line from start to finish—he was utterly hopeless.

So Bill Fox covered for him. Bill wrote all his speeches, memos, proposals, letters, and other material. As was traditional with us at Byoir in such situations, Bill did this quietly. The CIT management believed that Bill's fluid, clear prose was Fred Williams's.

Then the cozy arrangement came to an abrupt end. Bill Fox was transferred to another account.

During the short period when we were in the process of assigning and briefing another account executive, Fred Williams was on his own. It was then that he got shot down.

It was annual report time, and the corporation's annual report was in its final-proof stage. Much of it had been written by Bill Fox, though Fred Williams had been getting the credit. The report was nearly ready for the printer, but some last-minute changes were still being made.

At about eleven o'clock one morning, a few days after Bill Fox had left, Williams was called up to the office of the company's chairman and CEO, Walter Holmes, Jr. Holmes said there was one section of the report, dealing with a subsidiary, that would have to be rewritten. He explained what the problems were and detailed the changes that must be made, adding that speed was essential as the printer's deadline was very near. Therefore, Holmes said, it would be helpful if Fred could have the rewrite ready right after lunch.

Several hours passed. At about half past two in the afternoon, Holmes called downstairs to his PR man's office and asked when the copy would be ready.

Williams replied that he didn't know. Puzzled, Holmes asked why not. After some bluffing, the PR man finally blurted out that he couldn't do the rewrite.

Still more puzzled, Holmes asked what the problem was. Fred simply said again that he couldn't do it.

Dumbfounded, Holmes hung up his phone. Then he picked it up again and called me. He told me of his strange experience with Fred Williams and asked me if I could come to the CIT offices in a hurry. When I arrived, I took on the rewrite job and found it to be perfectly straightforward and simple—the kind of task most PR professionals do as routinely as tying shoelaces. By five o'clock that afternoon I had finished it, Holmes had approved it, and it was on its way to the printer.

Meanwhile, Holmes had been making inquiries, seeking an explanation of the perplexing episode earlier in the day. He learned the truth—that his PR chief couldn't write and that Byoir had been covering for him.

Before I left CIT's offices that day, Holmes asked me to give top priority to finding a new vice president of public relations. This time, he said with a wry smile, he and his colleagues would listen more carefully to reports from Byoir.

Of all the background elements that go to make a well-qualified public-relations professional, the most important by far is news media experience.
    —A story of Arthur Andersen & Company at tax time

This is another story of a mistake made in hiring a PR person. But the mistake this time, unfortunately, was the Byoir organization's.

Rules, they say, are made to be broken. Perhaps that is true in some circumstances. But I've learned over the years that it isn't usually a good idea to break one's own rules. Almost inevitably, one comes to regret it.

A firm rule in our organization, going back to the early days when Carl Byoir first began promoting Cuba's tourist trade in 1930, was that staff people we hired to do PR work must have at least three years of solid media experience. This meant work on a newspaper or magazine, or in a radio station—or, in later years, on television.

It was a good rule. It helped us maintain a high-quality staff not only at our New York headquarters but in regional offices and other outposts scattered about the country. But in 1981 we made an exception.

We had gone to work in 1980 for Arthur Andersen & Company, the biggest of the Big Eight accounting firms. Andersen's main offices were in Chicago, but for a time we serviced the account principally from New York. Then in 1981, when a management upheaval at Andersen produced a lot of changes, we decided (for reasons that aren't relevant to this story) that it would make more sense from now on to handle the account from our Chicago office. So we asked our Chicago office chief to recruit an experienced account executive.

After about two weeks, the Chicago manager phoned to tell me he had a fine prospect, a man with good experience in a Chicago PR agency who had also recently received an MBA degree, from the highly respected University of Chicago. He supposedly knew a lot about business and money—knowledge that would be helpful in serving a company like Andersen, with its diverse list of clients. The Chicago manager and his colleagues recommended strongly that he be hired.

Our normal routine in a situation like this would have been to invite the candidate to New York, where he and his qualifications would be scrutinized by a special screening committee. We had had this system in force since 1959. But in this particular case we were up against fierce time pressure. Because of the management upheaval at Andersen, the company was in dire need of good public-relations guidance. Executives were pressing us daily for help, but our response, I felt, was less useful than it might have been. We needed an account executive in the hot spot, and we needed him yesterday.

And so we broke our rule. In fact, we broke two. Not only did we fail to subject the candidate to the standard New York screening, but we also failed to check thoroughly enough into his background. He spoke vaguely of knowing a lot about the news media, so we let it go at that. We didn't check to see whether he actually had the required three years of solid experience. My New York colleagues and I simply approved the Chicago recommendation over the phone.

At first everybody was quite pleased with our catch. The new man was personally pleasant, bright, diligent. He wrote good proposals and was good at presenting them to the client. His writing was a bit too heavily laden with business jargon—almost always true of new MBAs—but it was basically a good workmanlike breed of prose, and only a little pencil editing was required to turn it into plain English.

But after a couple of months I began to feel uneasy. Something was missing.

Coverage. The new account executives didn't seem to be generating stories about Andersen in the business and financial press. I looked in vain for the company's name in all the usual places—the *Wall Street Journal*, the business pages of the *New York Times* and other big-city dailies, magazines like *Business Week* and *Fortune*, the TV business news reports. Nothing. Arthur Andersen & Company might almost have passed out of existence.

My philosophy of management called for constructive criticism. I've never found it does much good simply to read somebody a list of his or her failings. It's vastly more useful, I think, to offer specific suggestions for improvement. So that is what I did. It was early January, the beginning of the income-tax worry season, when I phoned the new man in Chicago. I suggested that he talk to a tax expert at Andersen and develop half a dozen good strong tax stories to offer to editors between now and April 15—stories on changes in the tax law, perhaps, or anything else that might seem newsworthy. Editors are always hungry for tax stories during the worry season.

The account man agreed. A few days later he had a two-hour session with an income-tax specialist at Andersen and went away with a thick sheaf of notes.

Two weeks went by and nothing happened. The Andersen tax specialist was puzzled. He had understood that the purpose of the two-hour interview was to generate newsworthy stories and he expected that he would be given an opportunity to review those stories before they were released to the media. But so far, no stories. Indeed, the tax specialist hadn't heard a peep from the account executive since the interview. What was going on? I then made my regular weekly trip to Chicago.

The puzzled tax man talked to another Andersen executive, who spoke to me. Equally mystified, I went to see the account executive.

"I hear you had a good two-hour session with an income-tax guy at Andersen," I said. "He says you took a lot of notes."

"Yes," the account man replied.

"Well, everyone is a bit mystified. When are we going to see the results? The stories?"

"Oh, I'm afraid there won't be any. I didn't see anything newsworthy in the material I collected."

I thought: *Oh-oh.*

I asked to see the man's notes, which at least he had had typed. I took them away and looked them over and several dandy story possibilities jumped up at me. Some were stories that could be tailored to fit two or more different kinds of market—not just the financial press but women's magazines, too, for example. There are not many nonfiction editors who will scorn a good tax story at tax time.

Admittedly much of the material in the notes *was* lacking in news appeal. The Andersen tax specialist had simply spewed forth everything he knew, without being selective. It is not easy to pluck out strong, lively stories, but people in the media learn how to do it, and they do it every day.

It was obvious that our new account man had not had much, if any, media experience.

I carried his notes back to New York and turned them over to some skilled people in our financial news department, with brief instructions. Within two days I was able to mail five fine tax pieces to the specialist at Andersen for his approval. We got excellent coverage.

We replaced the account executive promptly. The new incumbent was a former reporter and a good one. We weren't going to make the same mistake twice.

CHAPTER 11

THE POWER OF PUBLIC RELATIONS

Public relations can do many different jobs—often with astonishing effect.

Public relations, properly applied, can overcome the mightiest of opponents—even when that opponent has a head start.
                    —A story of AT&T and an epic battle

ONE OF the most titanic struggles I was ever involved in during my entire time at Byoir was a fight we had with the telecommunications colossus, AT&T. Not only did that gigantic company have much more money at its disposal than did our client, but it also had a substantial head start. Despite those two handicaps, we defeated our opponent completely through outstanding public relations.

That defeat led to radical changes in telephone service and other aspects of telecommunications in America. Hardly a man or woman in the nation hasn't been affected by those changes in one way or another.

The episode is a classic example of the power of public relations.

It took place in the middle 1970s, but its roots went back to 1968. In that year, Congress passed a bill that had the effect of ending Ma Bell's long-held monopoly of the $31 billion-a-year United States telecommunications industry. The bill opened the door for others besides AT&T to provide long-distance phone service, manufacture phones and related equipment, and so on. However, the bill didn't make it easy for others to get into these businesses, and at first few did. Initially Ma Bell lost less than 5 percent of its business to competitors.

But the competition was growing slowly and stubbornly, and there were indications that under certain conditions it might increase substantially in the future. Hence, when John D. DeButts was installed as AT&T's chairman and CEO in 1972, he announced that it would be his main goal to regain the monopoly for the Bell system and its 1800 "independent" affiliates.

DeButts quickly launched an aggressive and highly effective campaign to achieve this goal. The leitmotif of the campaign was an old home truth that had always made good sense to most Americans—"If it ain't broke, don't fix it." It was unarguably true that America had the best phone system in the world, better than anything in western Europe or Japan, and so far superior to Communist countries' systems that there wasn't even any comparison. DeButts therefore asked the question, "If we've got something that works so well, why tinker with it?"

He played on fears of the unknown. The Bell monopoly was safe and familiar, he told people. If competitors were allowed to come in the door, who knew what the results might be? The system might be wrecked. Service might deteriorate.

What DeButt's campaigners didn't mention, of course, was the opposite and in fact more likely possibility—competition might make the system still better, simultaneously bringing prices down.

But the campaign gained support rapidly. In 1976, due in large measure to AT&T's lobbying efforts, legislation in its favor was introduced in Congress. The proposed legislation was called the Consumer Communications Reform Act, and its thrust was to restore Ma Bell's monopoly more or less as it had existed before 1968. Popularly known as the Bell Bill, it had widespread support from many political and other groups, including the Communications Workers of America, a very powerful union.

Encouraged, AT&T poured more and more money into its campaign, determined to see the bill passed into law. By midsummer 1976, a startling fact came to light—some 120 members of Congress were on the public record as favoring the bill.

That was when Harold Geneen swung into action.

Geneen, chairman and CEO of ITT, had long hoped to make his company a major competitor of Ma Bell in some areas of its business. He now saw that he would have to move fast if he wanted any slice of the pie at all, let alone a large slice.

He told his public-affairs chief, Edward J. ("Ned") Gerrity, to find a high-powered PR firm to handle the fight. Gerrity immediately came to see me. When asked if I thought we could take on Ma Bell, I said yes. He explained that it was Geneen's idea that we wouldn't work directly for ITT but for the Washington-based North American Telephone Association (NATA), a group of companies like ITT, mainly manufacturers of communications equipment. Many of these companies had entered the business in 1968, many were relatively small, and many stood to be wiped out if the Bell Bill became law. NATA had a very small PR budget and had been completely overwhelmed by the size of John DeButts's assault. Ned Gerrity told me ITT would pay the bill for our services, since NATA couldn't.

We had a proposed plan of action ready within a week. A contract was signed two days later, and we went to work. Ned and his top assistant, Juan Cappello, were very helpful throughout the entire campaign.

Our specific objectives were to turn public and legislative opinion around and get the Bell Bill defeated. Our three key targets were labor, legislators, and private and commercial phone customers.

Next we identified some actual and potential allies. Two big allies were the Federal Communications Commission and the President's Office of Telecommunications Policy, both of which were on record as finding nothing to praise in the Bell Bill. We felt the United States public itself was a potential ally, for Americans have always reacted with suspicion to any suggestion of monopoly. If we could once show the public that the Bell Bill would create a monopoly, and that phone users would probably lose as a result, then we stood to pick up widespread support. So we aimed our efforts at both general public media and at consumer groups such as Common Cause and large organizations such as the General Federation of Women's Clubs. With congressional hearings on the Bell Bill scheduled to start in September 1976, we made it one of our first items of business to set up a major news conference. At this conference, held in Washington, D.C., we saw to it that NATA's opposition to the Bell Bill—and the reasons behind it—were announced. Not only did the conference attract a lot of media coverage, but it drew a good number of political leaders, too. In the very act of announcing we were entering the fight, we struck a telling blow.

Then we devloped four main ways of getting our message across to our target audiences. They were:

1. Placing favorable news and feature stories in newspapers and magazines.
2. Getting our story told on radio and TV.
3. Operating a speakers' bureau. Through this bureau we sent NATA spokespeople out on literally hundreds of speaking engagements during the three-year course of our campaign. Many of these appearances were local in scope and were reported only in local media—but we felt that community-oriented affairs of this kind, with neighbor speaking to neighbor, would be highly effective in building up the grass-roots support we needed.
4. Sending four Byoir staff people out for direct, face-to-face talks with editors, reporters, editorial writers, TV and radio producers, free lance journalists, and other members of the news media.

All these efforts produced good results, but the most powerfully effective were the last two, the speakers' bureau and the personal contacts. You'll recall the lesson I drew from an earlier story—that personal appearances and face-to-face contacts, though expensive when compared to most other means of getting a public-relations message across, tend to produce the fastest, most visible results.

It worked again in the AT&T case. The roving NATA speakers and the Byoir face-to-face travelers—particularly the latter—produced incredible coverage for our side of the story. The resulting articles were so one sided in our favor that politicians began to notice an abrupt shift in the wind, and they, too, one by one, began to support NATA. Naturally we reprinted what we considered the best editorials and political statements and sent them around to the press and broadcasting media.

Within a year of starting our campaign, we had AT&T worried. But the giant wasn't by any means ready to turn and run.

On the contrary, AT&T stepped up the intensity of its campaign. We never were quite sure how much money Ma Bell was spending, but we did know it was much more than we had and was increasing all the time. One staggeringly expensive AT&T move was a series of commercials on network TV, many of them aired in prime time. In these ads, John DeButts himself appeared, asserting that a ragtag crowd of competitors coming into the Bell System's nice tidy world would result in deteriorating service, higher prices, and a general breakdown of a smooth-working system. He ended each ad with the same words: "The System is the solution."

But the public wasn't listening.

By mid-1978, two years after we had entered the fight, it was apparent that AT&T's support was dwindling irrevocably and the Bell Bill was dying. Virtually all 120 legislators who had once actively favored the bill backed off. The bill finally died of neglect. It never came to a vote.

Bitterly disappointed, John DeButts announced that he would retire early. A whole new era of telecommunications was dawning. He wanted his company to be guided into that unknowable new era by a new executive team.

And so Ma Bell's monopoly ended for good, and today we enjoy a communications system of vastly greater capacity and scope than anything dreamed of in the 1970s. I've never seen a clearer illustration of the power of public relations.

---

*By using your imagination, you can make public
relations do the same job as advertising—and maybe
do it better.*
       —A story of Schaeffer Pen and a new-product
                                        campaign

The old Schaeffer Pen Company developed a highly appealing
new product in the early 1950s. In that era, ballpoint pens
were neither as ubiquitous nor as reliable as they are today, and
most people rightly distrusted them. The majority still preferred
reliable old fountain pens, which had to be filled with ink
periodically.

The drawback of fountain pens was, of course, that they were
messy, difficult to fill and often leaked ink onto one's clothes.
Ink-stained fingers and splashed desktops were commonly listed
among life's inescapable irritations, like taxes and mosquitos.

Then Schaeffer developed a fountain pen with so efficient a
filling mechanism that the job could be done while wearing
white gloves. The company, a Byoir client, asked our organization
to introduce the product to the United States market without
any advertising.

A few at Byoir were surprised by the assignment. Shouldn't a
new-product introduction campaign properly include a job for
advertising?

Well, maybe. Then again, maybe not.

It was true, then as now, that new-product campaigns are tradi-
tionally considered primarily advertising's domain. When a company invents something new and useful, the first thought in
every executive's mind is "Buy TV time! Buy space in magazines!" Public relations may then be used as an adjunct, but it is
nearly always advertising that takes on most of the responsibility
for exposing the new product's attractions to the buying public.

But the Schaeffer Pen story was different. Here was a case in
which public relations was being asked to lead the way, with

advertising in a follow-up role. Did we want the job? Even more to the point, could we do it?

The answer to both questions was yes.

We began with a series of press conferences in about ten major cities across the country. At these we handed out feature stories on the new pen and on writing instruments in general, also providing still photos and film clips showing people with white gloves filling the new pen. We worked hard to make our stories and presentations lively and interesting, to convince editors and reporters that this was a gold mine of good feature material. We weren't conning them—it *was* a gold mine. This phase of our efforts began to generate widespread coverage before the new pen was available in stores.

To keep the public's interest alive, we also developed a special promotion. We hid samples of the new pen in New York and other cities, and through the media we provided artful and mysterious clues as to where these pens could be found. People who found them could collect generous prizes from Schaeffer. This promotion stirred up a gratifying amount of excitement in the media and, in consequence, among the public.

The end results were still more gratifying. Before a single print ad had been published or TV commercial broadcast, Schaeffer received 45,000 letters asking when and where the new pen could be purchased. When the pen finally did hit the market, with public relations and advertising now working side by side to promote it, it was an instant best-seller. The white-glove pen was the most successful new-product campaign in Schaeffers's history.

Among the major selling points of public relations is that it is cheaper than advertising, and often much more effective.
—A story of Woolworth and a faulty utility light

Late in the 1970s a Florida man, using a portable electric utility light or trouble light in his attic, was electrocuted and killed. It was determined that the light was faulty. His family got in touch with the Consumer Product Safety Commission (CPSC) in Washington and urged that the public be warned against using this brand of utility light.

CPSC studied the matter and agreed that the light was dangerous. The commission then contacted the light's manufacturer, a New Jersey company, as well as some large chain stores where the light was sold, and demanded remedial action. Among the chains was Byoir's old client Woolworth.

The remedial action sought by CPSC was going to be very expensive. The commission wanted the light's manufacturer and the store chains to take out ads in major newspapers across the country and also on radio and prime-time TV, warning people to get rid of those utility lights or turn them in for refunds. The cost of the proposed ads worked out to something like $8 million–10 million.

I first asked Woolworth whether the lights were indeed as hazardous as CPSC claimed, and was told that we would have a difficult time proving otherwise. The danger might be remote, but it plainly did exist. So there was nothing to do but take our lumps, take them quickly, and get the whole unhappy episode behind us as fast as possible.

But then I asked myself, Why does it have to cost us so much? Instead of buying all that advertising space and time, why can't we accomplish the same purpose with a major, well-publicized press conference?

We took this question to court. The judge listened to arguments from our side about the efficiency of good public relations compared to paid ads. He thought for a while, then said, "All right. I'll give you one week to show what you can do."

Just one week. That wasn't much time. Luckily, the Byoir organization was a well-oiled machine that could produce results fast when it had to.

We set up a massive press conference in Washington, D.C., and made sure, of course, that dozens of key print and electronic journalists were invited. We publicized the conference with every means at our disposal—phone, mail, telegrams, personal visits, and drinks and lunches. As a result, the conference was a thundering success. It received widespread coverage in print, on radio, and on TV.

But we didn't stop there. We mailed stories about the faulty utility light to every daily newspaper in the United States, and to the news directors of literally hundreds of TV and radio stations. And of course we arranged to have the results monitored so that we would know when and where our story appeared.

At the end of the week we prepared a huge map of the country, and on this map we placed symbols showing where the story had been carried in print, on radio, and on television. We took this very impressive map to court and showed it to the judge. We had copies of major newspaper stories with us, and, to impress the judge still further, we played samples of radio and TV news programs that carried our story and warning to consumers.

The judge took it all in. Then he picked up his gavel, rapped it on his bench, and said, "Case dismissed."

Our efforts cost money, of course, but nowhere near the $8 million–10 million that would have gone into paid ads. It was a clear, concise demonstration of the power of good public relations.

As a rule, the results of public-relations work tend to blossom slowly. But good PR can also be used with stunning effect in very fast-moving emergencies.
—A story of CIT Financial and a stock-price plunge

This story is an outstanding example of how public relations can be the only solution to a serious and panicky problem. It is also an example of how rapidly good PR can do its job—provided you are willing to work fast.

Nobody who is unwilling to endure late nights, skipped meals, and stomach-churning deadlines belongs in the PR business. This is a story of PR at its most taxing—PR testing individual judgment, speed, and stamina to the utmost.

The story took place in the 1960s, but its origins went all the way back to the middle 1930s, when Thurman Arnold, the aggressive and reform-minded United States attorney general under President Roosevelt, obtained a court order requiring major automobile manufacturers to divest themselves of their financing subsidiaries. At that time, General Motors, Ford, and Chrysler—the Big Three—all had such subsidiaries and made a good deal of money from them. If you wanted to buy a Ford car, for example, you could get a loan from Ford's own finance company. You paid a stiff rate of interest, of course, and Ford thus made money not only from the sale of the car, but also from your interest payments.

Chrysler and Ford complied with that court order in the 1930s and closed down their financing operations. This left their dealers without any convenient loan arrangement to offer prospective buyers. To replace the lost in-house financing, many of Chrysler's dealers worked out a special arrangement with the Commerical Credit Corporation (CCC) of Baltimore. Similarly, many of Ford's dealers established a relationship with the Universal CIT Credit Corporation, which was the auto-financing subsidiary of CIT Financial.

Both CCC and CIT had previously offered auto loans, but because of competition from the Big Three, they had been pretty much restricted to cars of smaller manufacturers. The Thurman Arnold court order was a grand boost for CCC and CIT.

However, it was not as big a boost as it might have been. Alone among the Big Three, General Motors decided to fight the court order. The huge automaker announced that it was not going to close down its highly profitable financing subsidiary, General Motors Acceptance Corporation (GMAC).

So GMAC kept operating while mighty GM and a battery of lawyers took the case to court. The case dragged on and on and on, lasting for years, then decades. It dragged on so long that almost everybody forgot about it.

And meanwhile, GMAC kept collecting all those monthly interest payments from millions of car buyers.

Sometime in the 1960s, Henry Ford II said, "Hey! Wait a minute!" Ford reminded the world that his gigantic competitor, GM, had somehow managed to fend off the United States government for nearly thirty years. The GMAC case was still stumbling through the courts, providing a nice steady living for a number of laywers and clerks but in general getting nowhere. In the meantime, GMAC's profits were flowing into GM's coffers and enriching the stockholders, while Ford and Chrysler, by promptly obeying that court order back in the 1930s, had cut themselves off from a lucrative source of income.

And so Henry Ford II began to talk about reestablishing Ford's own in-house finance company. He set up a committee to study the pros and cons. Rumors flew, and a yes decision seemed imminent.

If Ford did decide to restart an in-house loan operation, of course, that would be a potentially staggering blow to CIT, and in anticipation the common stock of CIT Financial, traded on the New York Stock Exchange, began to drop sharply in price. In one ten-day period it lost twelve points, about 40 percent of its value. It was in an apparent free fall with the bottom nowhere in sight. The stockholders were on the ragged edge of panic.

Worried, CIT's three top executives flew to Detroit and sought a meeting with executives of Ford. The news they heard was soothing. Contrary to the rumors circulating in Wall Street, they were told, Ford had no plans to start a new auto financing operation any time soon, and there was little likelihood of a decision either way until a lot more study had been completed. Moreover, even if Ford were to decide to go ahead with a new loan operation, setting it up and getting it rolling on a nation-wide basis would take still more years.

The CIT executives wanted this calming news conveyed immediately to the nervous stockholders. This was how I entered the story, since CIT Financial was a long-term Byoir client.

I went to a five-hour emergency meeting with the CIT executives, including Bill Wilson, vice president of public relations. We decided that the best approach would be to send the shareholders a letter as soon as possible giving them the reassuring word from Detroit and stressing that all CIT's subsidiaries were enjoying healthy revenues and profits. The letter would encourage them to hold onto their stock rather than dumping it at panic prices.

Bill Wilson and I left the meeting late that afternoon and went to his office, where we began to compose the letter. Our plan was to finish it before going home that night, so that it would be ready for the executives to review first thing in the morning. But things didn't work out that way.

At about six o'clock, a surprise phone call came in from a *Wall Street Journal* reporter. He told us that a story had just come over the wire from Detroit that Ford had announced plans to reestablish an auto-loan subsidiary as soon as possible. And, Ford had signed up a Universal CIT district manager to organize it and run it.

Bill Wilson and I stared at each other.

By this time, all the CIT executives had left the office. Bill and I talked over the frightening situation and quickly arrived at a decision on what we had to do. It would mean a night of fast, relentless work for the two of us, but there was no other solution.

We phoned each of the top three executives as soon as he arrived at his home. We broke the news and said we had no explanation of Ford's apparently sudden change of mind. Perhaps Ford's executives had deliberately hoodwinked us into a false sense of security, or perhaps they themselves had had no idea that a decision would be made so fast or what the decision would be. At any rate, we were now up against it. The story of Ford's decision would certainly be carried tomorrow in all the big financial papers and on radio and TV. If we didn't act fast, CIT's stockholders would almost inevitably panic.

Bill and I told the three executives that we had to get a reassuring statement to the media *now*. Our statement had to be on every editor's and writer's desk at the same time as the Ford announcement. We didn't want our story to be told in a leisurely follow-up the day after tomorrow, after possibly catastrophic damage was done. Together, our story and Ford's announcement would defuse one another.

The badly shaken executives agreed. But what did we suggest?

Bill and I had a plan worked out. We proposed that the letter to shareholders, already composed, be hand-delivered within the next few hours to all the big New York news media we could get to. So the executives must approve the letter right now, over the phone. They approved it fast, with only minor changes. And then, at about a quarter to seven, Bill Wilson and I hit the streets.

He covered the *Wall Street Journal*, the *Daily News*, *United Press International*, and several others. I hit the *New York Times*, the Associated Press, *Business Week*, and all the big TV and radio networks. It was an exhausting night, but by the time we finished, we were satisfied that every major story to be written or broadcast would have our version of the events to draw on.

As expected, the Ford story out of Detroit the next day received very heavy coverage. But as we had hoped, the CIT letter to shareholders was included as part of every major report on the affair. The points we made in the letter were fairly and accurately reported. Editors gave a particularly generous amount of space and emphasis to our statement that it would take years for Ford to organize a nationwide automobile finance company and get it running smoothly. During those years, it was suggested, CIT and other auto-finance companies would of couse be expected to develop programs and consumer inducements to enable them to compete effectively with the new Ford company.

The result in Wall Street exceeded our highest hopes. CIT stock never wavered. On the day those stories broke, it didn't lose so much as a fraction of a point. The panic was apparently laid to rest. In the following week, the stock's price began to rise rapidly, and within ten days or so it had regained the twelve points that had been knocked out of it by the rumors a short time back.

Ford did eventually get its car-loan operation going, and it succeeded. But as we had told CIT's worried shareholders in our letter, it did not bring about the doom of Universal CIT or anything so dramatic. CIT Financial continued to operate profitably. Indeed, shareholders who hung onto the stock through those dark days were ultimately to be rewarded very handsomely. The company was eventually acquired by RCA, which paid a generous thirty-dollar premium over the shares' market price. In time, RCA resold the company to Manufacturers Hanover, under whose aegis the old CIT still operates profitably today.

I will always remember that wild night in New York as one of the most taxing episodes, yet in the end one of the most satisfying, in my public-relations career.

PR can also be used—and often is—to promote a show-business event.
　　　　　—A story of Howard Hughes, Jane Russell,
　　　　　　　　and a specially designed brassiere

Howard Hughes was a man of immensely diversified interests, for many of which Byoir served as his public-relations counsel. But only once did he ask us to help him promote a movie.

The movie was *The Outlaw*, featuring the debut of a young actress named Jane Russell. On this fascinating and instructive project, I learned a profound truth about publicity—an in-person appearance by a celebrity, carefully prepared and professionally handled, can lure people more strongly than any amount of national publicity or advertising.

It is hard to say why this is so. If you see an actress in a movie or a magazine, you see her large, close-up. You see every separate eyelash. But if you go to see her on a stage, even if you can only afford to sit far away in the balcony, there is something magnetic about the experience, despite the size. There she is, in the flesh.

A little background on Howard Hughes's movie ventures may be useful to set the scene for this story. Hughes had gone into the movie business in the mid-1920s, when an actor friend got him to invest $50,000 in a film project. The movie was a flop, but Hughes found Hollywood to be a highly intriguing place, full of money and starlets, two attractions that he couldn't resist. He went into business as an independent producer and turned out half a dozen films before the Second World War, including two major hits, *Hell's Angels* and *Scarface*.

Then, just before the war, he began work on what was to be another big success, *The Outlaw*.

Success, however, was a long time coming. The early history of this film was discouraging, to say the least.

The movie's plot was barely noticeable, as Hughes himself acknowledged. It was just another horse opera dealing with Billy the Kid. But it had one feature that Hughes thought would propel it to great heights. This feature was its star—a young woman, hitherto unknown, who had been working as an obscure photographer's model until Hughes's restless eye spotted her. Her name was Jane Russell.

As an actress Jane Russell was at that time, to put it charitably, less than brilliant. She had a rather attractive face. But when she strove for the look of sultry passion that had been used so effectively by Jean Harlow (another Hughes discovery) in *Hell's Angels*, it somehow came across as a look of dyspepsia, and her voice had an irritatingly mechanical quality.

But she had something that more than made up for these
drawbacks—a mammary development the likes of which had
never before been exposed to the popeyed gaze of the movie-
going public. As one of my colleagues put it, "She had only two
things to recommend her. Either one would probably have been
enough."

The movie also starred Walter Huston and Thomas Mitchell,
but hardly anybody noticed. All eyes were on Jane Russell. To
enhance her charms, Hughes had a special brassiere designed
which exaggerated the actress's magnificent cleavage.

The Outlaw was in no sense a pornographic film—certainly not
by today's standards and not even by those of the World War II
era. It was really just a run-of-the-mill Western. But critics
quickly noticed, and commented on, the camera's tendency to
linger for what seemed like unnecessarily long periods of time
on that enhanced cleavage. It was this that made the film famous.

Hughes showed it first to a private audience in Los Angeles.
The reviews weren't particularly kind. There was also a strong
feeling that the film wouldn't get past the censors.

Hughes then made a prescient decision. Guessing that sexual
taboos, beginning to change in the turbulent wartime society,
would eventually loosen enough so that he could show *The
Outlaw* without important opposition, he ordered the film shelved.
It stayed shelved until 1943, when Hughes began releasing it to
only three or four cities per year, until 1948, when it finally went
out on general release.

Hughes called in the Byoir organization to handle promotion
of the movie once he was ready to show it all over the country.

History has lost the name of the PR genius who first suggested
the idea of a city-by-city tour for Jane Russell. Maybe it was
Hughes himself. Maybe it was a Byoir staffer. Or maybe the
idea simply sprang up in the group mind without having an
individual author. At any rate, the decision was made to introduce the film on a one-city-at-a-time basis rather than nationally.

The plan called for the actress to travel to major cities with a
vaudeville comedian named Jack Beutel, well known at the time
but thoroughly forgotten since. In each city, this pair would
perform a live stage show for one week in a theater that was

adaptable for both stage and film purposes. Following the initial week, the film would then be shown in the same theater for as long as box-office receipts held up.

Byoir's assignment was to publicize the traveling show before it arrived in each city and to arrange interviews and photo sessions for Jane Russell during the big week. I was then working at Byoir's Chicago offices, so I got involved when the Russell-Beutel show came to the Windy City.

It has been reported in some versions of this epic tale that Hughes's PR agents—meaning me—hyped the publicity by posing as offended bluenoses, phoning the police and writing letters to the papers, demanding that the show be closed down in the name of public decency, thus adding to its allure. However, I can say from personal knowledge that we had no such program. We didn't need to. We were swamped with media requests for interviews, photos, and other material. We didn't have to use any trickery to hook the media. They came to us on their own.

The tour was a spectacular success. So was the movie. Critics panned it, but that made no difference whatever. The film had been so well promoted that it could hardly fail—and it didn't.

It was very profitable.

A good public-relations campaign can even give an old product new life.
                                   —A story of Cinderella

In the spring of 1984, Americans were startled to learn a new fact about aspirin from their newspapers, magazines, and TV programs. It turned out that this familiar over-the-counter drug, used for almost a hundred years for colds and headaches, could, besides relieving pain, help prevent heart attacks—particularly in patients who had already suffered a first attack.

This wasn't just a pitchman's claim. It was sober scientific fact, backed up by solid documentation widely accepted in the medical community.

The odd thing about this public revelation was that the evidence wasn't new. Cardiologists had noted aspirin's effectiveness against heart attack years before. Many tests had been conducted with appropriate safeguards, and the convincing results were known among medical people as far back as the late 1970s.

Why did these results suddenly burst into public view in 1984 after languishing in obscurity all those years? Credit Carl Byoir & Associates.

It all began when aspirin manufacturers got worried about the growing success of Tylenol and other nonaspirin analgesics. The manufacturers set up the Aspirin Foundation of America and hired the Byoir organization to generate new publicity for the old product—in particular, about its use for heart-attack victims.

The campaign was headed by a Byoir senior vice president, Howard Girsky, who set up a series of symposia at which cardiologists described their research on aspirin. The media were of course invited to these events, which took place in New York, Houston, London, and elsewhere.

To give the media an extra set of hard facts to talk about, Byoir conducted a poll of 1,000 cardiologists. We came up with results that surprised even our client, the Aspirin Foundation. It turned out that 67 percent of these physicians prescribed aspirin for first-time sufferers of heart attacks; 39 percent prescribed regular aspirin doses for people who had never had an attack, and 23 percent took daily doses themselves.

When we released these results at a symposium in New York, the coverage was enormous. We made the "Today" show on TV, health and science pages of major newspapers, and even some front pages. Thanks to Georgia Ingersoll, head of our magazine department, we made women's magazines such as *McCall's* and *Family Circle*. It seemed that suddenly every reading and TV-watching adult in the country knew about the use of aspirin in preventing heart attack.

Doctors, who had known about this use for years, were startled by the power of public relations in conveying the awareness so fast to the public. "For years, aspirin was the poor man on the druggist's shelf," said Dr. John Edmeads, a Toronto neurologist. "Now it is the wonder drug of the 1980s. Aspirin is a Cinderella story!"

And public relations was the fairy godmother.

EPILOGUE

THE FUTURE OF PUBLIC RELATIONS

IT MUST have become apparent by now that I am optimistic about the present and future of public relations. The profession has come a long way since I came into it in the 1940s, and with luck it will keep growing bigger and stronger in the years ahead.

Jack O'Dwyer, publisher of the leading PR newsletter, estimates there are some 300,000 men and women in the profession today—more than ever before. The demand for the kinds of services we provide is growing steadily. Business executives seem more keenly aware of the importance of effective communication with their various publics—customers, shareholders, legislators, employees, the general public. Indeed, I don't feel it is an exaggeration to say that a PR boom, started in the late 1970s, is under way.

There are many changes in the wind, and you are likely to see these altering the structure of the PR business in years to come. One important trend is the growing tendency of corporations to hire outside agencies rather than maintain large in-house PR staffs. A recent move by Monsanto is indicative of this trend. This big company had had its own PR staff for many years but had also used the services of Hill & Knowlton. But in 1987, Monsanto decided to pare its in-house staff radically and arranged for Hill & Knowlton to hire most of the former Monsanto PR employees. They kept doing substantially the same jobs, but as employees of the agency, not the client corporation.

This could be a useful turn of events. An agency such as Hill & Knowlton knows more about hiring and training good PR people than the average corporate executive who is made resonsible for such a staff. Moves such as Monsanto's could raise the caliber of professionalism in the PR business.

Another change in the wind is the growing consolidation of PR and advertising functions—the two great arms of the corporate communication business. More and more companies now prefer to hire double-duty agencies that can offer professional work in both fields. It is felt that the two functions can support and complement each other, so that the whole becomes greater than the sum of its parts.

I'm not perfectly sure about this reasoning. It may be valid in some cases. But what concerns me is that I sometimes see a mad scramble by PR and ad agencies to merge, thus creating the double-duty entities that the market demands.

These mergers may create strong new agencies as the trend continues, but a merger that isn't well handled can result in disaster. It was just such an unfortunate merger that caused the death of my own once-healthy agency, Carl Byoir & Associates. I want to tell the story of that disaster because it embodies a warning—there are dangers ahead if people don't walk into the future more carefully.

The Byoir organization was founded in 1930 in Havana. Carl Byoir had come from a family of Russian immigrants who had settled in Des Moines, Iowa, around the beginning of this century. Byoir went into journalism after leaving high school and quickly showed his fast-track orientation by becoming city editor of the Des Moines *Register* at age nineteen.

A little later he went to the University of Iowa. Before he graduated, he had accumulated something like $10,000—an enormous sum for a young man in those days before the First World War—by producing class yearbooks at his own college and others. He then went to New York and became a millionaire while still in his twenties, mainly by promoting a patent medicine that probably could not be sold legally today.

Byoir moved to Cuba for health reasons in late 1929, and,

with characteristic verve, quickly established himself as publicity agent for the island's tourist trade. The trade prospered so well under his guidance that the Cuban government wanted to hire him as a permanent minister of tourism, but he was too full of restless energy to settle down. He moved his staff back to the United States in the middle 1930s and began to expand Carl Byoir & Associates, the firm that I was to join after the Second World War.

It became one of the world's biggest and best-known public relations agencies. Our roster of clients, many of which you've encountered in this book, included blue-chip corporations and associations of the first rank. We attracted attention. Among those eying us were big ad agencies and others seeking a PR firm as a merger partner.

We had talks in the early 1970s with several ad agencies, all in the top twenty-five in terms of size but the talks never went anywhere. Then, in late 1977, we heard a proposal that we took seriously. It came from Arthur Schultz, chairman and CEO of a big Chicago-based ad agency named Foote, Cone & Belding.

Schultz told George Hammond, our chairman, and me that there were going to be more and more marriages of PR and ad agencies because the market demanded them. As a matter of fact, Schultz told us, FCB had recently failed to win Standard Oil of California as a client because a competing ad agency had a much bigger PR subsidiary.

Foote, Cone had seen this trend in the making as far back as the middle 1960s, Schultz said. His company had set up a small PR operation in London in 1965 and had added others since. FCB had acquired or established a total of seven PR operations in the United States and four abroad. But Schultz and his colleagues were dissatisfied with the results—and obviously, big prospective clients such as Standard Oil weren't much impressed either.

That was why Schultz wanted to explore the possibility of acquiring the Byoir organization. We were big, he pointed out; we were quality; and we had a client list that any agency would be proud to call its own.

To be specific, we were the third-biggest PR agency in the

nation. (The biggest was then Hill & Knowlton, the second was Burson-Marsteller.) We had eighty-five clients at the time and were growing fast. We had nine regional offices in the United States and subsidiaries and affiliates in London, Paris, Amsterdam, and dozens of other cities throughout the free world.

George Hammond and I agreed that Arthur Schultz's proposal was worth thinking about. We, too, had noticed the growing tendency of big business to seek combined advertising and PR help.

At many meetings over the next several months, details were worked out. And in April 1978, we were able to announce that Byoir had agreed to be acquired by Foote, Cone. The marriage, finalized on August 1 that year, was the biggest merger in the history of the communications field.

Things seemed to go well at first. It had been understood all along that although this was a merger of unequals—acquirer and acquired—Byoir was to be left to pursue its business in a more or less autonomous fashion. Indeed, Arthur Schultz had said in one of our early meetings that a major advantage of the marriage, to him, was that it would permit him to turn over all PR functions to the Byoir staff, while he and his colleagues could get back to what they did best, advertising.

It was a sensible approach, and that was how we arranged it in the beginning. Unfortunately the arrangement didn't last. After letting the Byoir staff run its own show for a while, the Foote Cone people, for reasons of their own, began to play a more and more active role in our affairs. Byoir staffers found themselves reporting to managers who may have been experts in the ad business but knew nothing about public relations. Understandably, frictions resulted.

The climax came in early March 1983 when the Foote Cone management abruptly fired twelve Byoir staff people, including two executive vice-presidents. The firing shocked the PR community and received wide coverage in the business press. Jack O'Dwyer referred to that day ever afterwards as Bloody Friday.

In the wake of that debacle, Foote, Cone then decided to eliminate our copy desk. The function of this desk, established by Carl Byoir in his firm's very earliest days, had been to edit press releases, feature stories, speeches, magazine articles, and all other written material we sent out. Editors and reporters around the country had felt for years—and had said publicly on many occasions—that Byoir copy was the cleanest in the business. We avoided "PR-speak," a peculiarly unattractive kind of language that all journalists recognize and detest.

PR-speak results from the efforts of inexperienced PR writers to inflate clients' images. Thus you will read of "optimum utilization" instead of "best use" because it sounds more important. In PR-speak people never "guess"; they always "estimate," because it sounds more solemn. This pompous, sludgy breed of language never got past our copy desk.

But now the copy desk was to be dismantled. The results were just as I had feared. Indeed, they were worse. At least our original Byoir staff had consisted of solidly qualified professionals; we never hired anybody who was incapable of putting together a good, straightforward, muscular piece of English prose. But Foote, Cone began bringing in people who had never logged much time at a typewriter keyboard. Instead of sending out material written in English, Byoir, for the first time in its history, now started sending out PR-speak.

Foote, Cone next started to lop off many of Byoir's fifteen specialized departments. These departments—TV-radio, magazines, financial, photo, lifestyles, labor relations, and so on—were staffed by people who knew their fields intimately, and were among the features that had attracted leading corporations to Byoir.

As these and other adverse changes were made, the morale of the original Byoir staff plummeted and turnover accelerated alarmingly. In the two years after Bloody Friday, five executive vice presidents left. So did eight senior vice-presidents, twenty-two vice presidents, half a dozen regional office managers, and many valued creative people. I left in mid-1984.

Jack O'Dwyer commented in his newsletter that there was no question in his mind that the Foote, Cone group "mismanaged" Byoir. He added, "The first mistake of the typical youth-worshipping ad execs was bringing in two PR executives, both in their early forties, as the new leadership . . . Veterans George

Hammond and Bob Wood were replaced after decades of experience, working closely with blue-chip corporate chairmen. The two new executives found themselves dealing with people much older and wiser than themselves."

As these bewildering changes took place and the once-proud Byoir staff deteriorated, clients began to desert the sinking company in droves. O'Dwyer reported that most of the biggest blue-chip clients pulled out during this troubled period in the mid-1980s. Among them were many of the companies you have encountered in this book:

- Hughes Aircraft, a client for 40 years.
- Hallmark, 37 years.
- RCA, 34 years.
- CIT Financial, 33 years.
- Borg Warner, 20 years.
- Also Arthur Andersen, ITT, Northeast Utilities, Ford Motor, Fireman's Fund, General Dynamics, Pepsico, and the Aspirin Foundation.

In August 1986, Foote, Cone & Belding sold the Byoir organization—or what was left of it—to Hill & Knowlton for a reported $12 million. Byoir was simply absorbed into the larger public-relations company and passed out of existence as a separate entity.

And thus did my company die.

There have been other mergers of advertising agencies and public relations firms in the years since, and the same kind of mistakes appear to have been made. Just as one example, the big ad agency Oglivy & Mather embarked on an aquisition program with the same idea Foote, Cone had: to create a double-duty agency. O&M acquired several respected PR companies, among them Dudly, Anderson & Yutzsy. But instead of putting a PR specialist in charge of the PR operation, Ogilvy appointed as manager a man who had no public relations experience. The results were "disappointing," as Jack O'Dwyer put it, and the man was dismissed after a year. Ogilvy has now installed an experienced public relations executive in the job. As of this writing, it is too early to tell whether the new man will be able to produce good results, but there is reason to be optimistic.

The moral of these stories is plain. Mergers between PR and ad agencies may produce useful results, but only if professionals in the two fields are left to run their own shops. It simply makes no sense to place advertising specialists in charge of PR specialists—or, for that matter, vice versa. If there are to be more of these mergers, which seems likely, ways must be found to let the two groups of professionals function side by side without getting in each other's way.

Can it be done? Is it reasonable to dream of a big, powerful, double-duty agency that runs efficiently?

As I said, I'm an optimist.

INDEX

Index